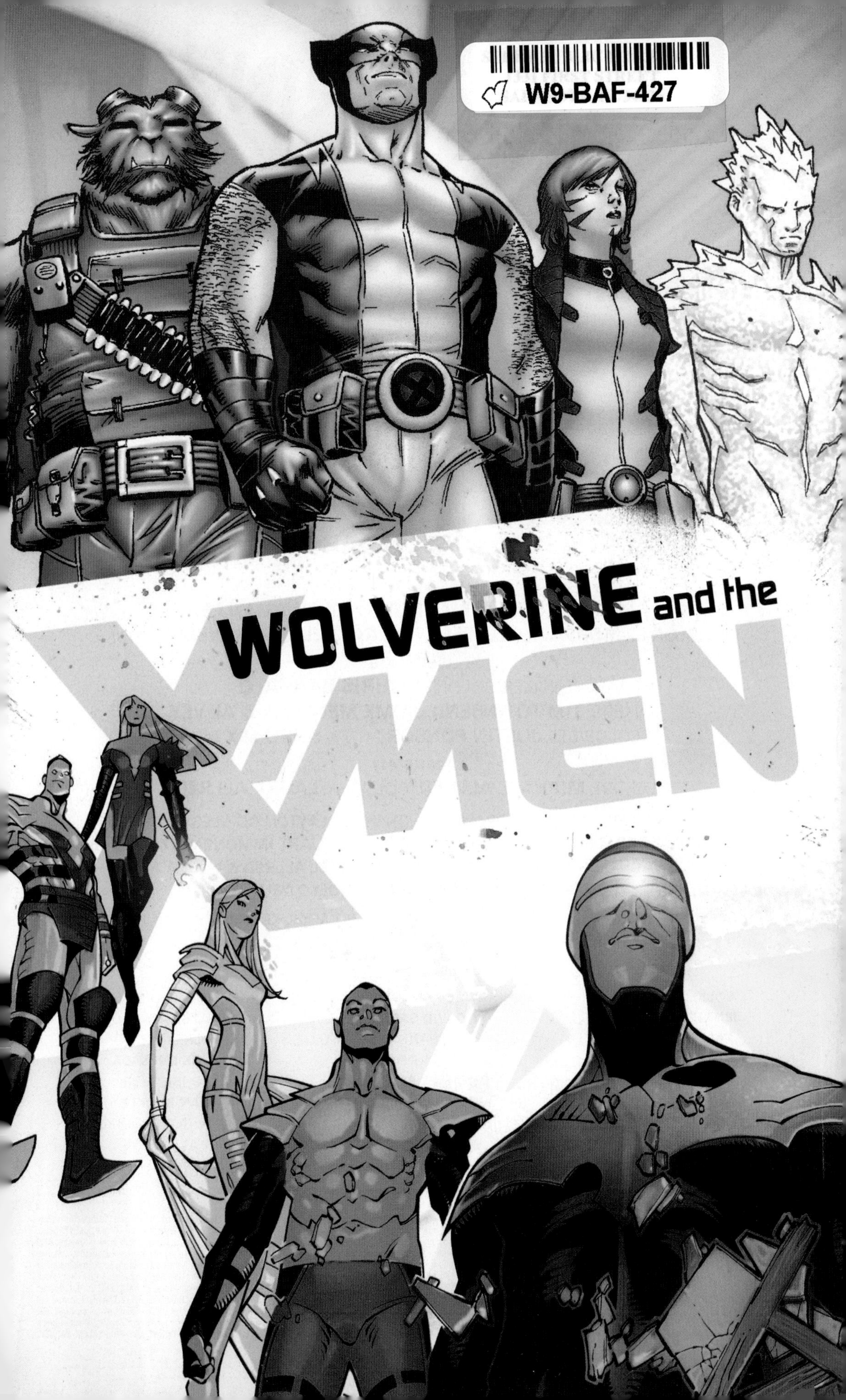
WOLVERINE and the
X-MEN

WOLVERINE and the X-MEN

WRITER: **JASON AARON**

ISSUES #14-15 & #18
PENCILER: **JORGE MOLINA** INKER: **NORMAN LEE**
COLORIST: **MORRY HOLLOWELL** WITH **RACHELLE ROSENBERG** (#18)

ISSUE #16
PENCILER/COLORIST: **CHRIS BACHALO**
INKERS: **TIM TOWNSEND, JAIME MENDOZA & AL VEY**
COLORISTS: **JUSTIN PONSOR** (#11) & **GURU-eFX** (#13)

ISSUE #17
ARTIST: **MICHAEL ALLRED** COLORIST: **LAURA ALLRED**

LETTERER: **CHRIS ELIOPOULOS** WITH **VC'S CLAYTON COWLES** (#17)
COVER ART: **NICK BRADSHAW & JUSTIN PONSOR** (#14), **STUART IMMONEN & MARTE GRACIA**
(#15), **CHRIS BACHALO & TIM TOWNSEND** (#16), **MICHAEL ALLRED & LAURA ALLRED** (#17)
AND **ED McGUINNESS & MORRY HOLLOWELL** (#18)

ASSISTANT EDITOR: **JORDAN D. WHITE** • ASSOCIATE EDITOR: **DANIEL KETCHUM** • EDITOR: **NICK LOWE**

COLLECTION EDITOR:
JENNIFER GRÜNWALD
ASSISTANT EDITORS:
ALEX STARBUCK
& NELSON RIBEIRO
EDITOR, SPECIAL PROJECTS:
MARK D. BEAZLEY
SENIOR EDITOR, SPECIAL PROJECTS:
JEFF YOUNGQUIST

SENIOR VICE PRESIDENT OF SALES:
DAVID GABRIEL
SVP OF BRAND PLANNING
& COMMUNICATIONS:
MICHAEL PASCIULLO
BOOK DESIGNER:
RODOLFO MURAGUCHI

EDITOR IN CHIEF:
AXEL ALONSO
CHIEF CREATIVE OFFICER:
JOE QUESADA
PUBLISHER:
DAN BUCKLEY
EXECUTIVE PRODUCER:
ALAN FINE

WOLVERINE & THE X-MEN BY JASON AARON VOL. 4. Contains material originally published in magazine form as WOLVERINE & THE X-MEN #14-18. First printing 2012. Hardcover ISBN# 978-0-7851-6542-2. Softcover ISBN# 978-0-7851-6543-9. Published by MARVEL WORLDWIDE, INC., a subsidiary of MARVEL ENTERTAINMENT, LLC. OFFICE OF PUBLICATION: 135 West 50th Street, New York, NY 10020. Copyright © 2012 and 2013 Marvel Characters, Inc. All rights reserved. Hardcover: $19.99 per copy in the U.S. and $21.99 in Canada (GST #R127032852). Softcover: $16.99 per copy in the U.S. and $18.99 in Canada (GST #R127032852). Canadian Agreement #40668537. All characters featured in this issue and the distinctive names and likenesses thereof, and all related indicia are trademarks of Marvel Characters, Inc. No similarity between any of the names, characters, persons, and/or institutions in this magazine with those of any living or dead person or institution is intended, and any such similarity which may exist is purely coincidental. **Printed in the U.S.A.** ALAN FINE, EVP - Office of the President, Marvel Worldwide, Inc. and EVP & CMO Marvel Characters B.V.; DAN BUCKLEY, Publisher & President - Print, Animation & Digital Divisions; JOE QUESADA, Chief Creative Officer; TOM BREVOORT, SVP of Publishing; DAVID BOGART, SVP of Operations & Procurement, Publishing; RUWAN JAYATILLEKE, SVP & Associate Publisher, Publishing; C.B. CEBULSKI, SVP of Creator & Content Development; DAVID GABRIEL, SVP of Publishing Sales & Circulation; MICHAEL PASCIULLO, SVP of Brand Planning & Communications; JIM O'KEEFE, VP of Operations & Logistics; DAN CARR, Executive Director of Publishing Technology; SUSAN CRESPI, Editorial Operations Manager; ALEX MORALES, Publishing Operations Manager; STAN LEE, Chairman Emeritus. For information regarding advertising in Marvel Comics or on Marvel.com, please contact Niza Disla, Director of Marvel Partnerships, at ndisla@marvel.com. For Marvel subscription inquiries, please call 800-217-9158. **Manufactured between 10/22/2012 and 12/3/2012 (hardcover), and 10/22/2012 and 4/29/2013 (softcover), by R.R. DONNELLEY, INC., SALEM, VA, USA.**

10 9 8 7 6 5 4 3 2 1

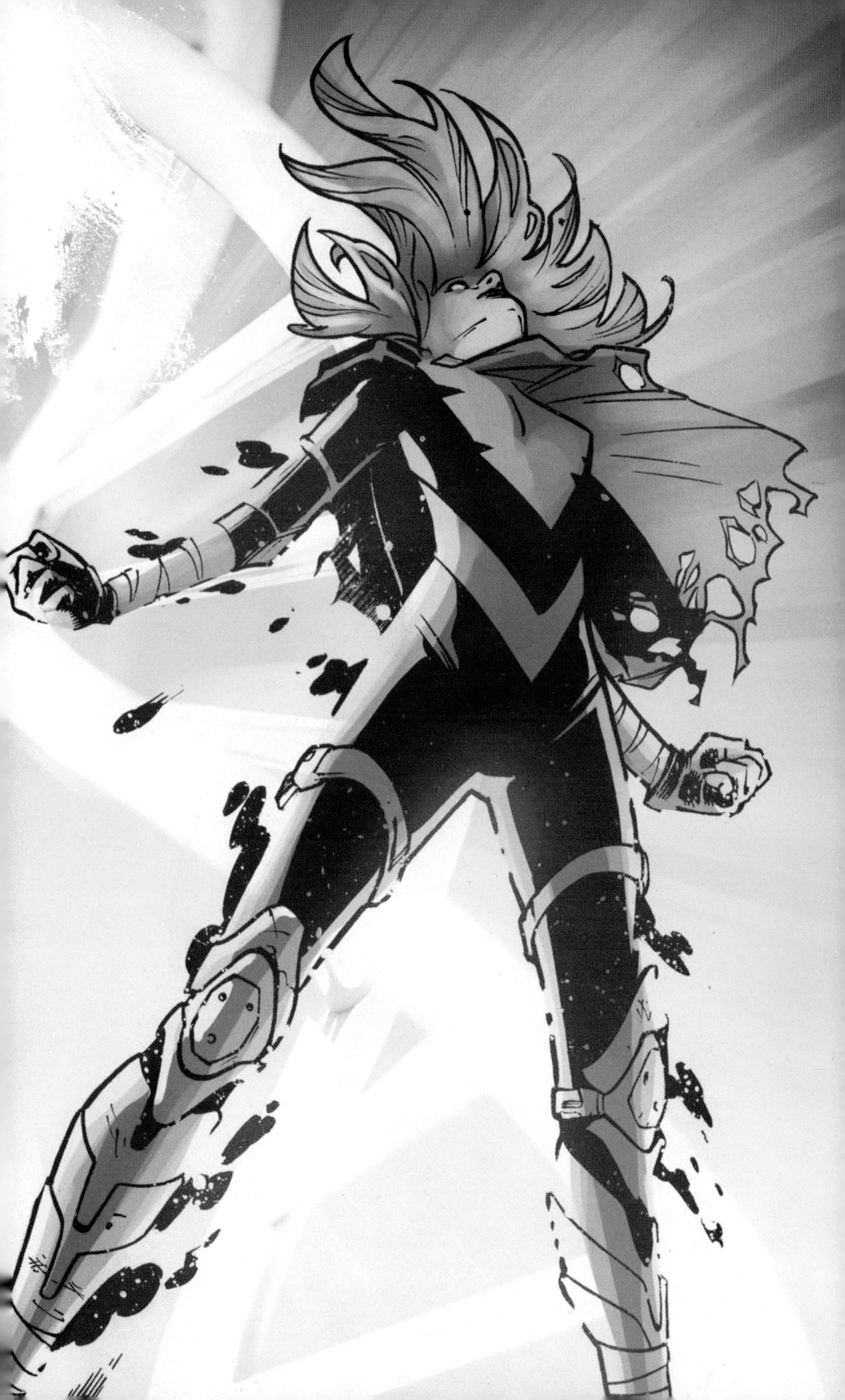

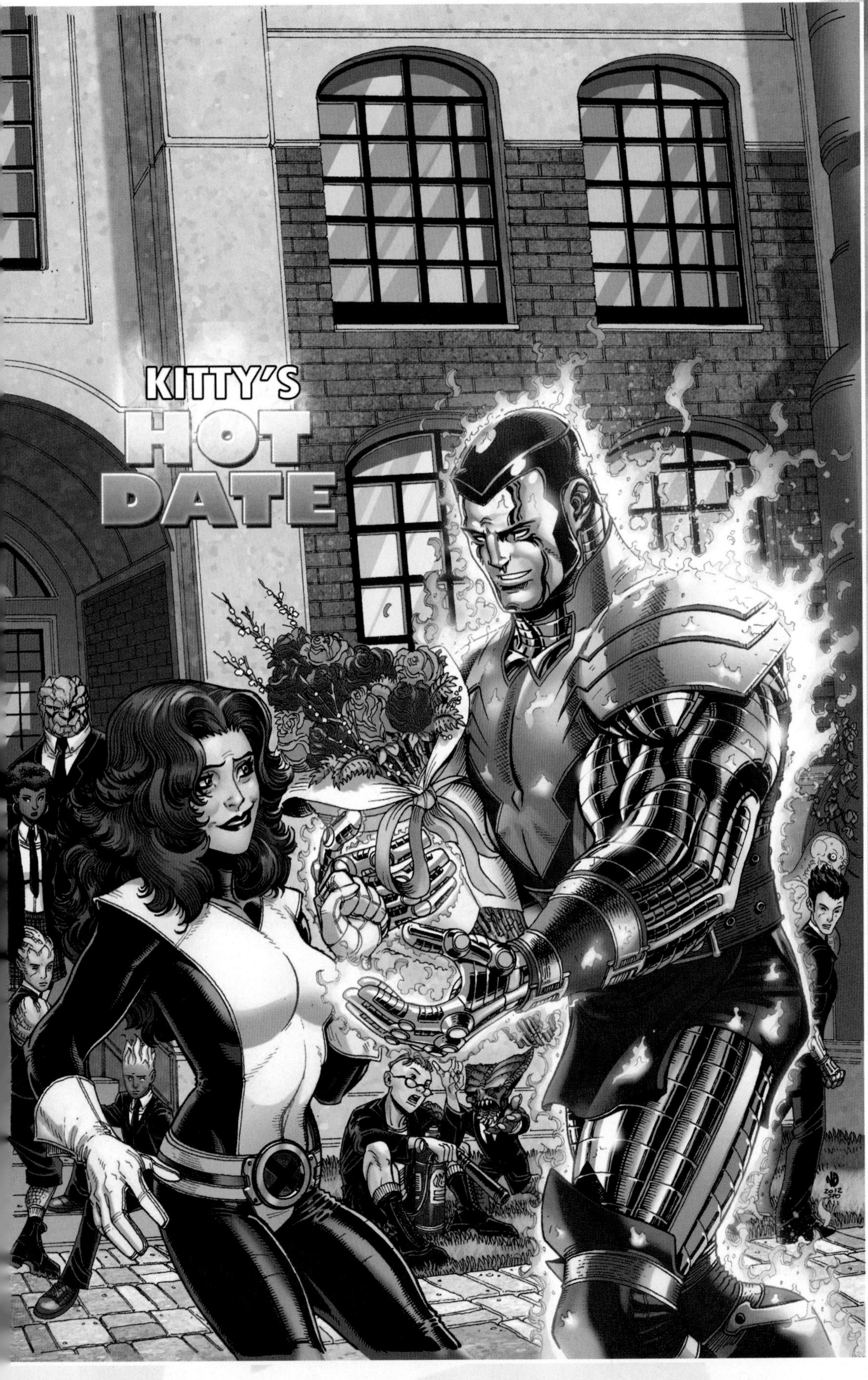
KITTY'S
HOT
DATE

WOLVERINE and the X-MEN

If you were born different with mutant super-powers, the Jean Grey School for Higher Learning is the school for you. Founded by Wolverine and staffed by experienced X-Men, you will learn everything you need to know to survive in a world that hates and fears you.

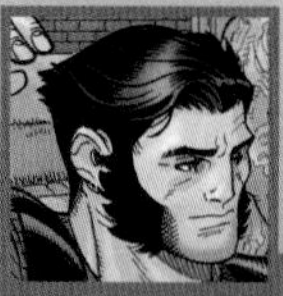

WOLVERINE
Clawed Headmaster

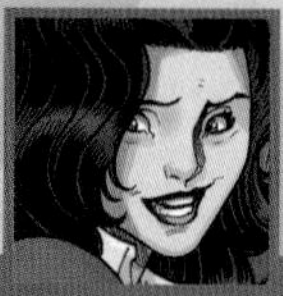

KITTY PRYDE
Phasing Headmistress

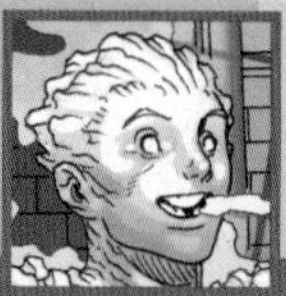

ICEMAN
Ice-Controlling Teacher

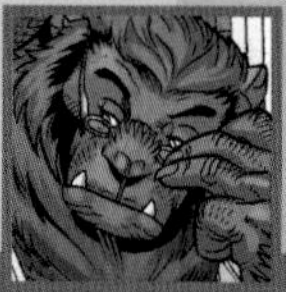

BEAST
Animalistic, Intellectual Vice-Principal

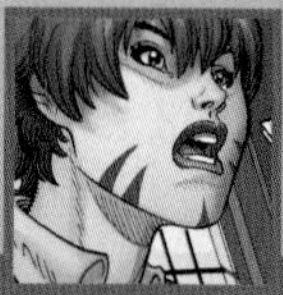

RACHEL GREY
Telekinetic, Telepathic Teacher

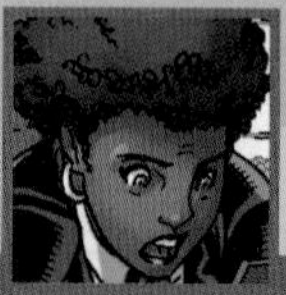

IDIE OKONKWO
Temperature-Controlling Student

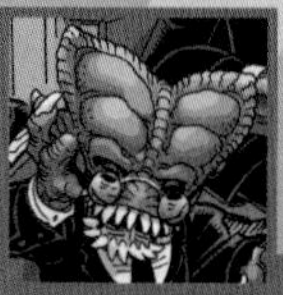

BROO
Alien Student

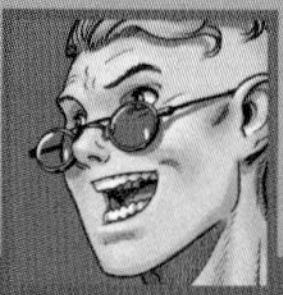

QUENTIN QUIRE
Telepathic Student

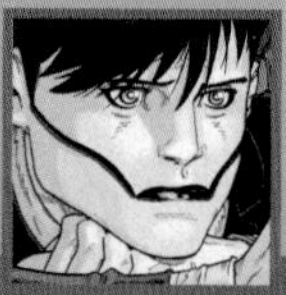

GENESIS
Flying, Eye-Blasting Student

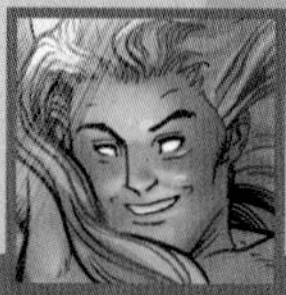

ANGEL
Metal-Winged Student

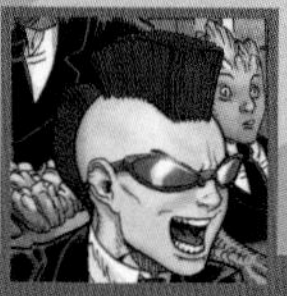

KID GLADIATOR
Superstrong Alien Student

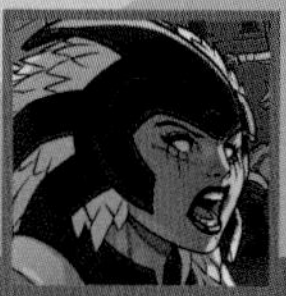

WARBIRD
Shi'ar Bodyguard

PREVIOUSLY

THE PHOENIX FORCE HAS RETURNED TO EARTH AND SPLIT BETWEEN FIVE HOSTS CYCLOPS, EMMA FROST, NAMOR, COLOSSUS AND MAGIK. NOW THE MOST POWERFU HEROES ON EARTH, THEY'RE UTILIZING THEIR POWER TOWARDS BOTH BETTERIN THE WORLD AND WAGING A MANHUNT FOR THE AVENGERS.

IN THE HISTORY OF THE X-MEN, KITTY PRYDE AND COLOSSUS HAVE BEEN ONE OF TH GROUP'S MOST PROMINENT COUPLES. THE PAIR FOUND THEMSELVES ON OPPOSIN SIDES OF THE X-MEN'S RECENT SCHISM, WITH COLOSSUS SIDING WITH CYCLOP AND KITTY HELPING WOLVERINE WITH HIS NEW SCHOOL. WILL COLOSSUS' NEV STATUS HELP THEM BRIDGE THIS CHASM?

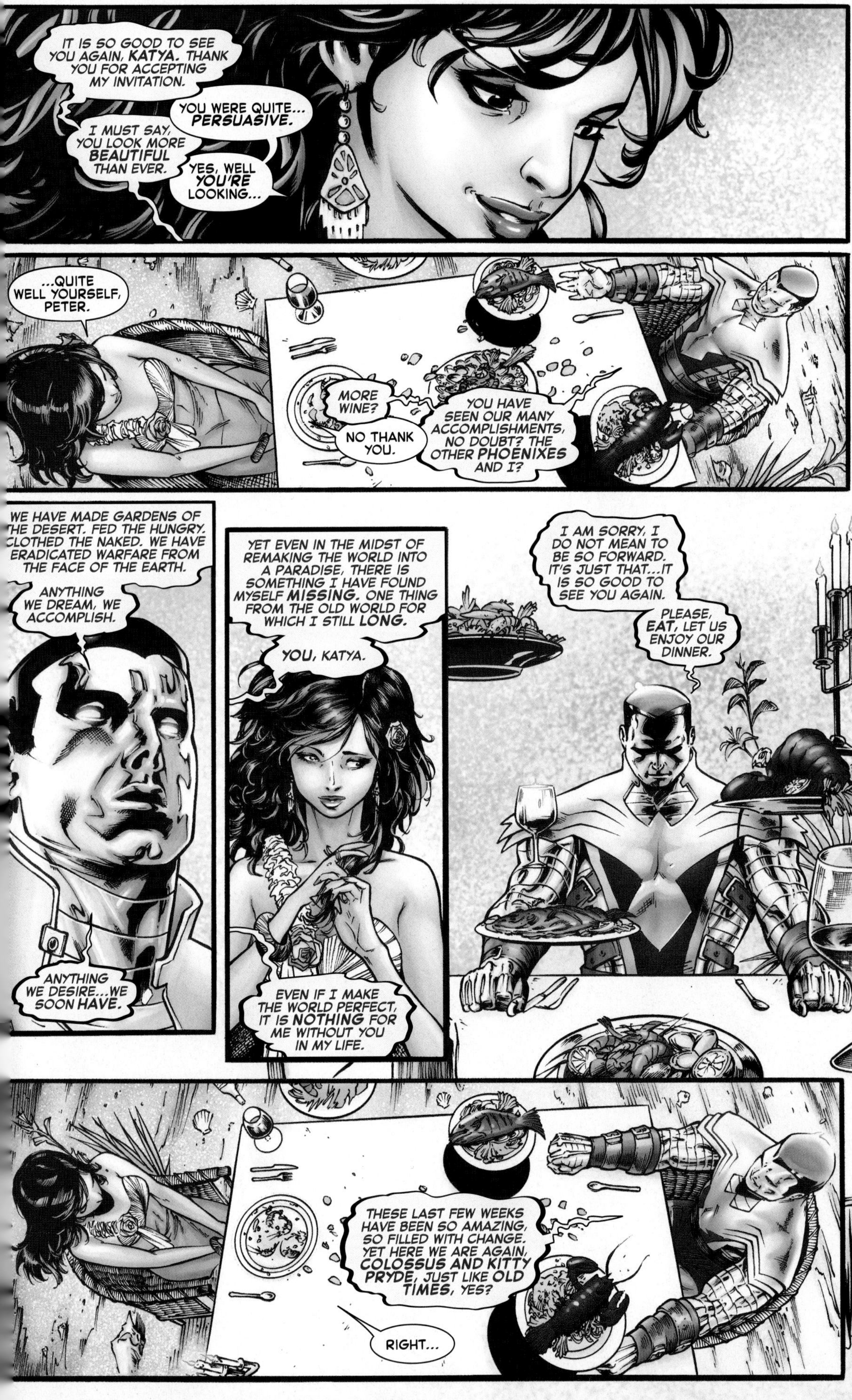
IT IS SO GOOD TO SEE YOU AGAIN, KATYA. THANK YOU FOR ACCEPTING MY INVITATION.
YOU WERE QUITE... PERSUASIVE.
I MUST SAY, YOU LOOK MORE BEAUTIFUL THAN EVER.
YES, WELL YOU'RE LOOKING...
...QUITE WELL YOURSELF, PETER.
MORE WINE?
NO THANK YOU.
YOU HAVE SEEN OUR MANY ACCOMPLISHMENTS, NO DOUBT? THE OTHER PHOENIXES AND I?
WE HAVE MADE GARDENS OF THE DESERT. FED THE HUNGRY. CLOTHED THE NAKED. WE HAVE ERADICATED WARFARE FROM THE FACE OF THE EARTH.
ANYTHING WE DREAM, WE ACCOMPLISH.
ANYTHING WE DESIRE...WE SOON HAVE.
YET EVEN IN THE MIDST OF REMAKING THE WORLD INTO A PARADISE, THERE IS SOMETHING I HAVE FOUND MYSELF MISSING. ONE THING FROM THE OLD WORLD FOR WHICH I STILL LONG.
YOU, KATYA.
EVEN IF I MAKE THE WORLD PERFECT, IT IS NOTHING FOR ME WITHOUT YOU IN MY LIFE.
I AM SORRY, I DO NOT MEAN TO BE SO FORWARD. IT'S JUST THAT...IT IS SO GOOD TO SEE YOU AGAIN.
PLEASE, EAT, LET US ENJOY OUR DINNER.
THESE LAST FEW WEEKS HAVE BEEN SO AMAZING, SO FILLED WITH CHANGE. YET HERE WE ARE AGAIN, COLOSSUS AND KITTY PRYDE, JUST LIKE OLD TIMES, YES?
RIGHT...

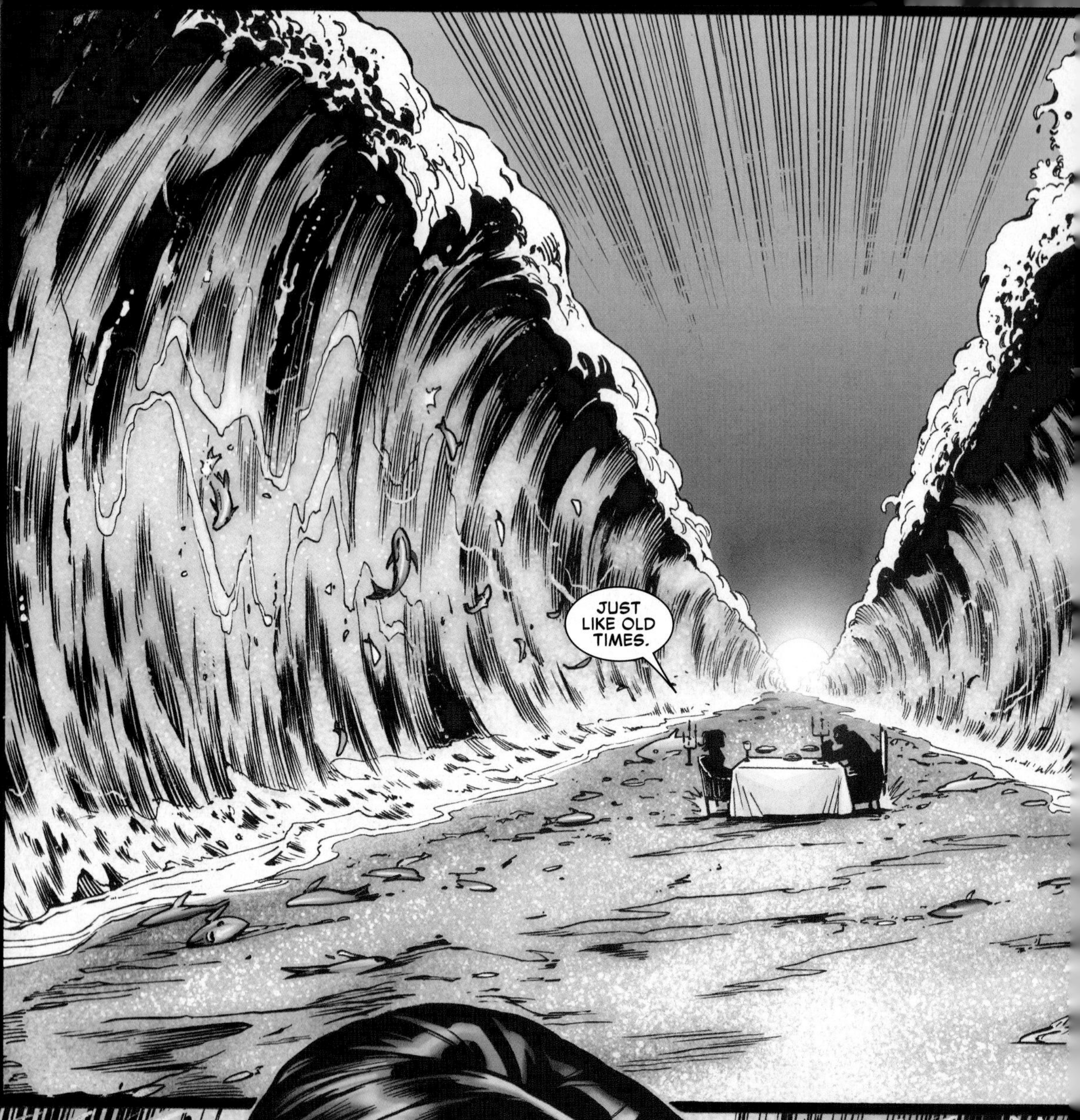
JUST LIKE OLD TIMES.

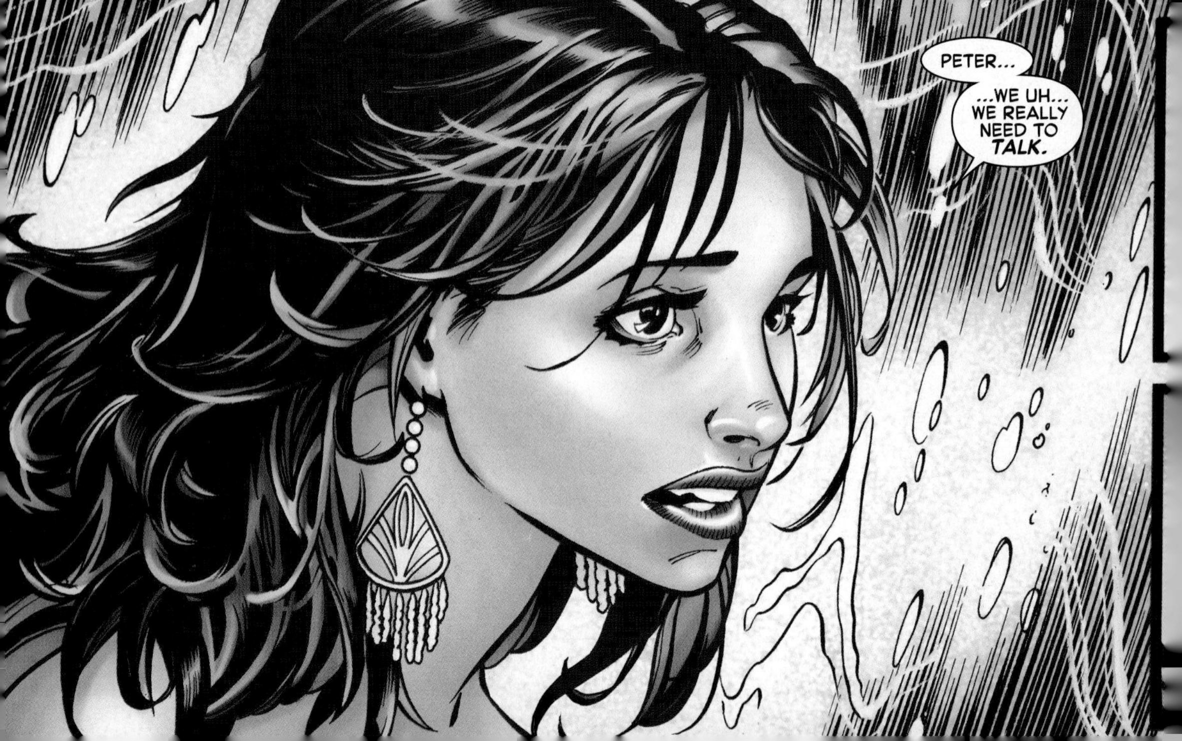
PETER...
...WE UH... WE REALLY NEED TO TALK.

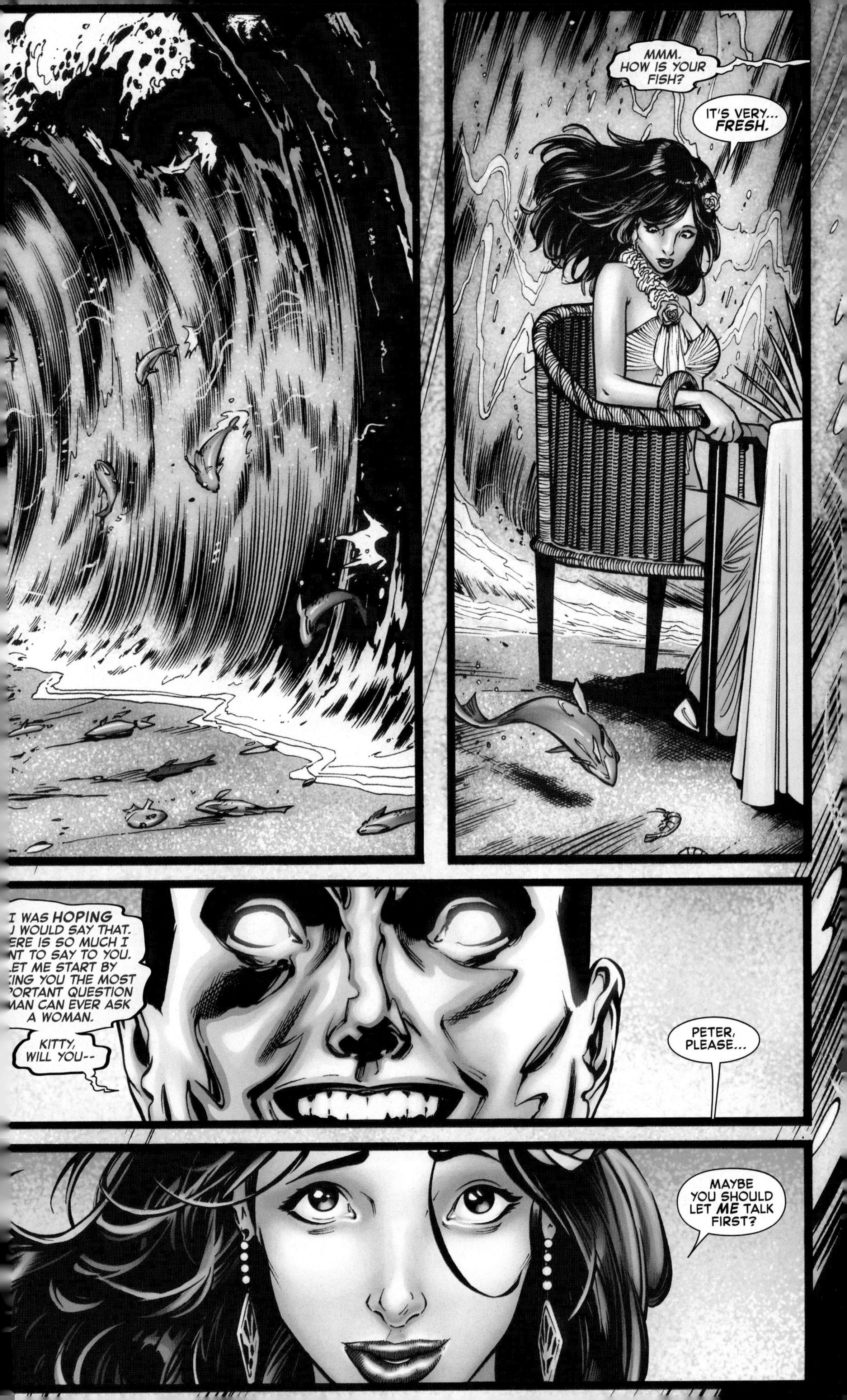
MMM. HOW IS YOUR FISH?
IT'S VERY... FRESH.
I WAS HOPING
U WOULD SAY THAT.
ERE IS SO MUCH I
NT TO SAY TO YOU.
LET ME START BY
KING YOU THE MOST
PORTANT QUESTION
MAN CAN EVER ASK
A WOMAN.
KITTY, WILL YOU--
PETER, PLEASE...
MAYBE YOU SHOULD LET ME TALK FIRST?

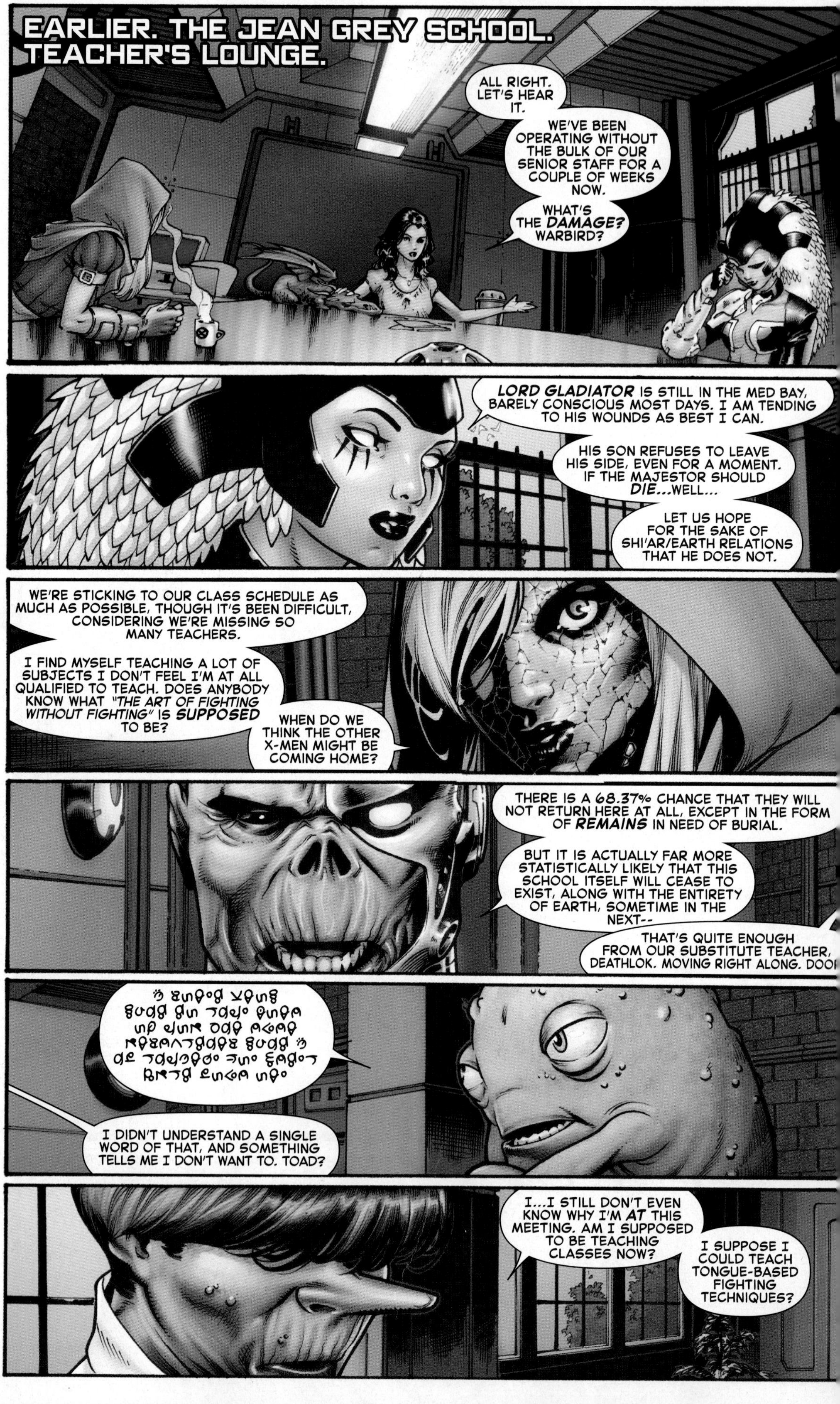
EARLIER. THE JEAN GREY SCHOOL. TEACHER'S LOUNGE.
ALL RIGHT. LET'S HEAR IT.
WE'VE BEEN OPERATING WITHOUT THE BULK OF OUR SENIOR STAFF FOR A COUPLE OF WEEKS NOW.
WHAT'S THE DAMAGE? WARBIRD?
LORD GLADIATOR IS STILL IN THE MED BAY, BARELY CONSCIOUS MOST DAYS. I AM TENDING TO HIS WOUNDS AS BEST I CAN.
HIS SON REFUSES TO LEAVE HIS SIDE, EVEN FOR A MOMENT. IF THE MAJESTOR SHOULD DIE...WELL...
LET US HOPE FOR THE SAKE OF SHI'AR/EARTH RELATIONS THAT HE DOES NOT.
WE'RE STICKING TO OUR CLASS SCHEDULE AS MUCH AS POSSIBLE, THOUGH IT'S BEEN DIFFICULT, CONSIDERING WE'RE MISSING SO MANY TEACHERS.
I FIND MYSELF TEACHING A LOT OF SUBJECTS I DON'T FEEL I'M AT ALL QUALIFIED TO TEACH. DOES ANYBODY KNOW WHAT "THE ART OF FIGHTING WITHOUT FIGHTING" IS SUPPOSED TO BE?
WHEN DO WE THINK THE OTHER X-MEN MIGHT BE COMING HOME?
THERE IS A 68.37% CHANCE THAT THEY WILL NOT RETURN HERE AT ALL, EXCEPT IN THE FORM OF REMAINS IN NEED OF BURIAL.
BUT IT IS ACTUALLY FAR MORE STATISTICALLY LIKELY THAT THIS SCHOOL ITSELF WILL CEASE TO EXIST, ALONG WITH THE ENTIRETY OF EARTH, SOMETIME IN THE NEXT--
THAT'S QUITE ENOUGH FROM OUR SUBSTITUTE TEACHER, DEATHLOK. MOVING RIGHT ALONG. DOO
I DIDN'T UNDERSTAND A SINGLE WORD OF THAT, AND SOMETHING TELLS ME I DON'T WANT TO. TOAD?
I...I STILL DON'T EVEN KNOW WHY I'M AT THIS MEETING. AM I SUPPOSED TO BE TEACHING CLASSES NOW?
I SUPPOSE I COULD TEACH TONGUE-BASED FIGHTING TECHNIQUES?

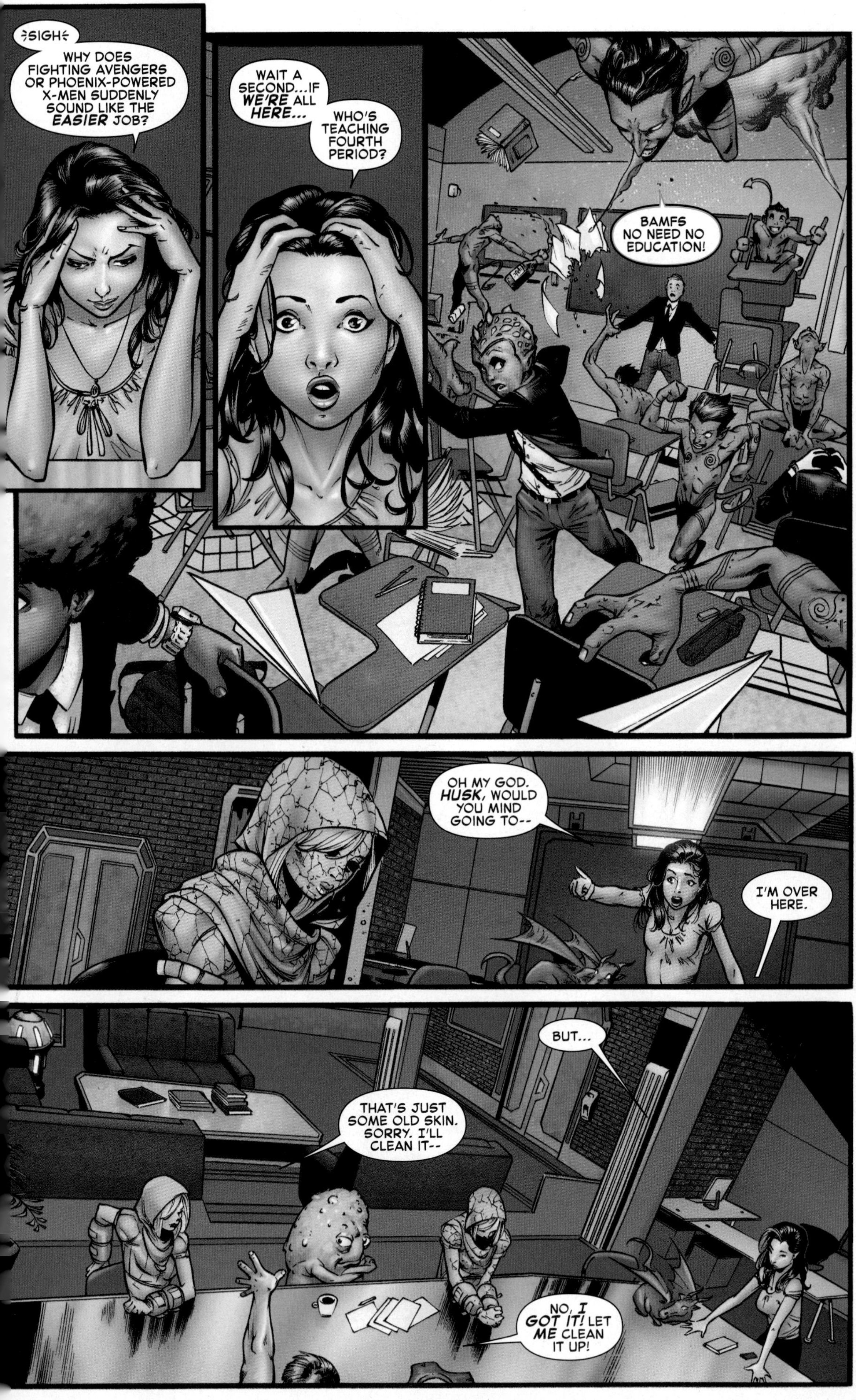

⁼SIGH⁼
WHY DOES FIGHTING AVENGERS OR PHOENIX-POWERED X-MEN SUDDENLY SOUND LIKE THE EASIER JOB?
WAIT A SECOND...IF WE'RE ALL HERE...
WHO'S TEACHING FOURTH PERIOD?
BAMFS NO NEED NO EDUCATION!
OH MY GOD. HUSK, WOULD YOU MIND GOING TO--
I'M OVER HERE.
BUT...
THAT'S JUST SOME OLD SKIN. SORRY. I'LL CLEAN IT--
NO, I GOT IT! LET ME CLEAN IT UP!

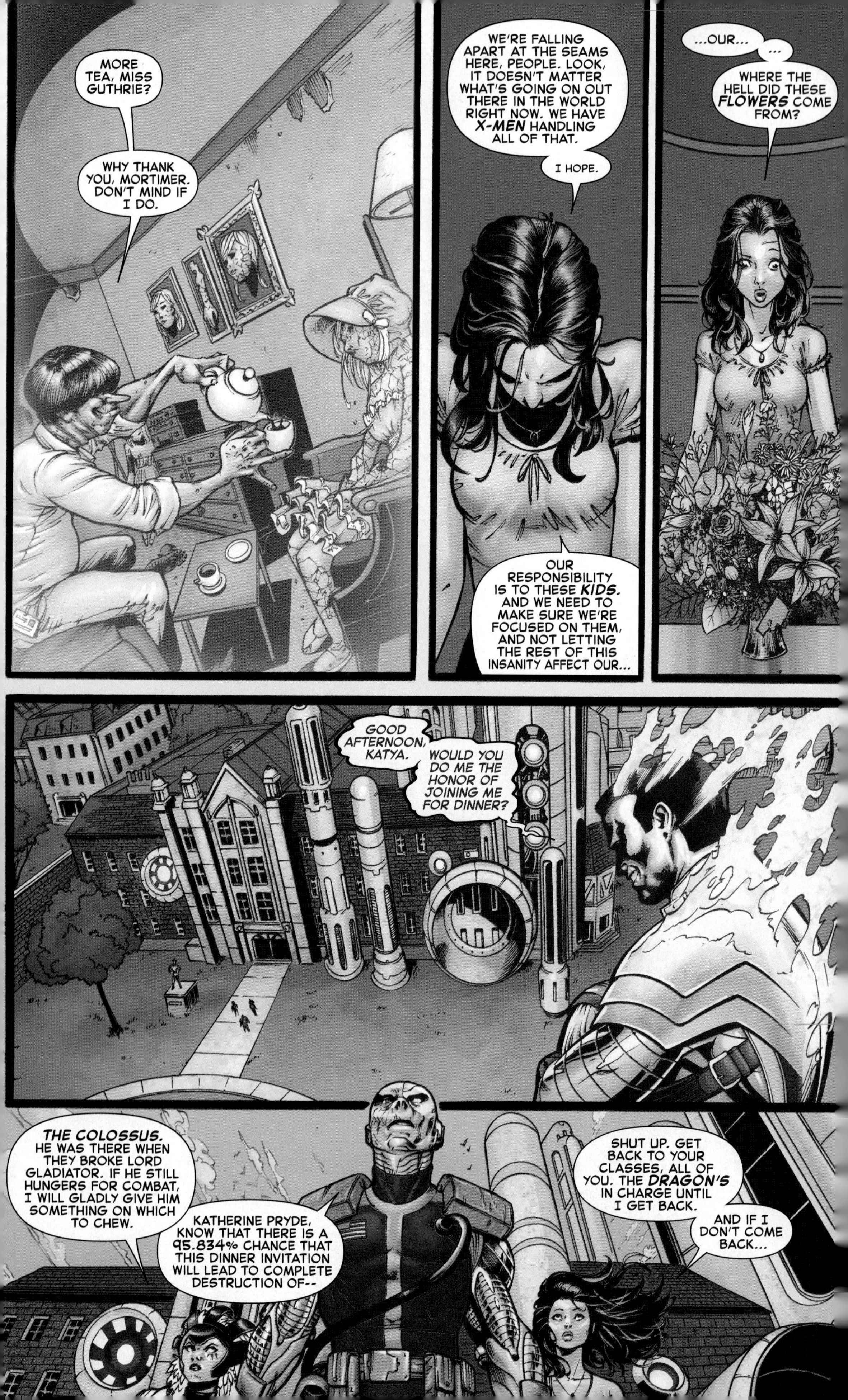
MORE TEA, MISS GUTHRIE?
WHY THANK YOU, MORTIMER. DON'T MIND IF I DO.
WE'RE FALLING APART AT THE SEAMS HERE, PEOPLE. LOOK, IT DOESN'T MATTER WHAT'S GOING ON OUT THERE IN THE WORLD RIGHT NOW. WE HAVE X-MEN HANDLING ALL OF THAT.
I HOPE.
OUR RESPONSIBILITY IS TO THESE KIDS. AND WE NEED TO MAKE SURE WE'RE FOCUSED ON THEM, AND NOT LETTING THE REST OF THIS INSANITY AFFECT OUR...
...OUR...
...
WHERE THE HELL DID THESE FLOWERS COME FROM?
GOOD AFTERNOON, KATYA.
WOULD YOU DO ME THE HONOR OF JOINING ME FOR DINNER?
THE COLOSSUS. HE WAS THERE WHEN THEY BROKE LORD GLADIATOR. IF HE STILL HUNGERS FOR COMBAT, I WILL GLADLY GIVE HIM SOMETHING ON WHICH TO CHEW.
KATHERINE PRYDE, KNOW THAT THERE IS A 95.834% CHANCE THAT THIS DINNER INVITATION WILL LEAD TO COMPLETE DESTRUCTION OF--
SHUT UP. GET BACK TO YOUR CLASSES, ALL OF YOU. THE DRAGON'S IN CHARGE UNTIL I GET BACK.
AND IF I DON'T COME BACK...

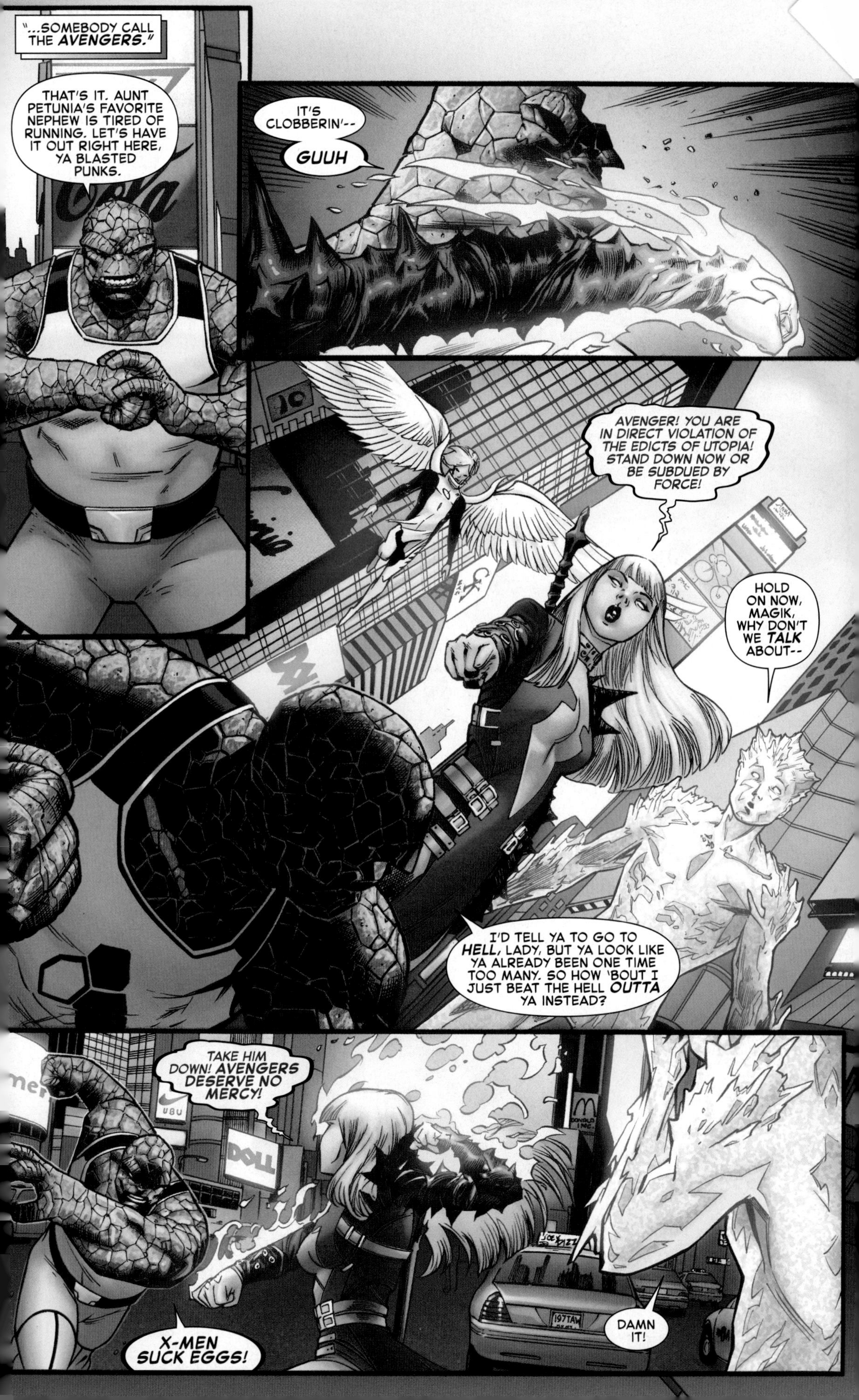
"...SOMEBODY CALL THE AVENGERS."
THAT'S IT. AUNT PETUNIA'S FAVORITE NEPHEW IS TIRED OF RUNNING. LET'S HAVE IT OUT RIGHT HERE, YA BLASTED PUNKS.
IT'S CLOBBERIN'--
GUUH
AVENGER! YOU ARE IN DIRECT VIOLATION OF THE EDICTS OF UTOPIA! STAND DOWN NOW OR BE SUBDUED BY FORCE!
HOLD ON NOW, MAGIK, WHY DON'T WE TALK ABOUT--
I'D TELL YA TO GO TO HELL, LADY, BUT YA LOOK LIKE YA ALREADY BEEN ONE TIME TOO MANY. SO HOW 'BOUT I JUST BEAT THE HELL OUTTA YA INSTEAD?
TAKE HIM DOWN! AVENGERS DESERVE NO MERCY!
X-MEN SUCK EGGS!
DAMN IT!

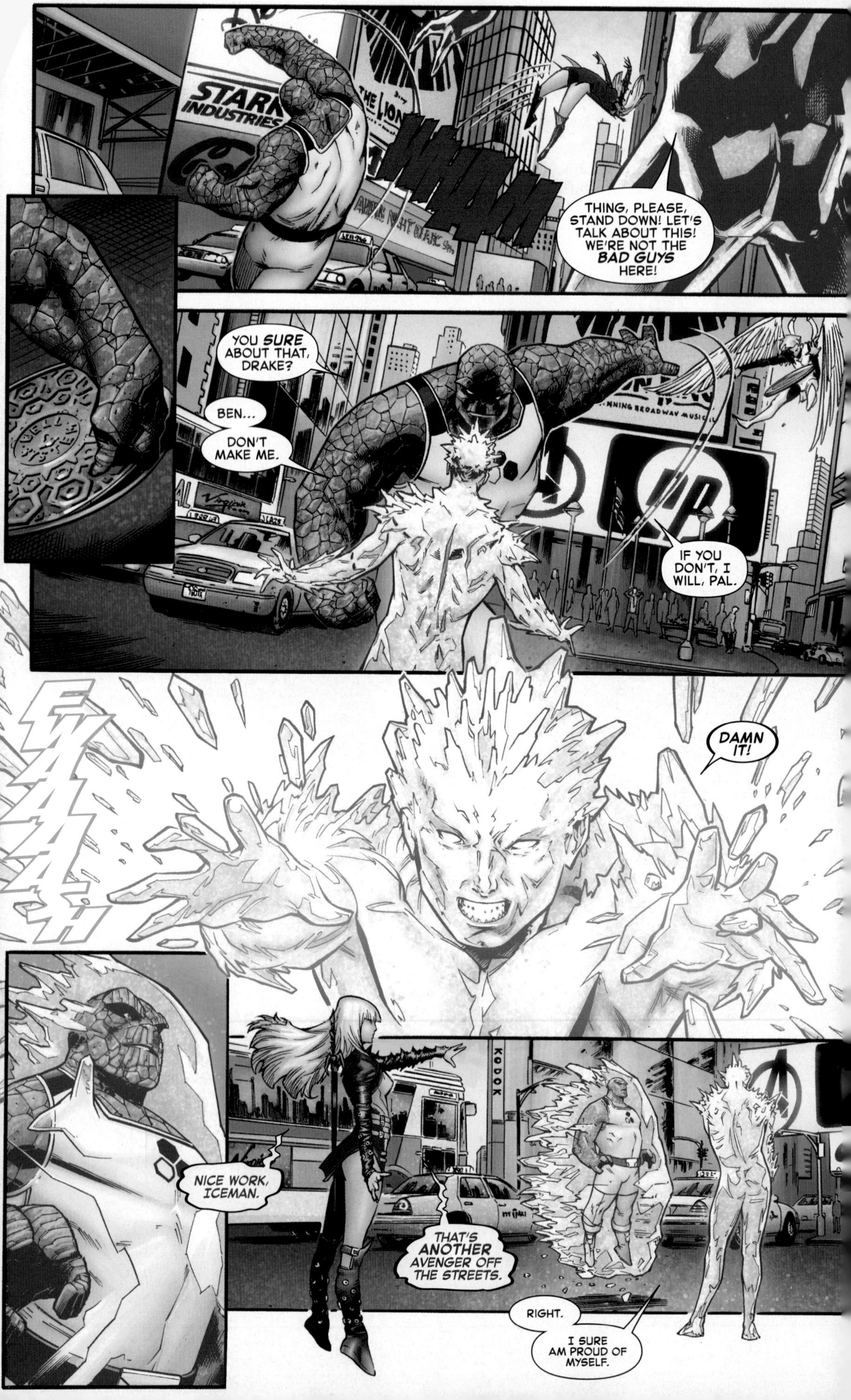

STARK INDUSTRIES
WHAM
THING, PLEASE, STAND DOWN! LET'S TALK ABOUT THIS! WE'RE NOT THE BAD GUYS HERE!
YOU SURE ABOUT THAT, DRAKE?
BEN...
DON'T MAKE ME.
IF YOU DON'T, I WILL, PAL.
FWAAAAH
DAMN IT!
KODOK
NICE WORK, ICEMAN.
THAT'S ANOTHER AVENGER OFF THE STREETS.
RIGHT.
I SURE AM PROUD OF MYSELF.

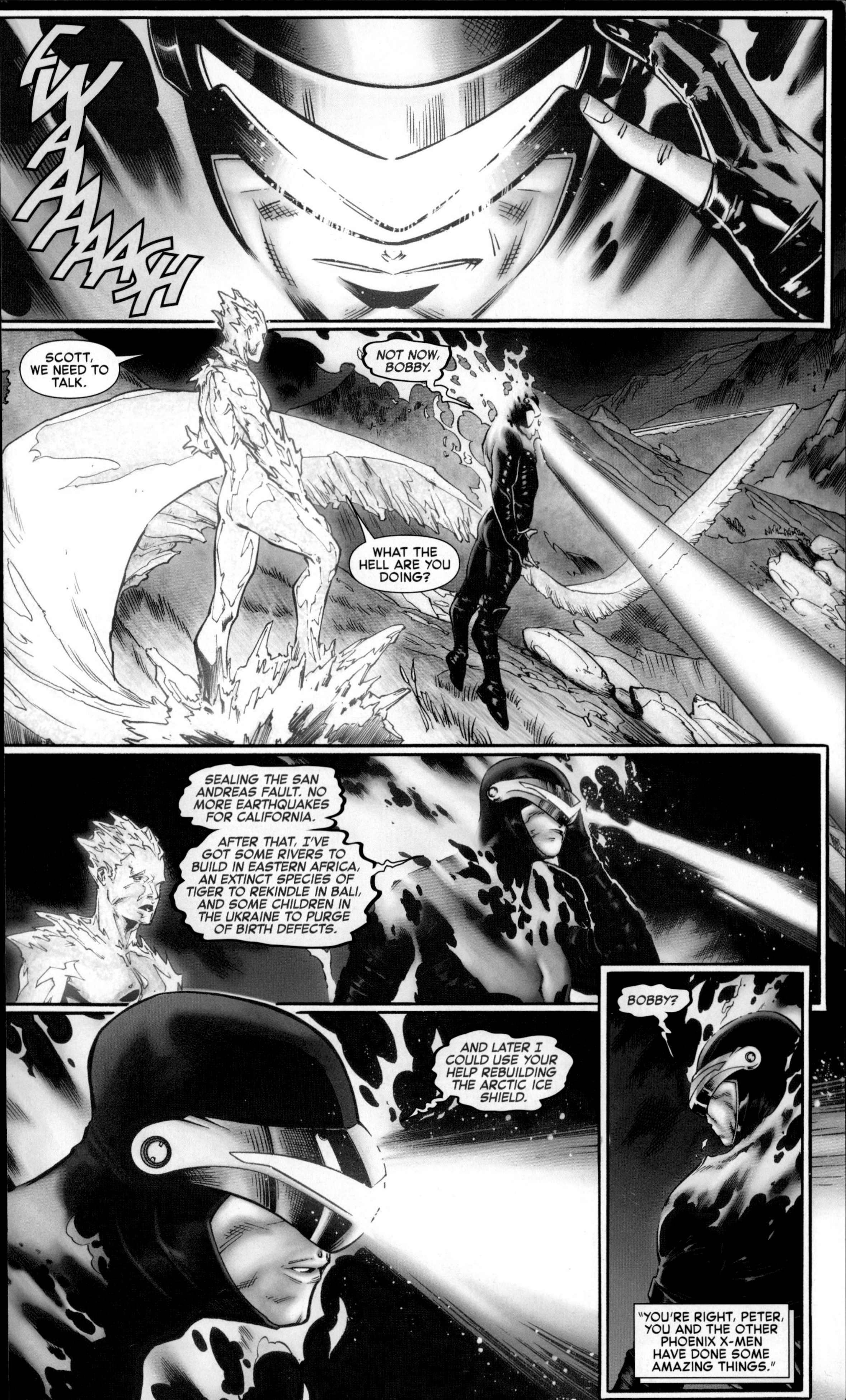
FWAAAAACH
SCOTT, WE NEED TO TALK.
NOT NOW, BOBBY.
WHAT THE HELL ARE YOU DOING?
SEALING THE SAN ANDREAS FAULT. NO MORE EARTHQUAKES FOR CALIFORNIA.
AFTER THAT, I'VE GOT SOME RIVERS TO BUILD IN EASTERN AFRICA, AN EXTINCT SPECIES OF TIGER TO REKINDLE IN BALI, AND SOME CHILDREN IN THE UKRAINE TO PURGE OF BIRTH DEFECTS.
AND LATER I COULD USE YOUR HELP REBUILDING THE ARCTIC ICE SHIELD.
BOBBY?
"YOU'RE RIGHT, PETER, YOU AND THE OTHER PHOENIX X-MEN HAVE DONE SOME AMAZING THINGS."

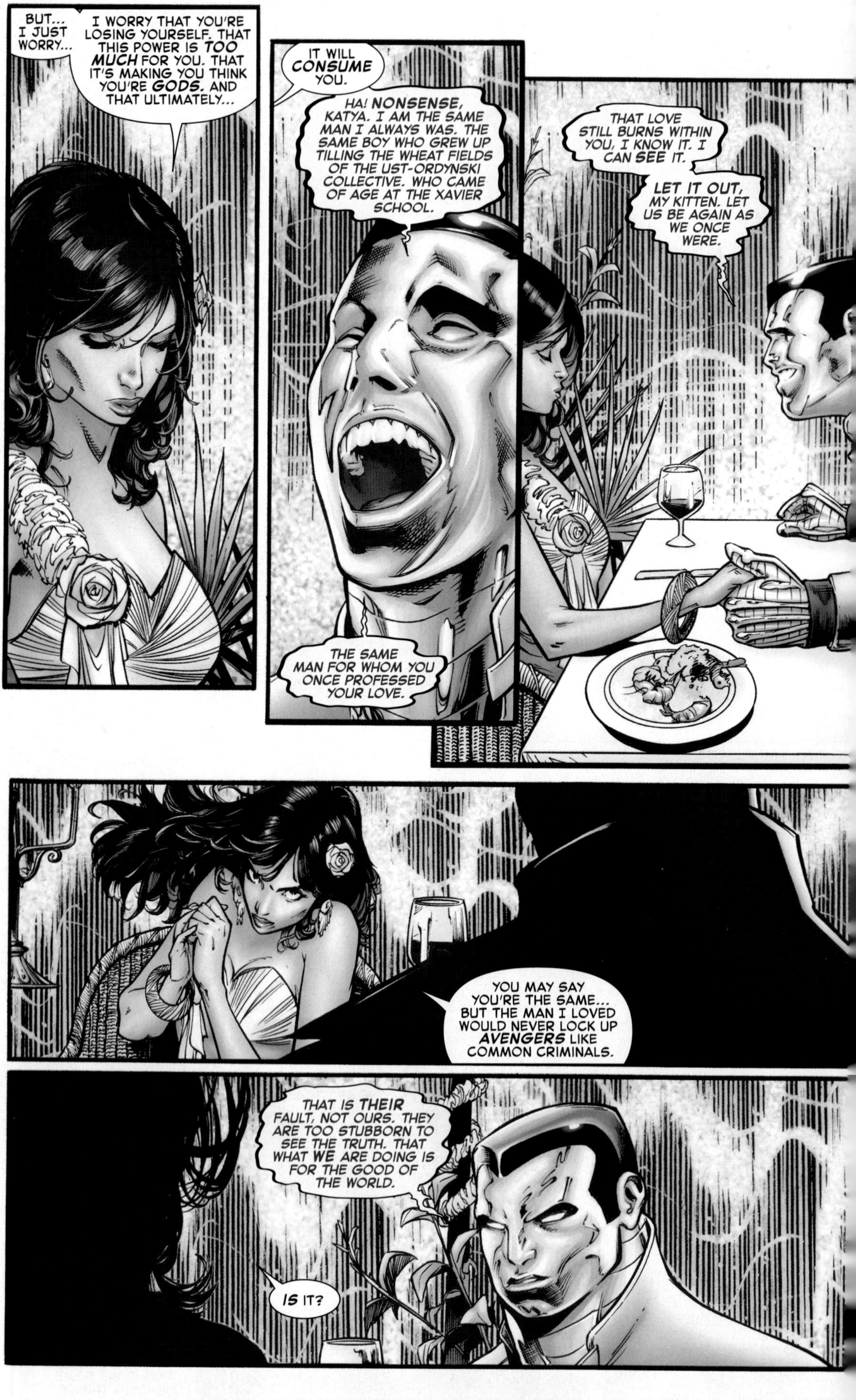
BUT... I JUST WORRY...
I WORRY THAT YOU'RE LOSING YOURSELF. THAT THIS POWER IS TOO MUCH FOR YOU. THAT IT'S MAKING YOU THINK YOU'RE GODS. AND THAT ULTIMATELY...
IT WILL CONSUME YOU.
HA! NONSENSE, KATYA. I AM THE SAME MAN I ALWAYS WAS. THE SAME BOY WHO GREW UP TILLING THE WHEAT FIELDS OF THE UST-ORDYNSKI COLLECTIVE. WHO CAME OF AGE AT THE XAVIER SCHOOL.
THE SAME MAN FOR WHOM YOU ONCE PROFESSED YOUR LOVE.
THAT LOVE STILL BURNS WITHIN YOU, I KNOW IT. I CAN SEE IT.
LET IT OUT, MY KITTEN. LET US BE AGAIN AS WE ONCE WERE.
YOU MAY SAY YOU'RE THE SAME... BUT THE MAN I LOVED WOULD NEVER LOCK UP AVENGERS LIKE COMMON CRIMINALS.
THAT IS THEIR FAULT, NOT OURS. THEY ARE TOO STUBBORN TO SEE THE TRUTH. THAT WHAT WE ARE DOING IS FOR THE GOOD OF THE WORLD.
IS IT?

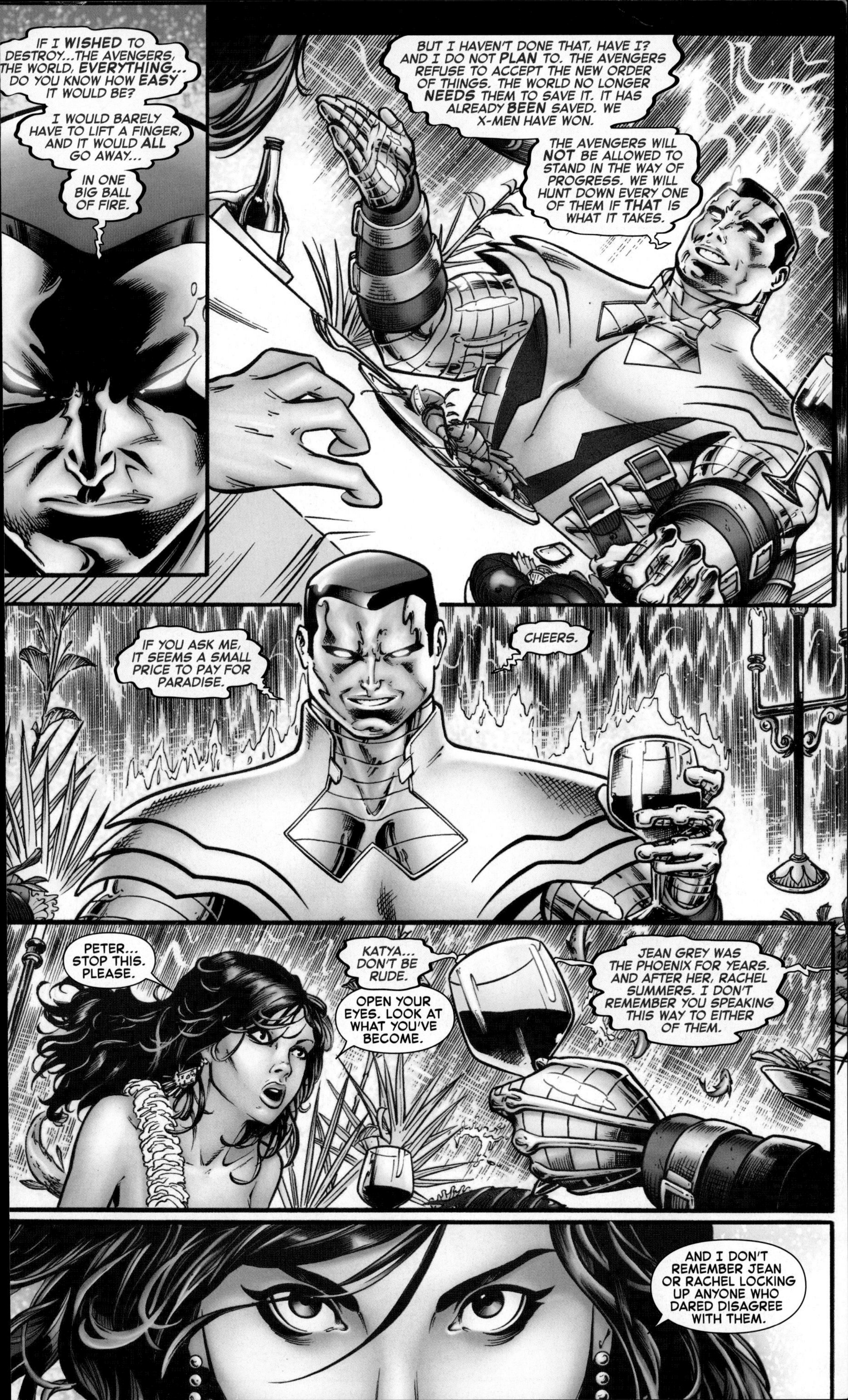
IF I WISHED TO DESTROY...THE AVENGERS, THE WORLD, EVERYTHING... DO YOU KNOW HOW EASY IT WOULD BE?
I WOULD BARELY HAVE TO LIFT A FINGER, AND IT WOULD ALL GO AWAY...
IN ONE BIG BALL OF FIRE.
BUT I HAVEN'T DONE THAT, HAVE I? AND I DO NOT PLAN TO. THE AVENGERS REFUSE TO ACCEPT THE NEW ORDER OF THINGS. THE WORLD NO LONGER NEEDS THEM TO SAVE IT. IT HAS ALREADY BEEN SAVED. WE X-MEN HAVE WON.
THE AVENGERS WILL NOT BE ALLOWED TO STAND IN THE WAY OF PROGRESS. WE WILL HUNT DOWN EVERY ONE OF THEM IF THAT IS WHAT IT TAKES.
IF YOU ASK ME, IT SEEMS A SMALL PRICE TO PAY FOR PARADISE.
CHEERS.
PETER... STOP THIS. PLEASE.
KATYA... DON'T BE RUDE.
OPEN YOUR EYES. LOOK AT WHAT YOU'VE BECOME.
JEAN GREY WAS THE PHOENIX FOR YEARS. AND AFTER HER, RACHEL SUMMERS. I DON'T REMEMBER YOU SPEAKING THIS WAY TO EITHER OF THEM.
AND I DON'T REMEMBER JEAN OR RACHEL LOCKING UP ANYONE WHO DARED DISAGREE WITH THEM.

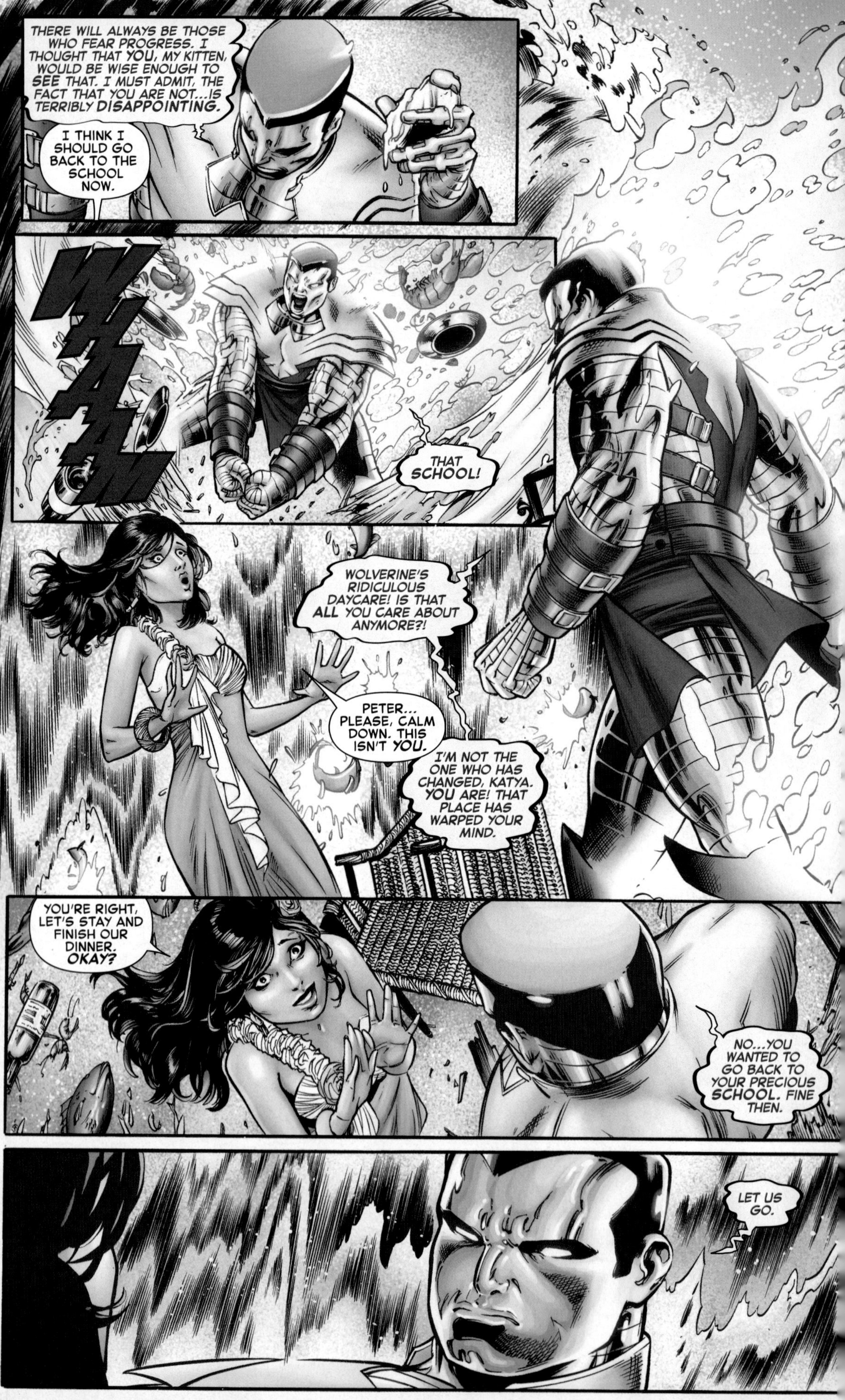

THERE WILL ALWAYS BE THOSE WHO FEAR PROGRESS. I THOUGHT THAT YOU, MY KITTEN, WOULD BE WISE ENOUGH TO SEE THAT. I MUST ADMIT, THE FACT THAT YOU ARE NOT...IS TERRIBLY DISAPPOINTING.
I THINK I SHOULD GO BACK TO THE SCHOOL NOW.
WHAM
THAT SCHOOL!
WOLVERINE'S RIDICULOUS DAYCARE! IS THAT ALL YOU CARE ABOUT ANYMORE?!
PETER... PLEASE, CALM DOWN. THIS ISN'T YOU.
I'M NOT THE ONE WHO HAS CHANGED, KATYA. YOU ARE! THAT PLACE HAS WARPED YOUR MIND.
YOU'RE RIGHT, LET'S STAY AND FINISH OUR DINNER. OKAY?
NO...YOU WANTED TO GO BACK TO YOUR PRECIOUS SCHOOL. FINE THEN.
LET US GO.

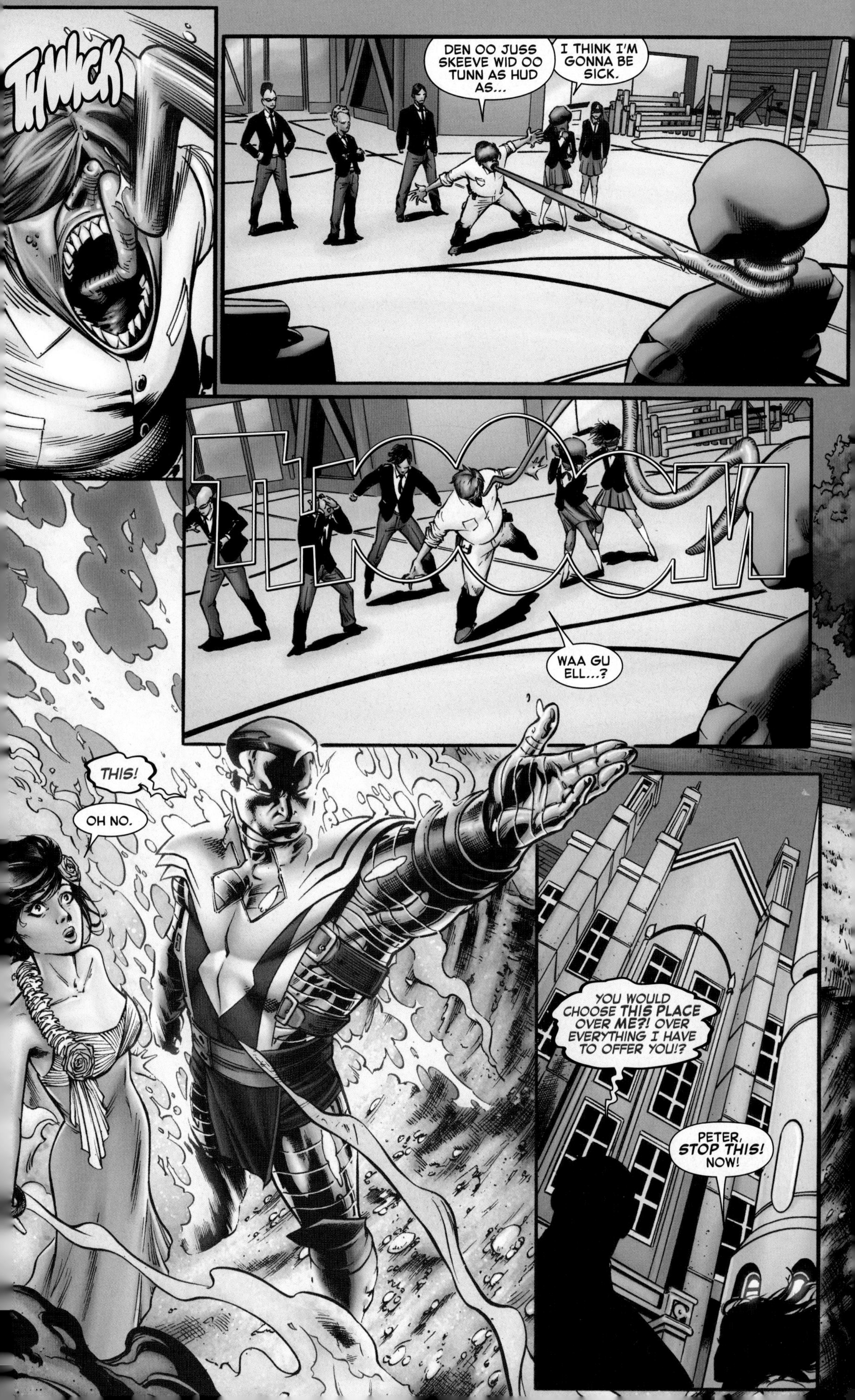
THWICK
DEN OO JUSS SKEEVE WID OO TUNN AS HUD AS...
I THINK I'M GONNA BE SICK.
THOOOM
WAA GU ELL...?
THIS!
OH NO.
YOU WOULD CHOOSE THIS PLACE OVER ME?! OVER EVERYTHING I HAVE TO OFFER YOU!?
PETER, STOP THIS! NOW!

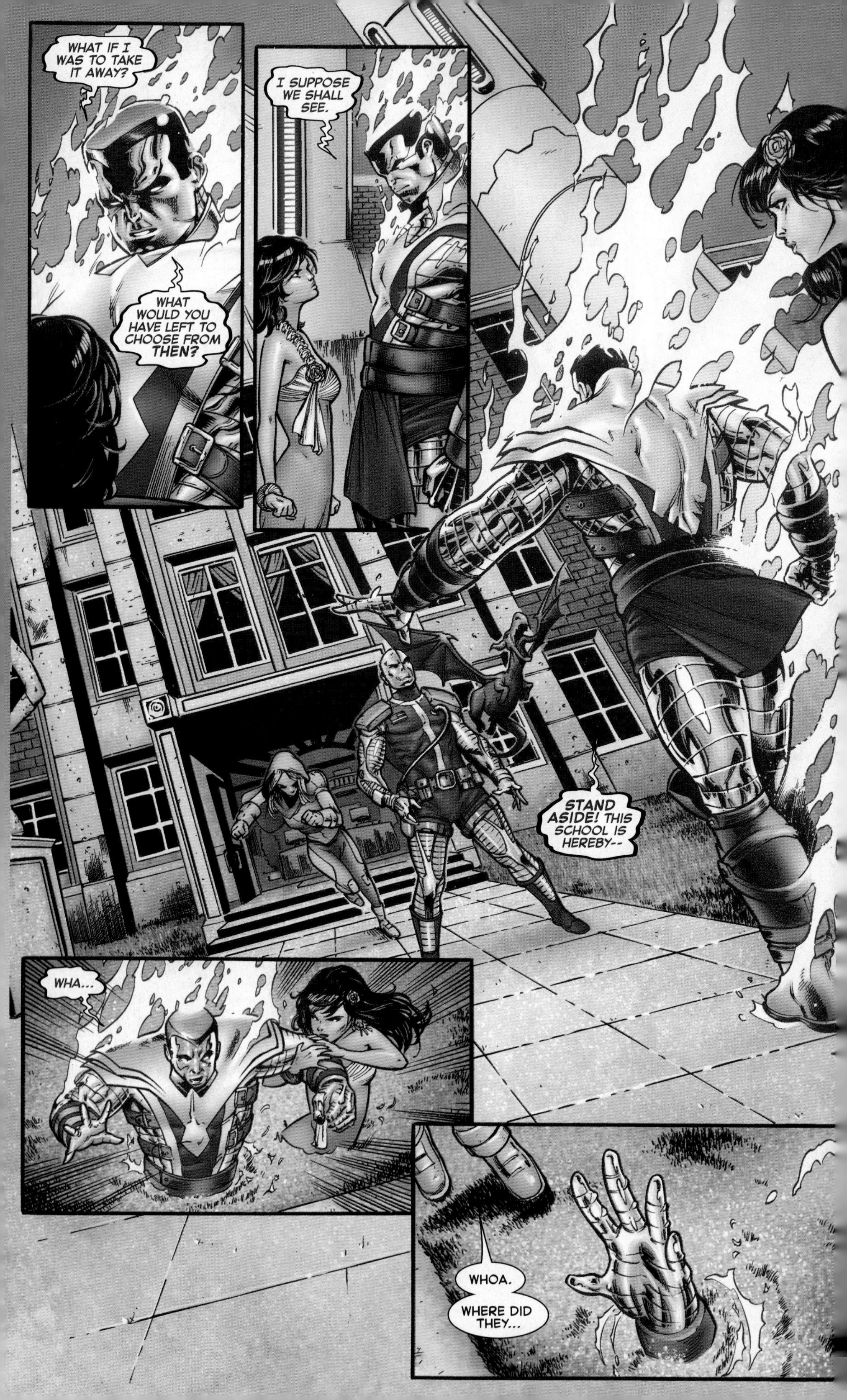
WHAT IF I WAS TO TAKE IT AWAY?
WHAT WOULD YOU HAVE LEFT TO CHOOSE FROM THEN?
I SUPPOSE WE SHALL SEE.
STAND ASIDE! THIS SCHOOL IS HEREBY--
WHA...
WHOA.
WHERE DID THEY...

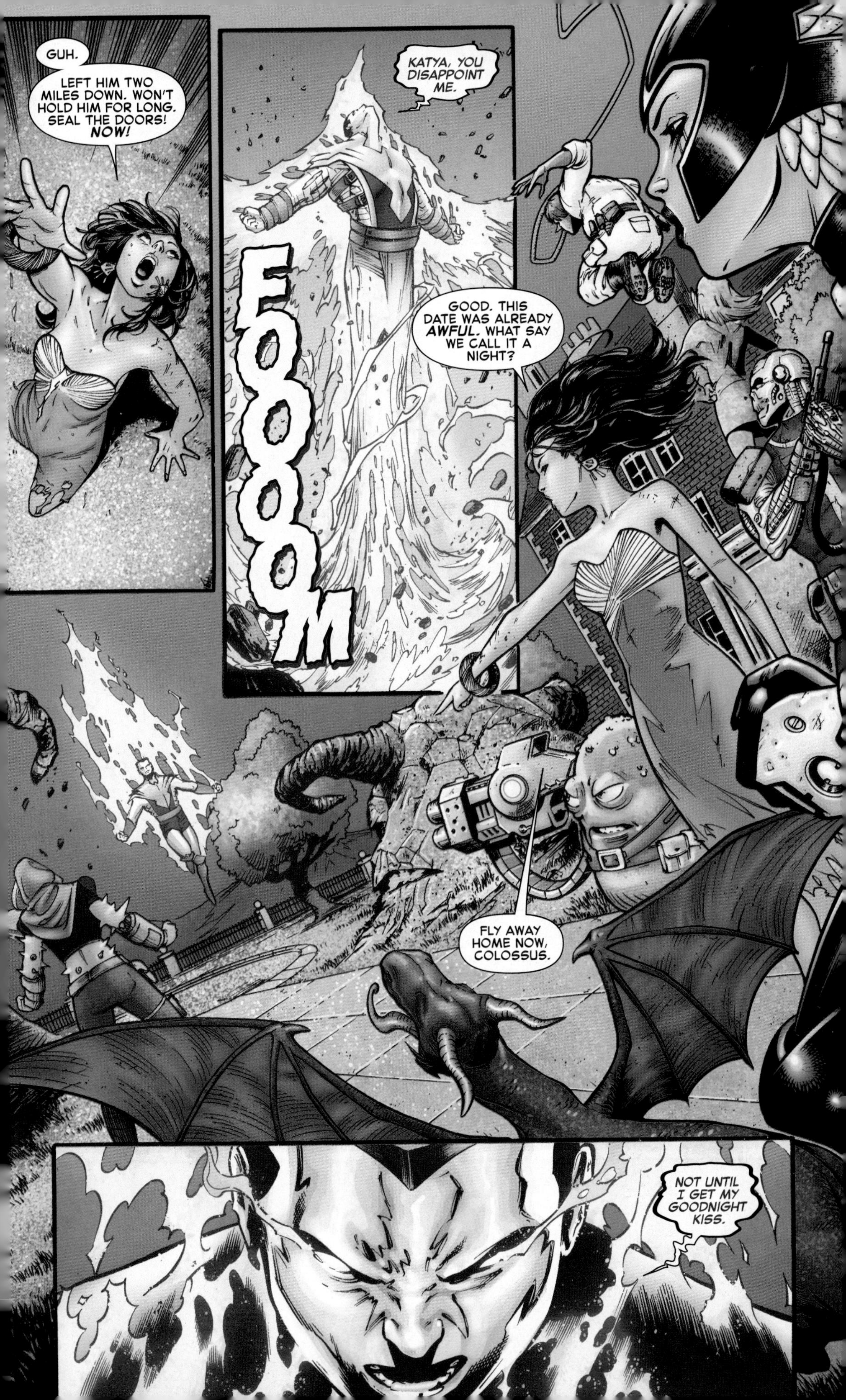
GUH.
LEFT HIM TWO MILES DOWN. WON'T HOLD HIM FOR LONG. SEAL THE DOORS! NOW!
KATYA, YOU DISAPPOINT ME.
FOOOOOM
GOOD. THIS DATE WAS ALREADY AWFUL. WHAT SAY WE CALL IT A NIGHT?
FLY AWAY HOME NOW, COLOSSUS.
NOT UNTIL I GET MY GOODNIGHT KISS.

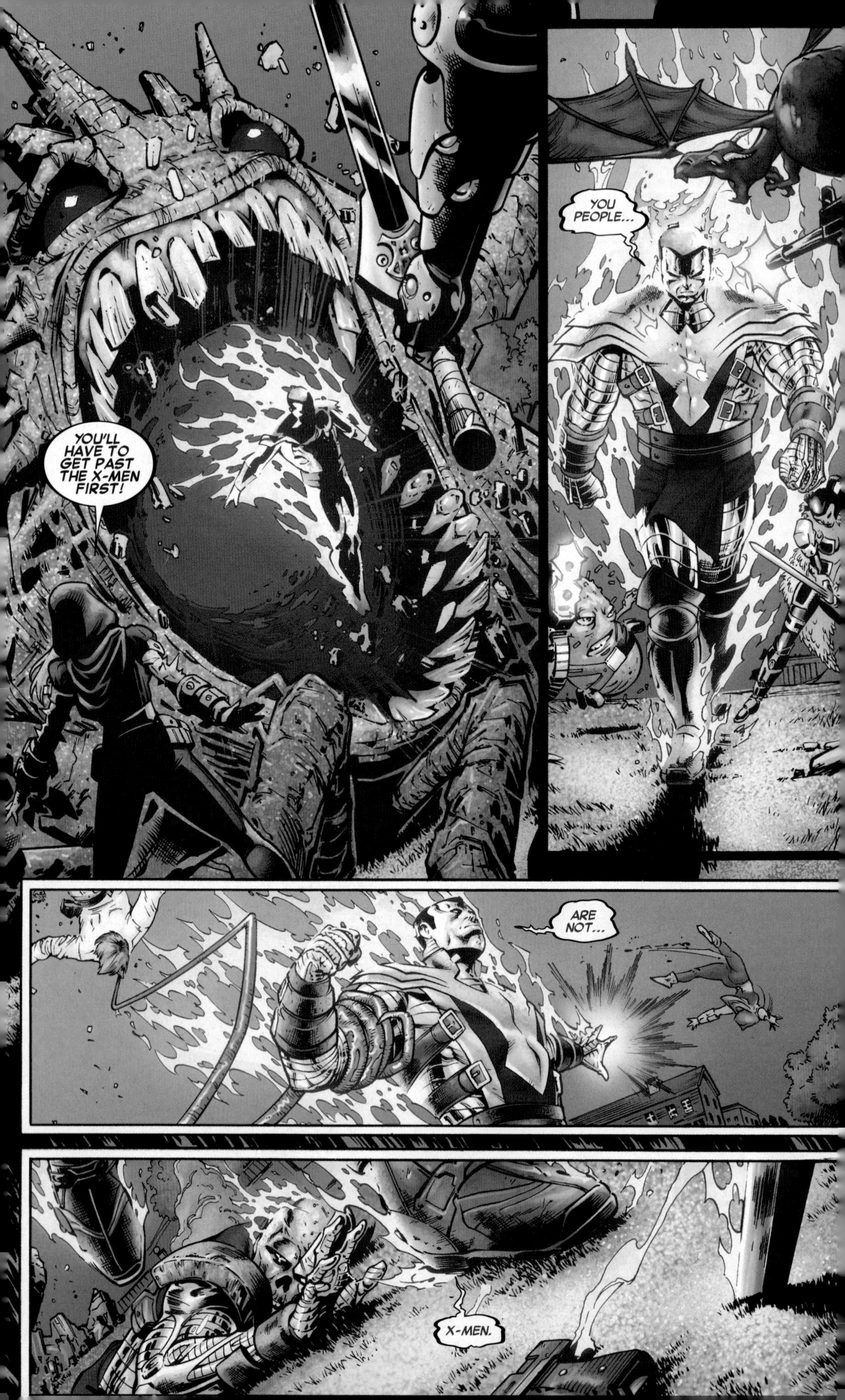
YOU'LL HAVE TO GET PAST THE X-MEN FIRST!
YOU PEOPLE...
ARE NOT...
X-MEN.

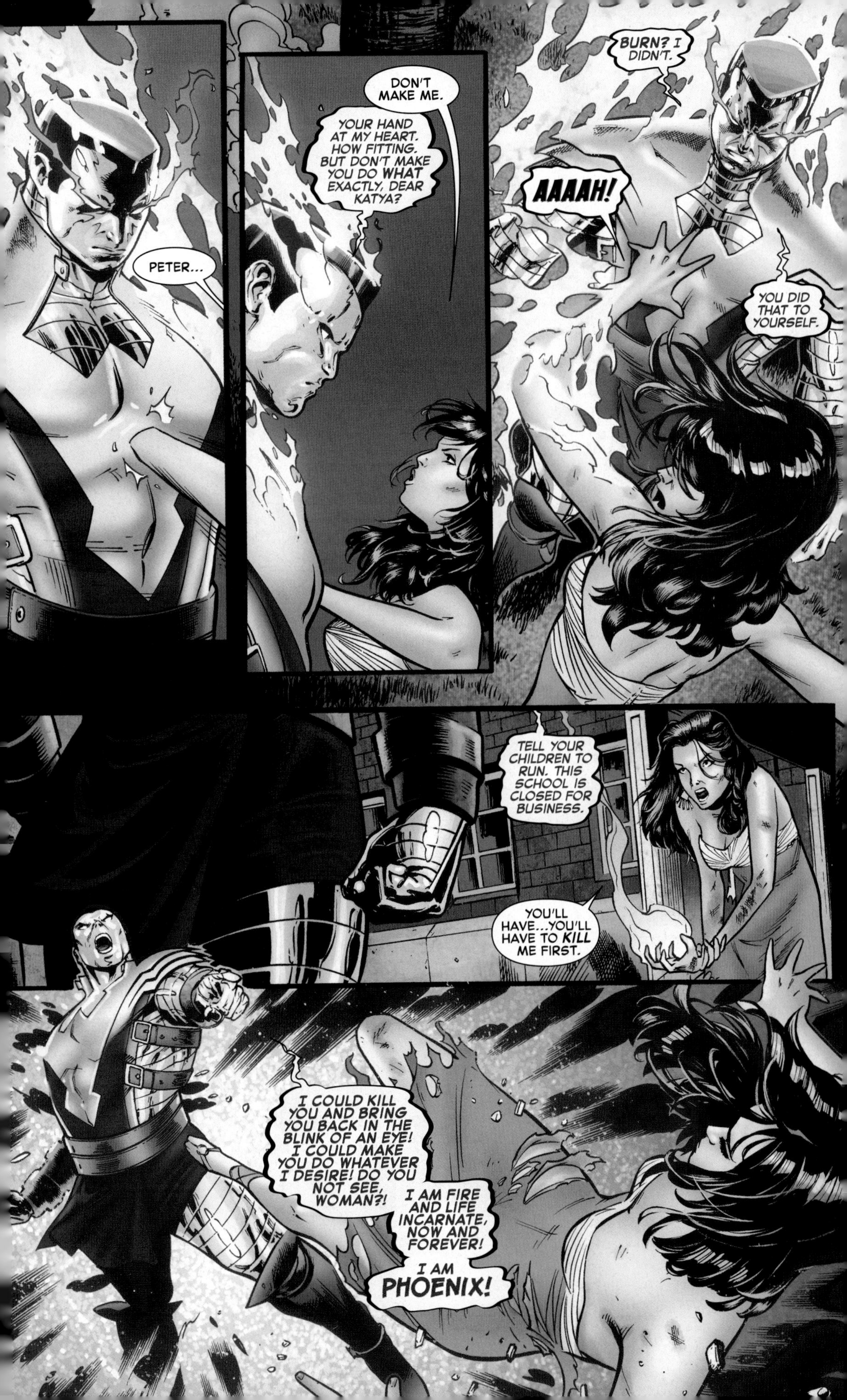
PETER...
DON'T MAKE ME.
YOUR HAND AT MY HEART. HOW FITTING. BUT DON'T MAKE YOU DO WHAT EXACTLY, DEAR KATYA?
BURN? I DIDN'T.
AAAAH!
YOU DID THAT TO YOURSELF.
TELL YOUR CHILDREN TO RUN. THIS SCHOOL IS CLOSED FOR BUSINESS.
YOU'LL HAVE...YOU'LL HAVE TO KILL ME FIRST.
I COULD KILL YOU AND BRING YOU BACK IN THE BLINK OF AN EYE! I COULD MAKE YOU DO WHATEVER I DESIRE! DO YOU NOT SEE, WOMAN?!
I AM FIRE AND LIFE INCARNATE, NOW AND FOREVER!
I AM PHOENIX!

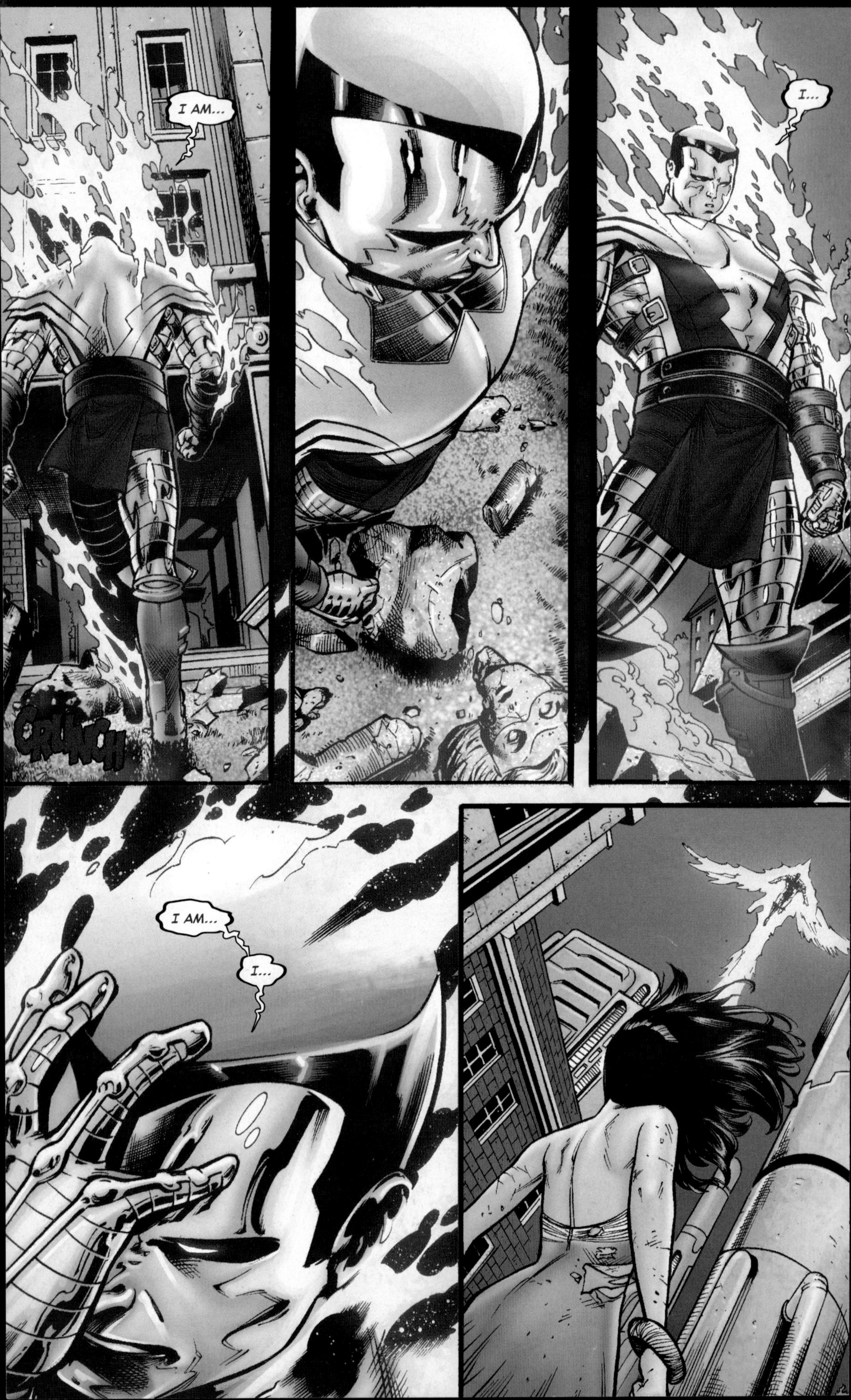

I AM...
CRUNCH
I...
I AM...
I...

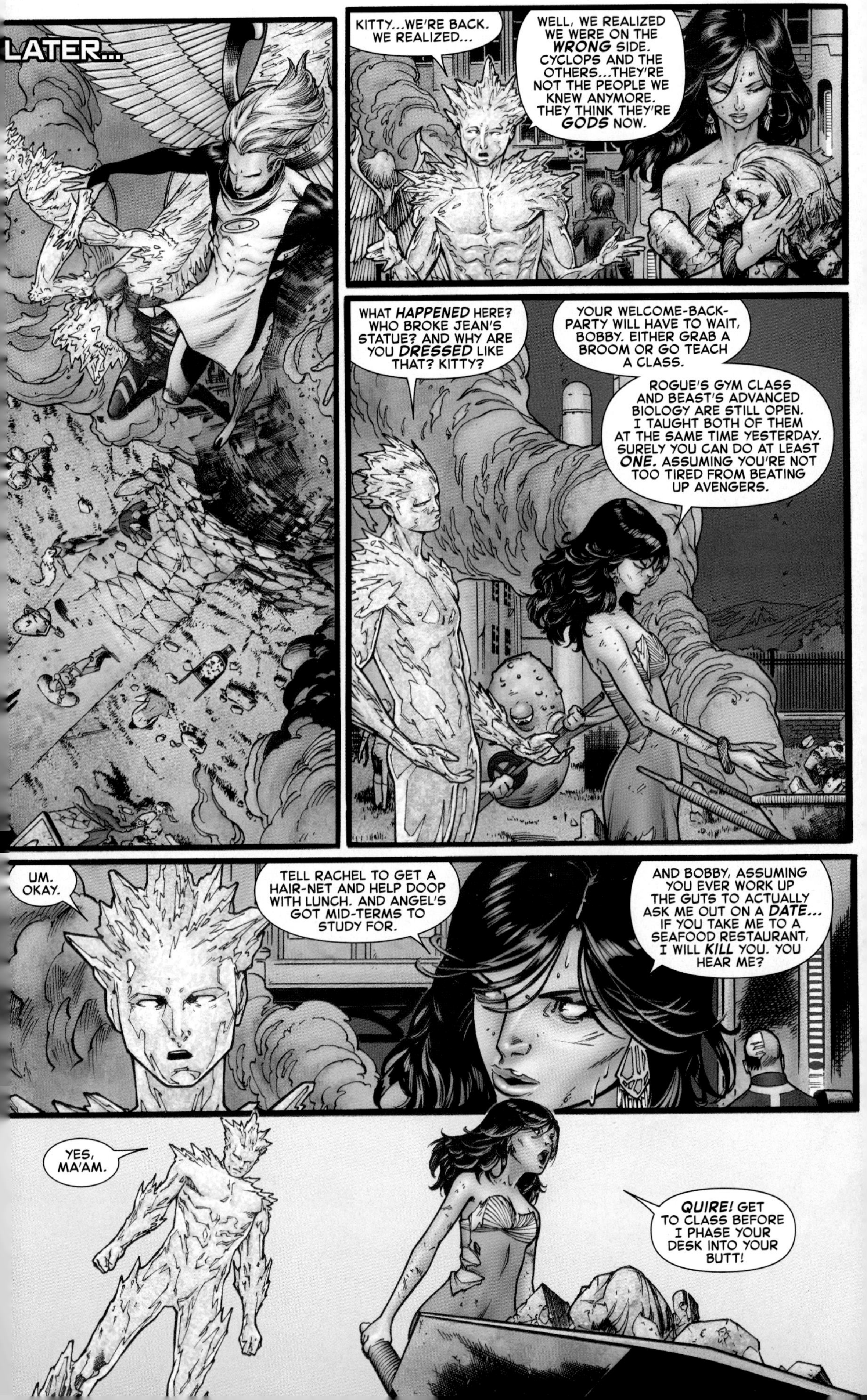
LATER...
KITTY...WE'RE BACK. WE REALIZED...
WELL, WE REALIZED WE WERE ON THE WRONG SIDE. CYCLOPS AND THE OTHERS...THEY'RE NOT THE PEOPLE WE KNEW ANYMORE. THEY THINK THEY'RE GODS NOW.
WHAT HAPPENED HERE? WHO BROKE JEAN'S STATUE? AND WHY ARE YOU DRESSED LIKE THAT? KITTY?
YOUR WELCOME-BACK-PARTY WILL HAVE TO WAIT, BOBBY. EITHER GRAB A BROOM OR GO TEACH A CLASS.
ROGUE'S GYM CLASS AND BEAST'S ADVANCED BIOLOGY ARE STILL OPEN. I TAUGHT BOTH OF THEM AT THE SAME TIME YESTERDAY. SURELY YOU CAN DO AT LEAST ONE. ASSUMING YOU'RE NOT TOO TIRED FROM BEATING UP AVENGERS.
UM. OKAY.
TELL RACHEL TO GET A HAIR-NET AND HELP DOOP WITH LUNCH. AND ANGEL'S GOT MID-TERMS TO STUDY FOR.
AND BOBBY, ASSUMING YOU EVER WORK UP THE GUTS TO ACTUALLY ASK ME OUT ON A DATE... IF YOU TAKE ME TO A SEAFOOD RESTAURANT, I WILL KILL YOU. YOU HEAR ME?
YES, MA'AM.
QUIRE! GET TO CLASS BEFORE I PHASE YOUR DESK INTO YOUR BUTT!

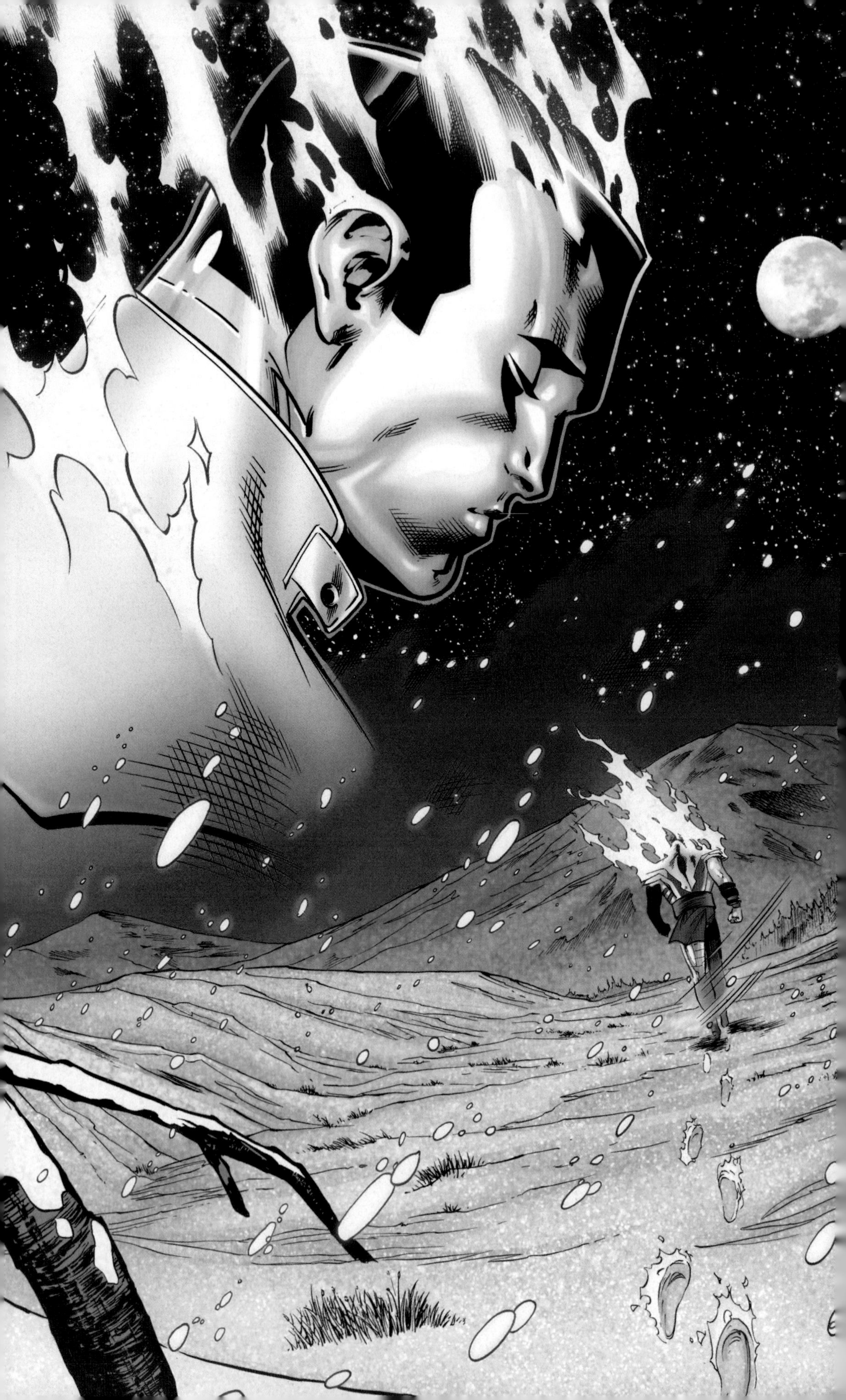

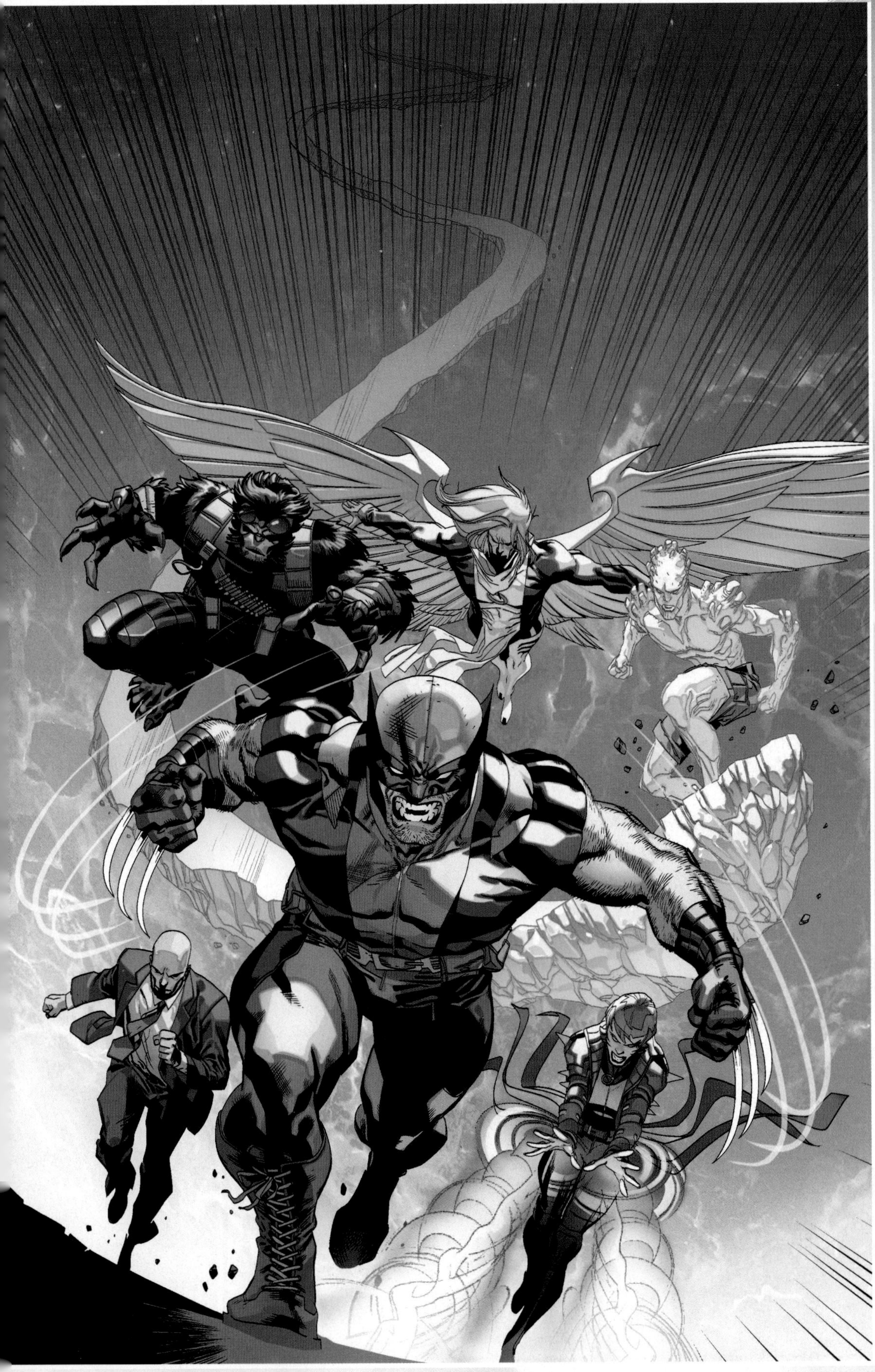

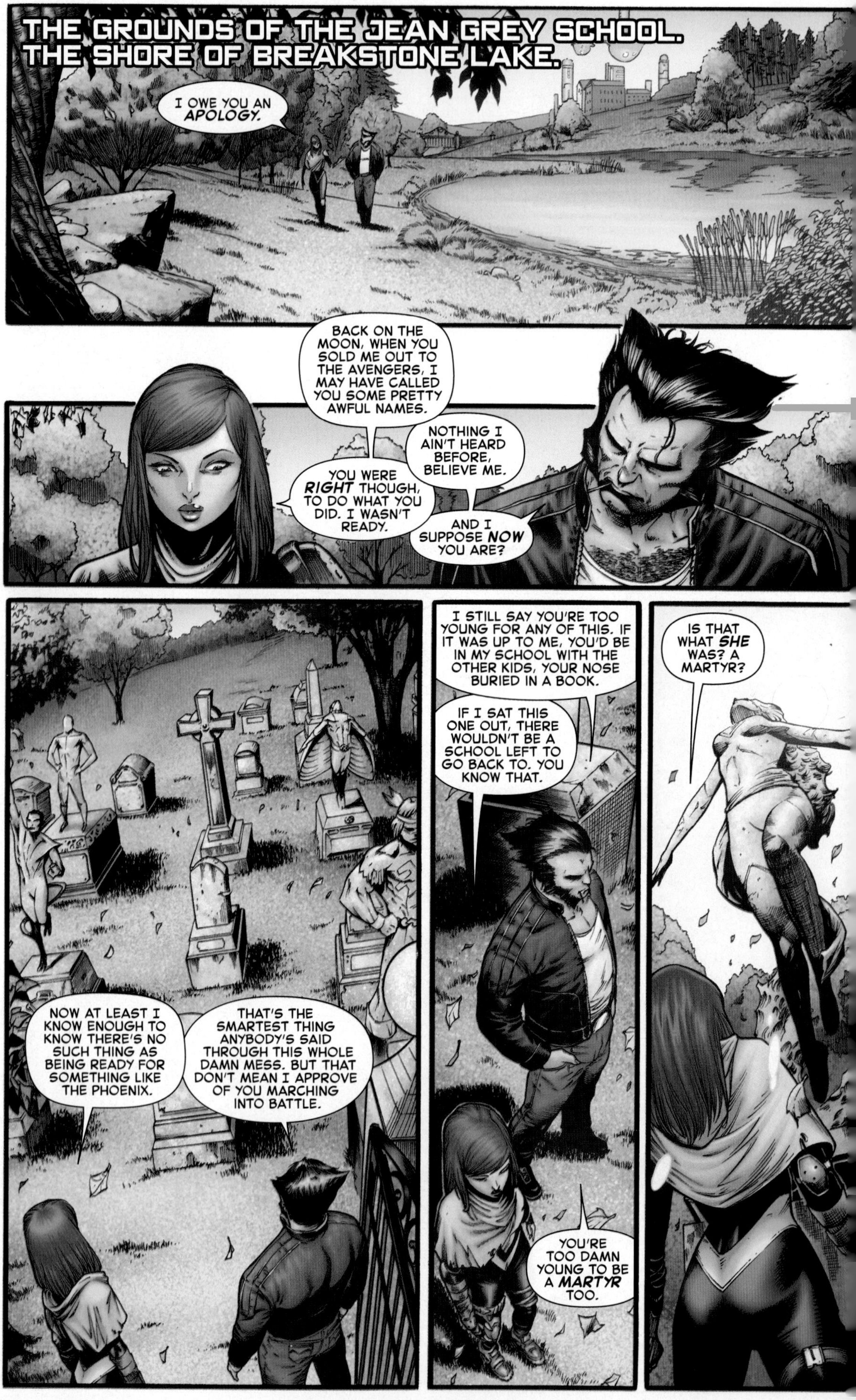
THE GROUNDS OF THE JEAN GREY SCHOOL. THE SHORE OF BREAKSTONE LAKE.
I OWE YOU AN *APOLOGY.*
BACK ON THE MOON, WHEN YOU SOLD ME OUT TO THE AVENGERS, I MAY HAVE CALLED YOU SOME PRETTY AWFUL NAMES.
NOTHING I AIN'T HEARD BEFORE, BELIEVE ME.
YOU WERE *RIGHT* THOUGH, TO DO WHAT YOU DID. I WASN'T READY.
AND I SUPPOSE *NOW* YOU ARE?
NOW AT LEAST I KNOW ENOUGH TO KNOW THERE'S NO SUCH THING AS BEING READY FOR SOMETHING LIKE THE PHOENIX.
THAT'S THE SMARTEST THING ANYBODY'S SAID THROUGH THIS WHOLE DAMN MESS. BUT THAT DON'T MEAN I APPROVE OF YOU MARCHING INTO BATTLE.
I STILL SAY YOU'RE TOO YOUNG FOR ANY OF THIS. IF IT WAS UP TO ME, YOU'D BE IN MY SCHOOL WITH THE OTHER KIDS, YOUR NOSE BURIED IN A BOOK.
IF I SAT THIS ONE OUT, THERE WOULDN'T BE A SCHOOL LEFT TO GO BACK TO. YOU KNOW THAT.
YOU'RE TOO DAMN YOUNG TO BE A *MARTYR* TOO.
IS THAT WHAT *SHE* WAS? A MARTYR?

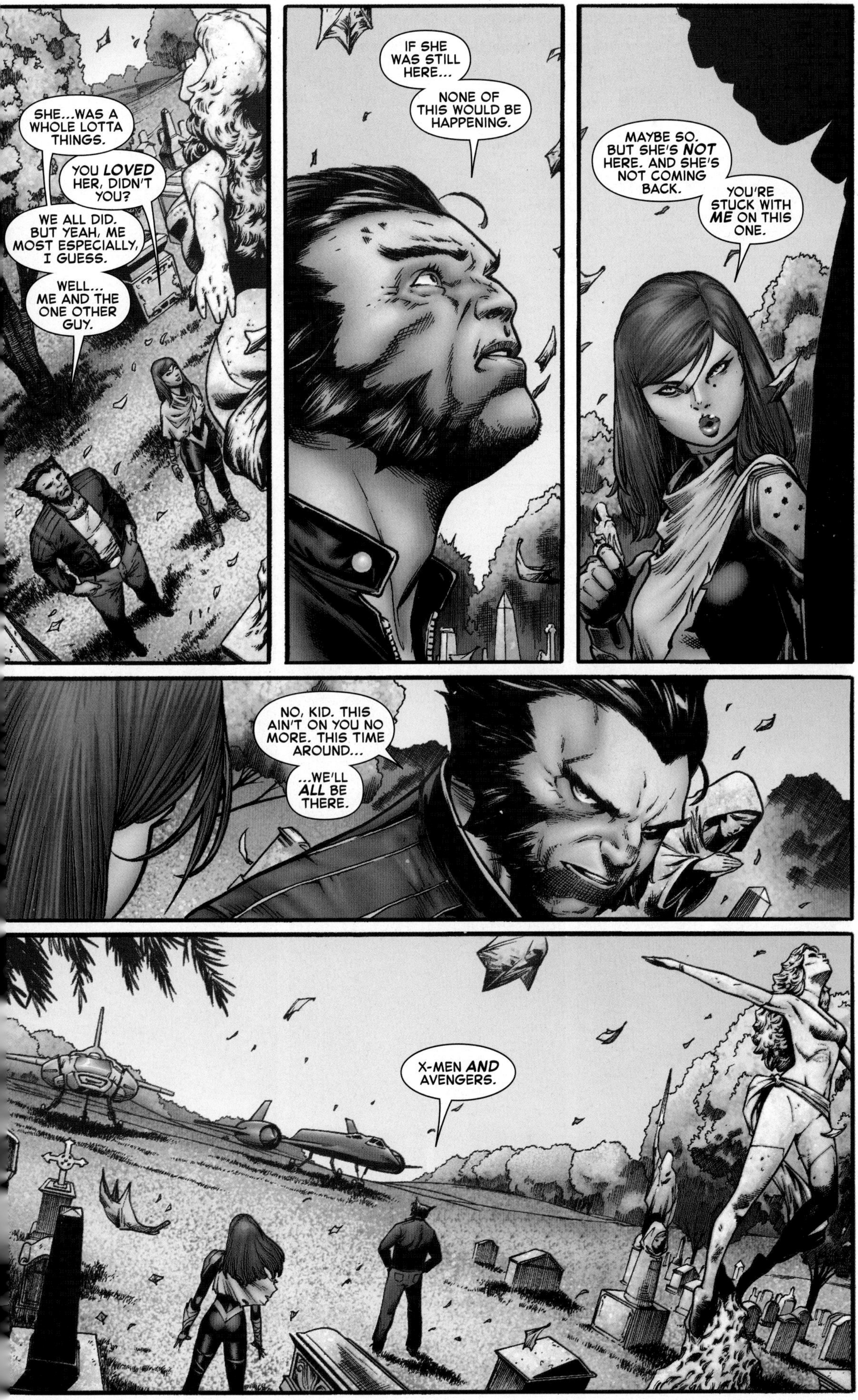
SHE...WAS A WHOLE LOTTA THINGS.
YOU LOVED HER, DIDN'T YOU?
WE ALL DID. BUT YEAH, ME MOST ESPECIALLY, I GUESS.
WELL... ME AND THE ONE OTHER GUY.
IF SHE WAS STILL HERE...
NONE OF THIS WOULD BE HAPPENING.
MAYBE SO. BUT SHE'S NOT HERE. AND SHE'S NOT COMING BACK.
YOU'RE STUCK WITH ME ON THIS ONE.
NO, KID. THIS AIN'T ON YOU NO MORE. THIS TIME AROUND...
...WE'LL ALL BE THERE.
X-MEN AND AVENGERS.

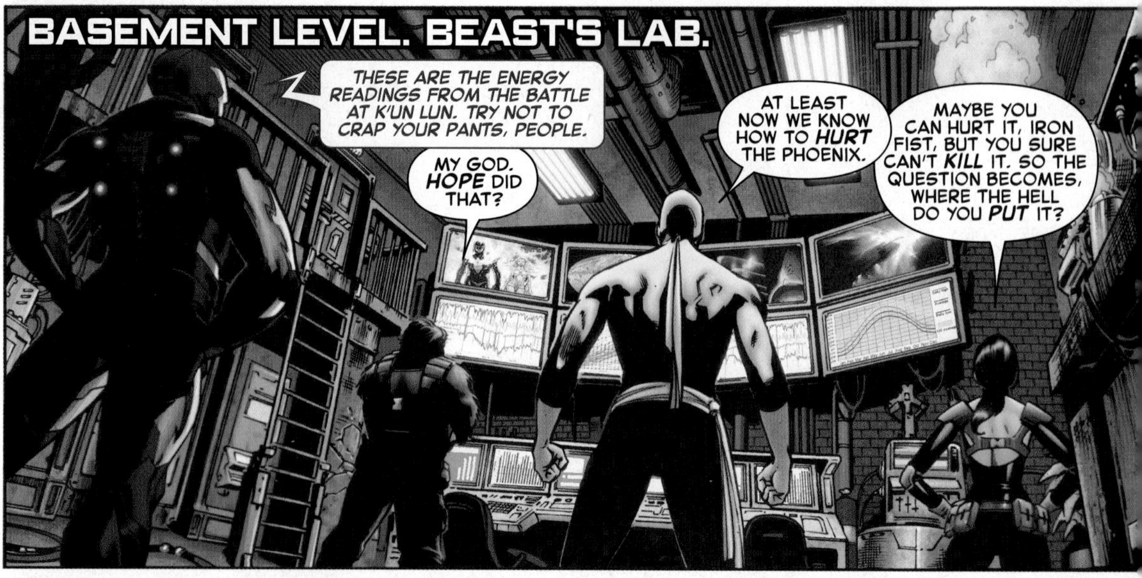
BASEMENT LEVEL. BEAST'S LAB.
THESE ARE THE ENERGY READINGS FROM THE BATTLE AT K'UN LUN. TRY NOT TO CRAP YOUR PANTS, PEOPLE.
MY GOD. HOPE DID THAT?
AT LEAST NOW WE KNOW HOW TO HURT THE PHOENIX.
MAYBE YOU CAN HURT IT, IRON FIST, BUT YOU SURE CAN'T KILL IT. SO THE QUESTION BECOMES, WHERE THE HELL DO YOU PUT IT?

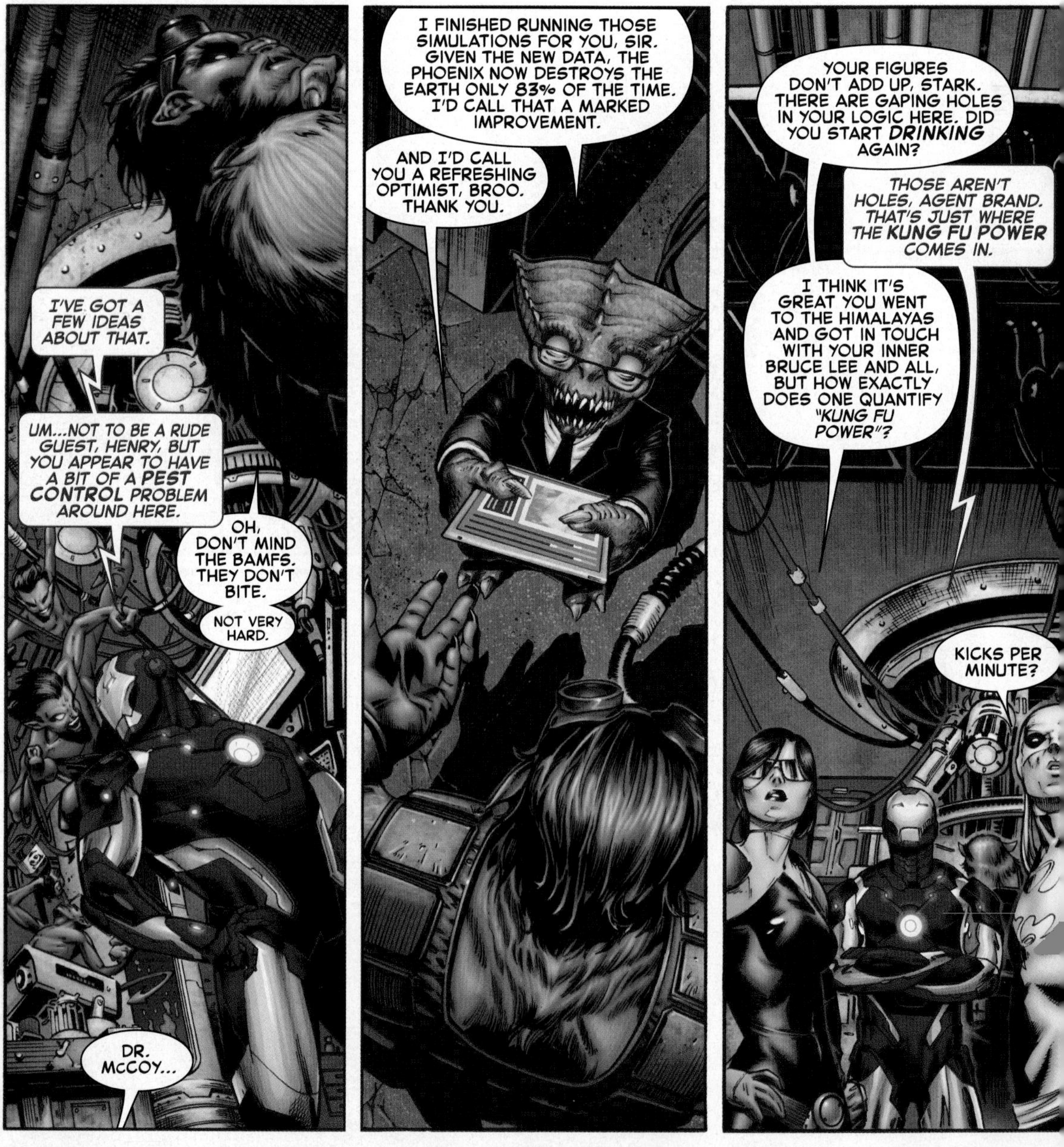
I'VE GOT A FEW IDEAS ABOUT THAT.
UM...NOT TO BE A RUDE GUEST, HENRY, BUT YOU APPEAR TO HAVE A BIT OF A PEST CONTROL PROBLEM AROUND HERE.
OH, DON'T MIND THE BAMFS. THEY DON'T BITE.
NOT VERY HARD.
DR. McCOY...
I FINISHED RUNNING THOSE SIMULATIONS FOR YOU, SIR. GIVEN THE NEW DATA, THE PHOENIX NOW DESTROYS THE EARTH ONLY 83% OF THE TIME. I'D CALL THAT A MARKED IMPROVEMENT.
AND I'D CALL YOU A REFRESHING OPTIMIST, BROO. THANK YOU.
YOUR FIGURES DON'T ADD UP, STARK. THERE ARE GAPING HOLES IN YOUR LOGIC HERE. DID YOU START DRINKING AGAIN?
THOSE AREN'T HOLES, AGENT BRAND. THAT'S JUST WHERE THE KUNG FU POWER COMES IN.
I THINK IT'S GREAT YOU WENT TO THE HIMALAYAS AND GOT IN TOUCH WITH YOUR INNER BRUCE LEE AND ALL, BUT HOW EXACTLY DOES ONE QUANTIFY "KUNG FU POWER"?
KICKS PER MINUTE?

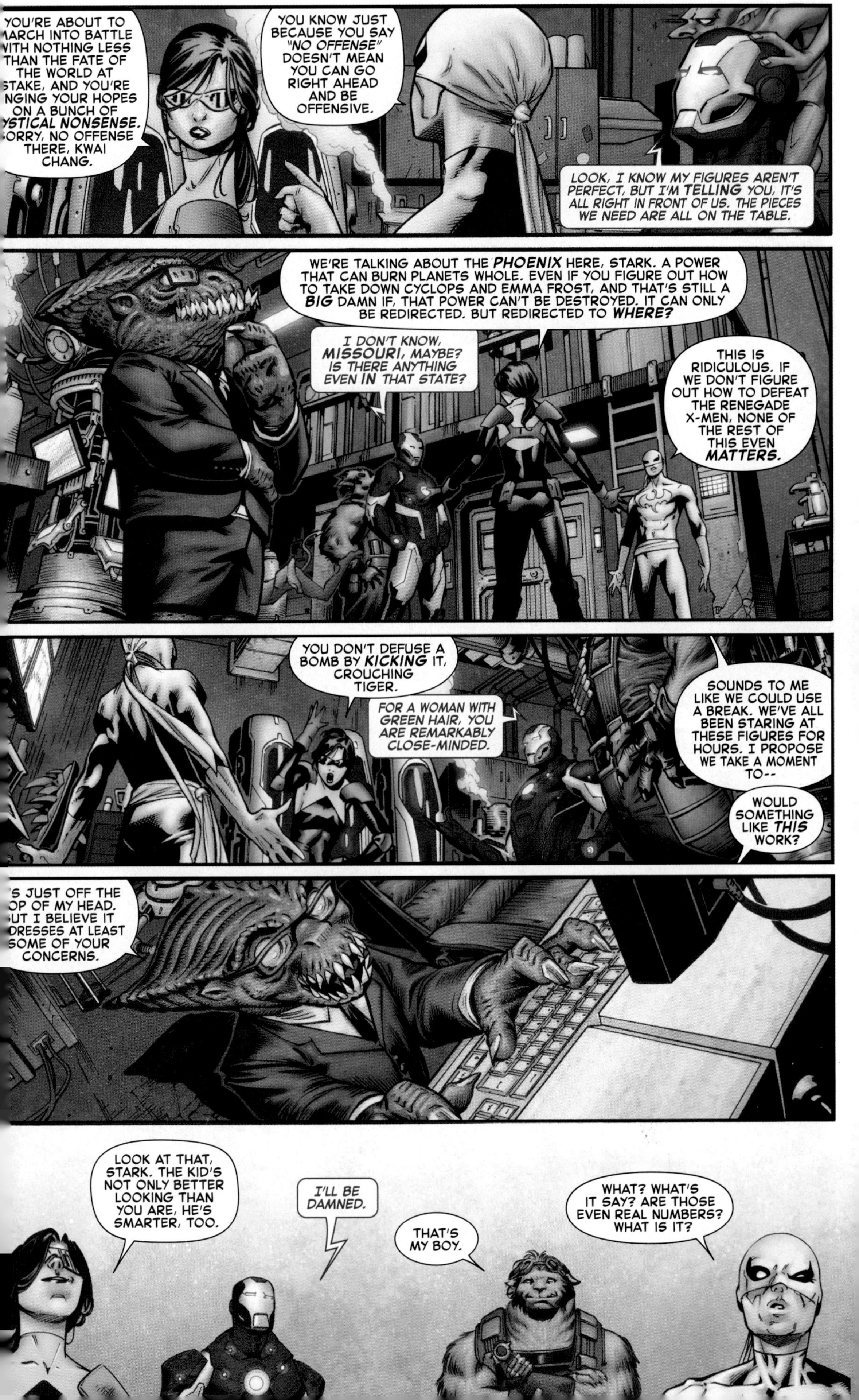
YOU'RE ABOUT TO MARCH INTO BATTLE WITH NOTHING LESS THAN THE FATE OF THE WORLD AT STAKE, AND YOU'RE NGING YOUR HOPES ON A BUNCH OF YSTICAL NONSENSE. ORRY, NO OFFENSE THERE, KWAI CHANG.
YOU KNOW JUST BECAUSE YOU SAY "NO OFFENSE" DOESN'T MEAN YOU CAN GO RIGHT AHEAD AND BE OFFENSIVE.
LOOK, I KNOW MY FIGURES AREN'T PERFECT, BUT I'M TELLING YOU, IT'S ALL RIGHT IN FRONT OF US. THE PIECES WE NEED ARE ALL ON THE TABLE.
WE'RE TALKING ABOUT THE PHOENIX HERE, STARK. A POWER THAT CAN BURN PLANETS WHOLE. EVEN IF YOU FIGURE OUT HOW TO TAKE DOWN CYCLOPS AND EMMA FROST, AND THAT'S STILL A BIG DAMN IF, THAT POWER CAN'T BE DESTROYED. IT CAN ONLY BE REDIRECTED. BUT REDIRECTED TO WHERE?
I DON'T KNOW, MISSOURI, MAYBE? IS THERE ANYTHING EVEN IN THAT STATE?
THIS IS RIDICULOUS. IF WE DON'T FIGURE OUT HOW TO DEFEAT THE RENEGADE X-MEN, NONE OF THE REST OF THIS EVEN MATTERS.
YOU DON'T DEFUSE A BOMB BY KICKING IT, CROUCHING TIGER.
FOR A WOMAN WITH GREEN HAIR, YOU ARE REMARKABLY CLOSE-MINDED.
SOUNDS TO ME LIKE WE COULD USE A BREAK. WE'VE ALL BEEN STARING AT THESE FIGURES FOR HOURS. I PROPOSE WE TAKE A MOMENT TO--
WOULD SOMETHING LIKE THIS WORK?
'S JUST OFF THE OP OF MY HEAD. UT I BELIEVE IT DRESSES AT LEAST SOME OF YOUR CONCERNS.
LOOK AT THAT, STARK. THE KID'S NOT ONLY BETTER LOOKING THAN YOU ARE, HE'S SMARTER, TOO.
I'LL BE DAMNED.
THAT'S MY BOY.
WHAT? WHAT'S IT SAY? ARE THOSE EVEN REAL NUMBERS? WHAT IS IT?

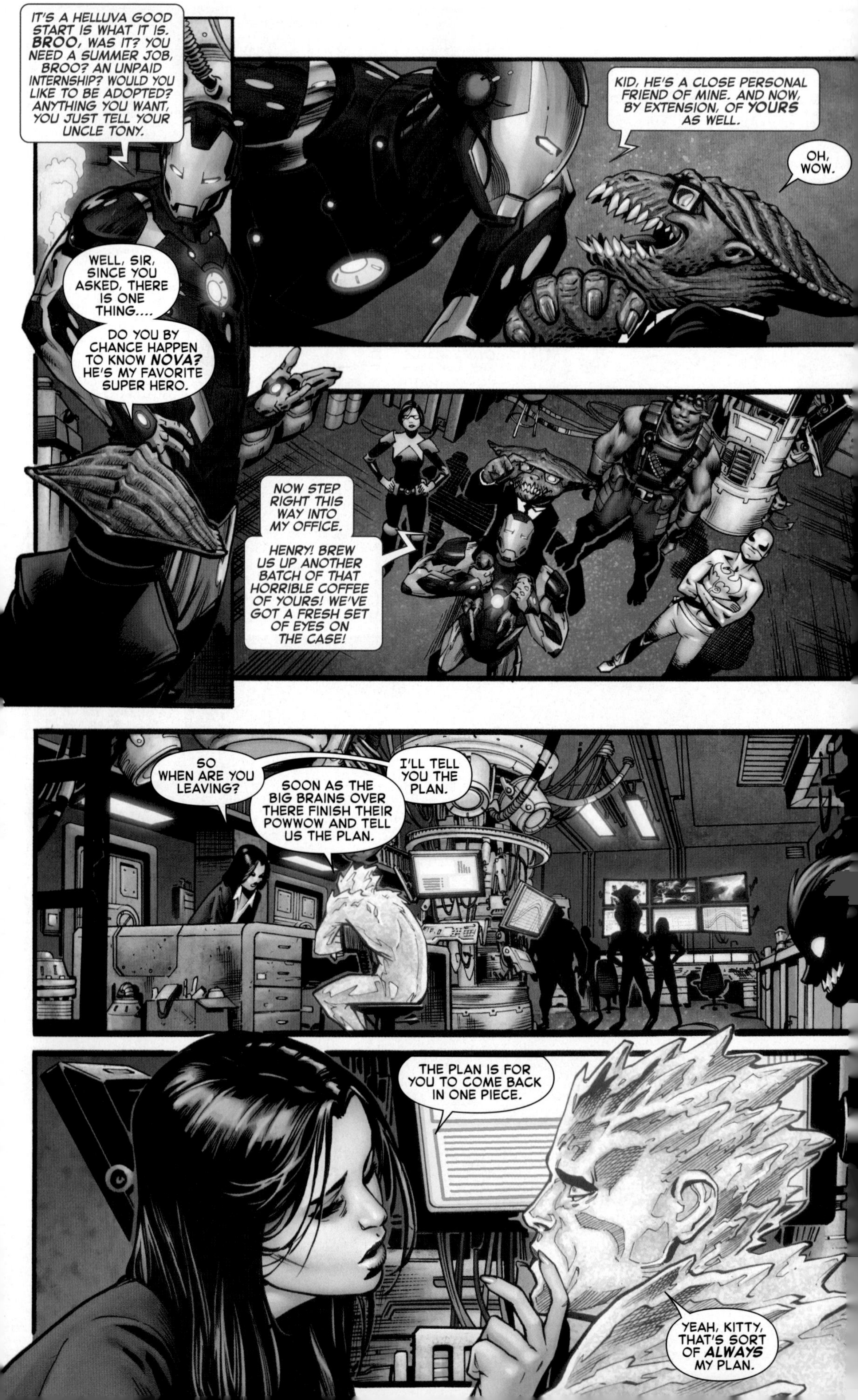
IT'S A HELLUVA GOOD START IS WHAT IT IS. BROO, WAS IT? YOU NEED A SUMMER JOB, BROO? AN UNPAID INTERNSHIP? WOULD YOU LIKE TO BE ADOPTED? ANYTHING YOU WANT, YOU JUST TELL YOUR UNCLE TONY.
KID, HE'S A CLOSE PERSONAL FRIEND OF MINE. AND NOW, BY EXTENSION, OF YOURS AS WELL.
OH, WOW.
WELL, SIR, SINCE YOU ASKED, THERE IS ONE THING....
DO YOU BY CHANCE HAPPEN TO KNOW NOVA? HE'S MY FAVORITE SUPER HERO.
NOW STEP RIGHT THIS WAY INTO MY OFFICE.
HENRY! BREW US UP ANOTHER BATCH OF THAT HORRIBLE COFFEE OF YOURS! WE'VE GOT A FRESH SET OF EYES ON THE CASE!
SO WHEN ARE YOU LEAVING?
SOON AS THE BIG BRAINS OVER THERE FINISH THEIR POWWOW AND TELL US THE PLAN.
I'LL TELL YOU THE PLAN.
THE PLAN IS FOR YOU TO COME BACK IN ONE PIECE.
YEAH, KITTY, THAT'S SORT OF ALWAYS MY PLAN.

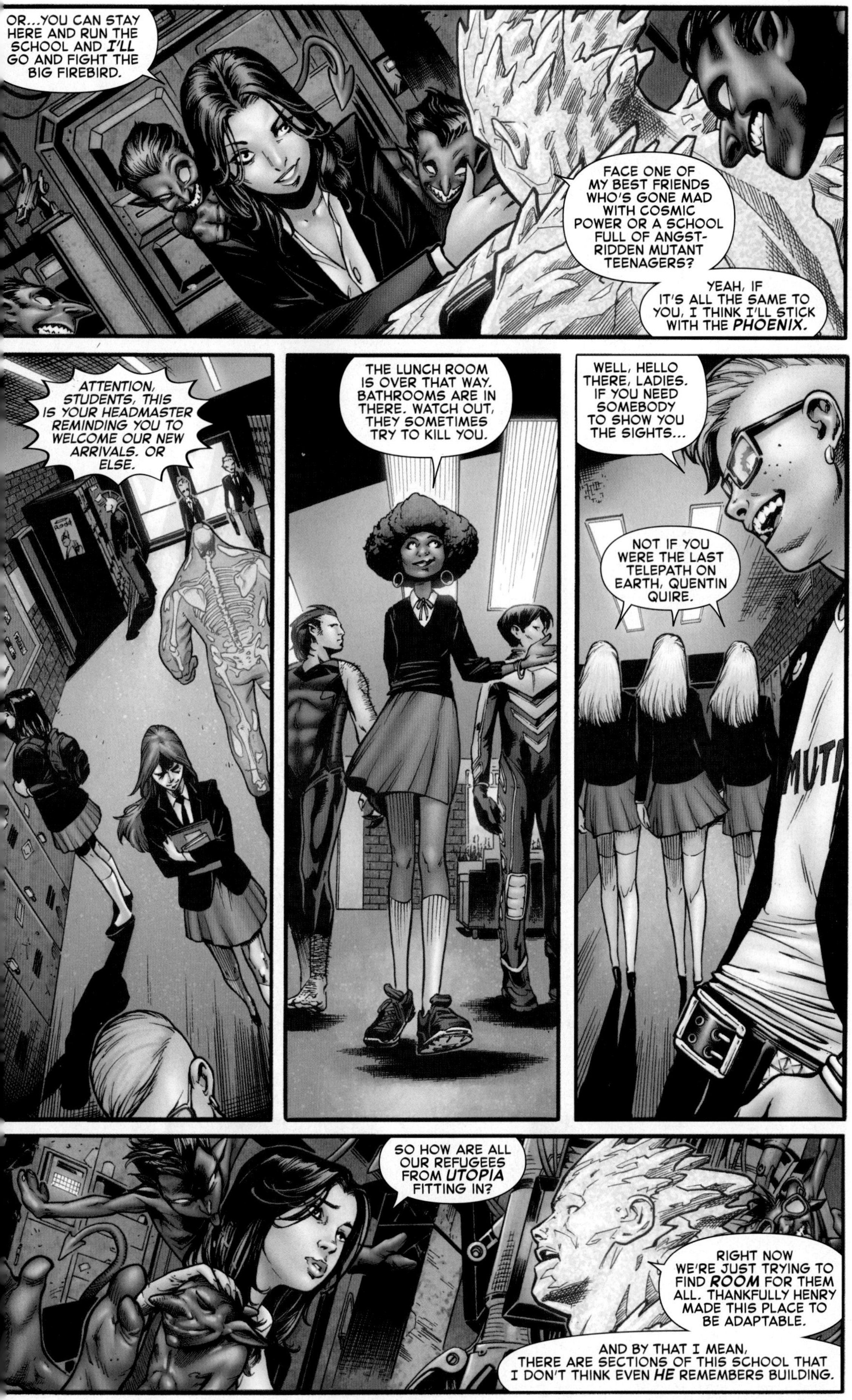
OR...YOU CAN STAY HERE AND RUN THE SCHOOL AND I'LL GO AND FIGHT THE BIG FIREBIRD.
FACE ONE OF MY BEST FRIENDS WHO'S GONE MAD WITH COSMIC POWER OR A SCHOOL FULL OF ANGST-RIDDEN MUTANT TEENAGERS?
YEAH, IF IT'S ALL THE SAME TO YOU, I THINK I'LL STICK WITH THE PHOENIX.
ATTENTION, STUDENTS, THIS IS YOUR HEADMASTER REMINDING YOU TO WELCOME OUR NEW ARRIVALS. OR ELSE.
THE LUNCH ROOM IS OVER THAT WAY. BATHROOMS ARE IN THERE. WATCH OUT, THEY SOMETIMES TRY TO KILL YOU.
WELL, HELLO THERE, LADIES. IF YOU NEED SOMEBODY TO SHOW YOU THE SIGHTS...
NOT IF YOU WERE THE LAST TELEPATH ON EARTH, QUENTIN QUIRE.
SO HOW ARE ALL OUR REFUGEES FROM UTOPIA FITTING IN?
RIGHT NOW WE'RE JUST TRYING TO FIND ROOM FOR THEM ALL. THANKFULLY HENRY MADE THIS PLACE TO BE ADAPTABLE.
AND BY THAT I MEAN, THERE ARE SECTIONS OF THIS SCHOOL THAT I DON'T THINK EVEN HE REMEMBERS BUILDING.

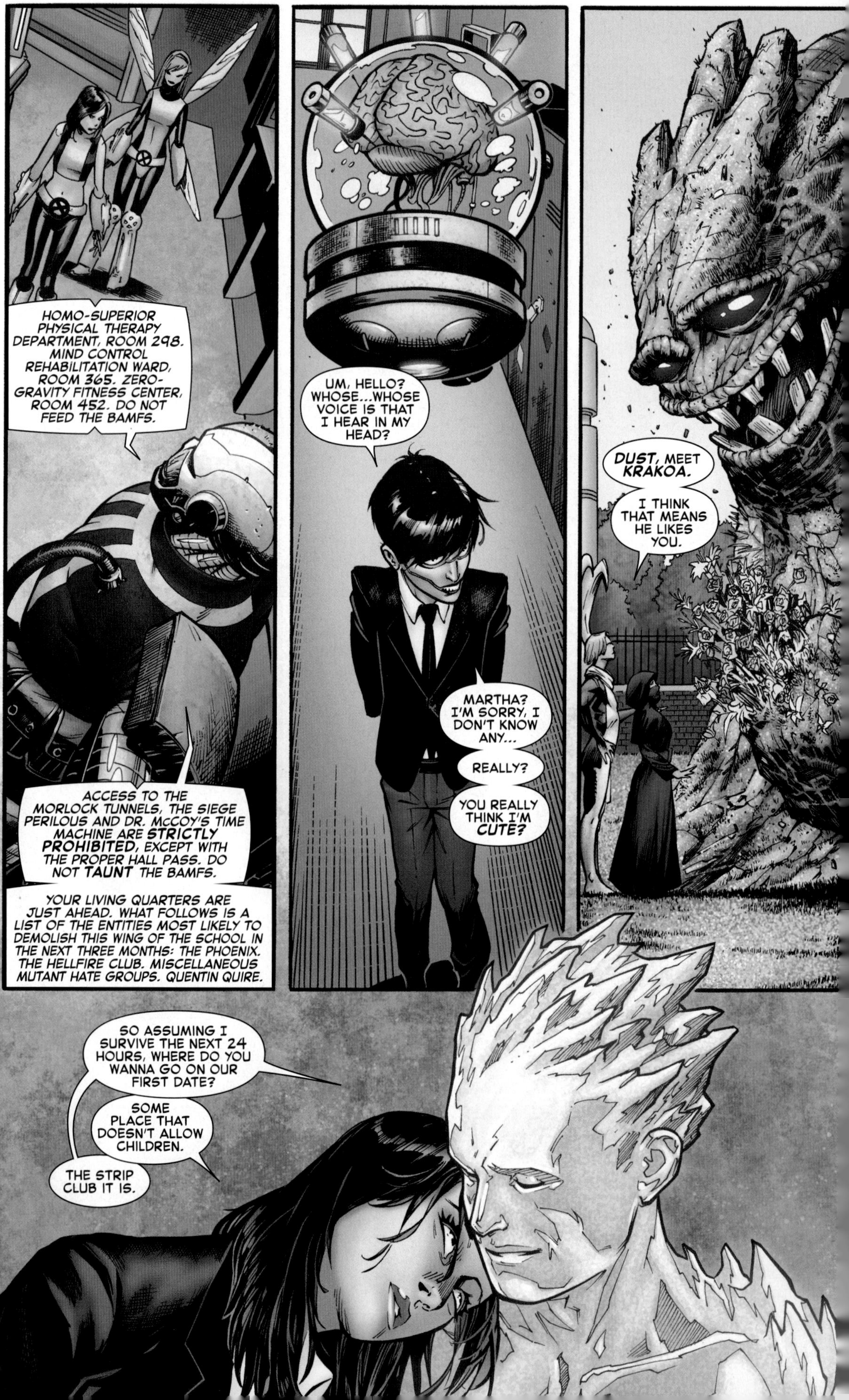
HOMO-SUPERIOR PHYSICAL THERAPY DEPARTMENT, ROOM 298. MIND CONTROL REHABILITATION WARD, ROOM 365. ZERO-GRAVITY FITNESS CENTER, ROOM 452. DO NOT FEED THE BAMFS.
ACCESS TO THE MORLOCK TUNNELS, THE SIEGE PERILOUS AND DR. McCOY'S TIME MACHINE ARE STRICTLY PROHIBITED, EXCEPT WITH THE PROPER HALL PASS. DO NOT TAUNT THE BAMFS.
YOUR LIVING QUARTERS ARE JUST AHEAD. WHAT FOLLOWS IS A LIST OF THE ENTITIES MOST LIKELY TO DEMOLISH THIS WING OF THE SCHOOL IN THE NEXT THREE MONTHS: THE PHOENIX. THE HELLFIRE CLUB. MISCELLANEOUS MUTANT HATE GROUPS. QUENTIN QUIRE.
UM, HELLO? WHOSE...WHOSE VOICE IS THAT I HEAR IN MY HEAD?
MARTHA? I'M SORRY, I DON'T KNOW ANY...
REALLY?
YOU REALLY THINK I'M CUTE?
DUST, MEET KRAKOA.
I THINK THAT MEANS HE LIKES YOU.
SO ASSUMING I SURVIVE THE NEXT 24 HOURS, WHERE DO YOU WANNA GO ON OUR FIRST DATE?
SOME PLACE THAT DOESN'T ALLOW CHILDREN.
THE STRIP CLUB IT IS.

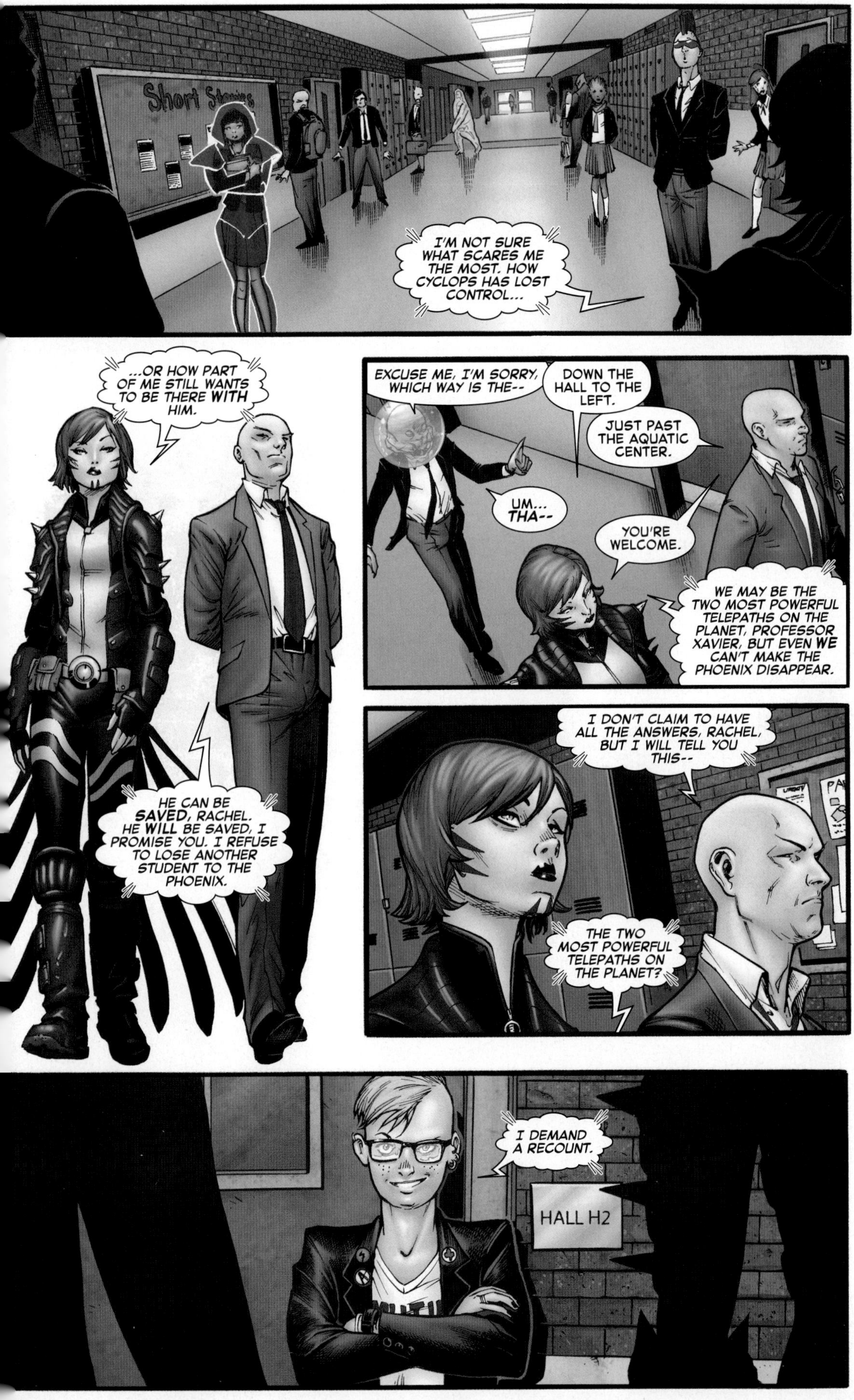
Short Stories
I'M NOT SURE WHAT SCARES ME THE MOST. HOW CYCLOPS HAS LOST CONTROL...
...OR HOW PART OF ME STILL WANTS TO BE THERE WITH HIM.
HE CAN BE SAVED, RACHEL. HE WILL BE SAVED, I PROMISE YOU. I REFUSE TO LOSE ANOTHER STUDENT TO THE PHOENIX.
EXCUSE ME, I'M SORRY, WHICH WAY IS THE--
DOWN THE HALL TO THE LEFT.
JUST PAST THE AQUATIC CENTER.
UM... THA--
YOU'RE WELCOME.
WE MAY BE THE TWO MOST POWERFUL TELEPATHS ON THE PLANET, PROFESSOR XAVIER, BUT EVEN WE CAN'T MAKE THE PHOENIX DISAPPEAR.
I DON'T CLAIM TO HAVE ALL THE ANSWERS, RACHEL, BUT I WILL TELL YOU THIS--
THE TWO MOST POWERFUL TELEPATHS ON THE PLANET?
I DEMAND A RECOUNT.
HALL H2

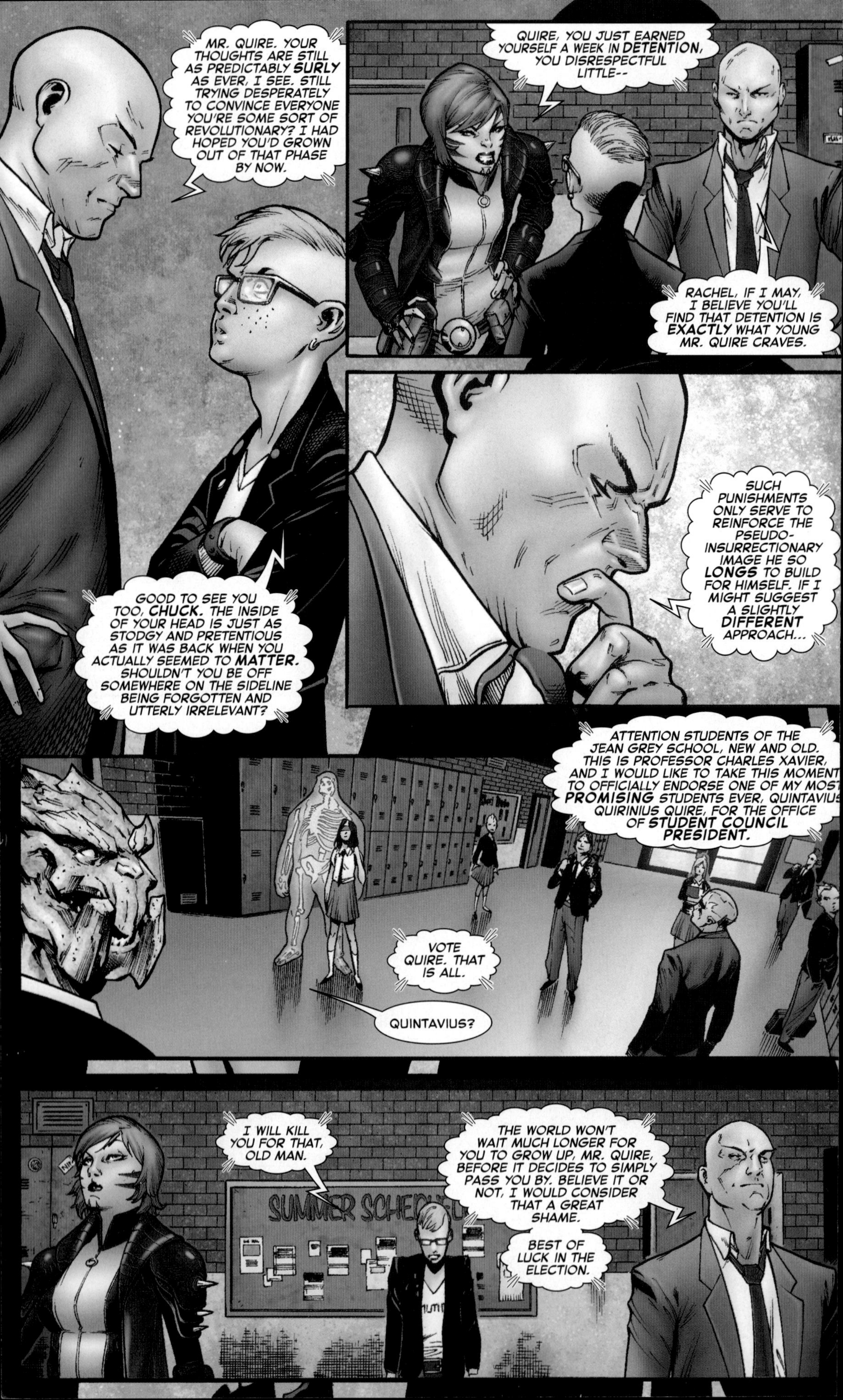

MR. QUIRE. YOUR THOUGHTS ARE STILL AS PREDICTABLY SURLY AS EVER, I SEE. STILL TRYING DESPERATELY TO CONVINCE EVERYONE YOU'RE SOME SORT OF REVOLUTIONARY? I HAD HOPED YOU'D GROWN OUT OF THAT PHASE BY NOW.
GOOD TO SEE YOU TOO, CHUCK. THE INSIDE OF YOUR HEAD IS JUST AS STODGY AND PRETENTIOUS AS IT WAS BACK WHEN YOU ACTUALLY SEEMED TO MATTER. SHOULDN'T YOU BE OFF SOMEWHERE ON THE SIDELINE BEING FORGOTTEN AND UTTERLY IRRELEVANT?
QUIRE, YOU JUST EARNED YOURSELF A WEEK IN DETENTION, YOU DISRESPECTFUL LITTLE--
RACHEL, IF I MAY, I BELIEVE YOU'LL FIND THAT DETENTION IS EXACTLY WHAT YOUNG MR. QUIRE CRAVES.
SUCH PUNISHMENTS ONLY SERVE TO REINFORCE THE PSEUDO-INSURRECTIONARY IMAGE HE SO LONGS TO BUILD FOR HIMSELF. IF I MIGHT SUGGEST A SLIGHTLY DIFFERENT APPROACH...
ATTENTION STUDENTS OF THE JEAN GREY SCHOOL, NEW AND OLD. THIS IS PROFESSOR CHARLES XAVIER, AND I WOULD LIKE TO TAKE THIS MOMENT TO OFFICIALLY ENDORSE ONE OF MY MOST PROMISING STUDENTS EVER, QUINTAVIUS QUIRINIUS QUIRE, FOR THE OFFICE OF STUDENT COUNCIL PRESIDENT.
VOTE QUIRE. THAT IS ALL.
QUINTAVIUS?
I WILL KILL YOU FOR THAT, OLD MAN.
SUMMER SCHEDULE
THE WORLD WON'T WAIT MUCH LONGER FOR YOU TO GROW UP, MR. QUIRE, BEFORE IT DECIDES TO SIMPLY PASS YOU BY. BELIEVE IT OR NOT, I WOULD CONSIDER THAT A GREAT SHAME.
BEST OF LUCK IN THE ELECTION.

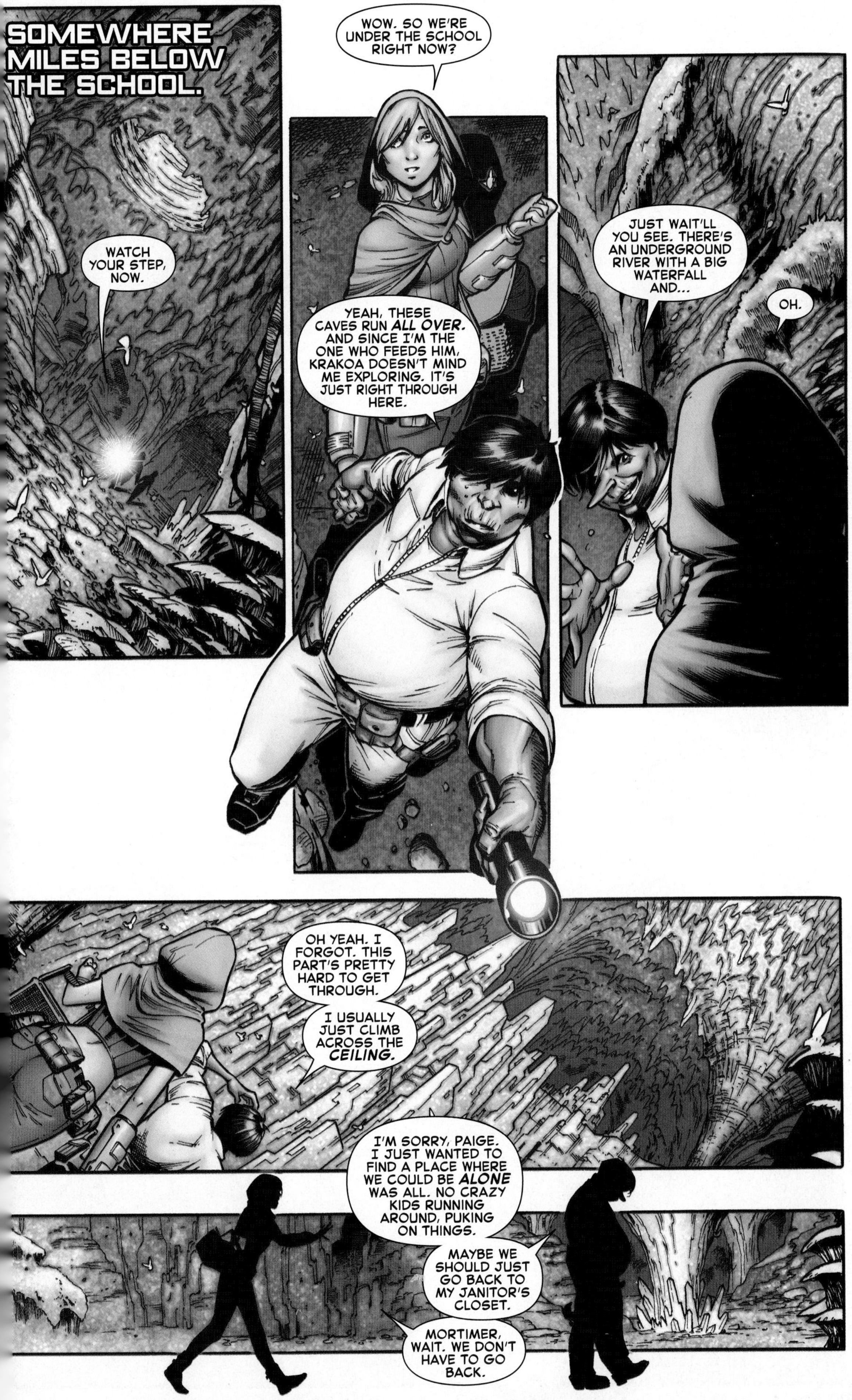
SOMEWHERE MILES BELOW THE SCHOOL.
WOW. SO WE'RE UNDER THE SCHOOL RIGHT NOW?
WATCH YOUR STEP, NOW.
YEAH, THESE CAVES RUN ALL OVER. AND SINCE I'M THE ONE WHO FEEDS HIM, KRAKOA DOESN'T MIND ME EXPLORING. IT'S JUST RIGHT THROUGH HERE.
JUST WAIT'LL YOU SEE. THERE'S AN UNDERGROUND RIVER WITH A BIG WATERFALL AND...
OH.
OH YEAH. I FORGOT. THIS PART'S PRETTY HARD TO GET THROUGH.
I USUALLY JUST CLIMB ACROSS THE CEILING.
I'M SORRY, PAIGE. I JUST WANTED TO FIND A PLACE WHERE WE COULD BE ALONE WAS ALL. NO CRAZY KIDS RUNNING AROUND, PUKING ON THINGS.
MAYBE WE SHOULD JUST GO BACK TO MY JANITOR'S CLOSET.
MORTIMER, WAIT. WE DON'T HAVE TO GO BACK.

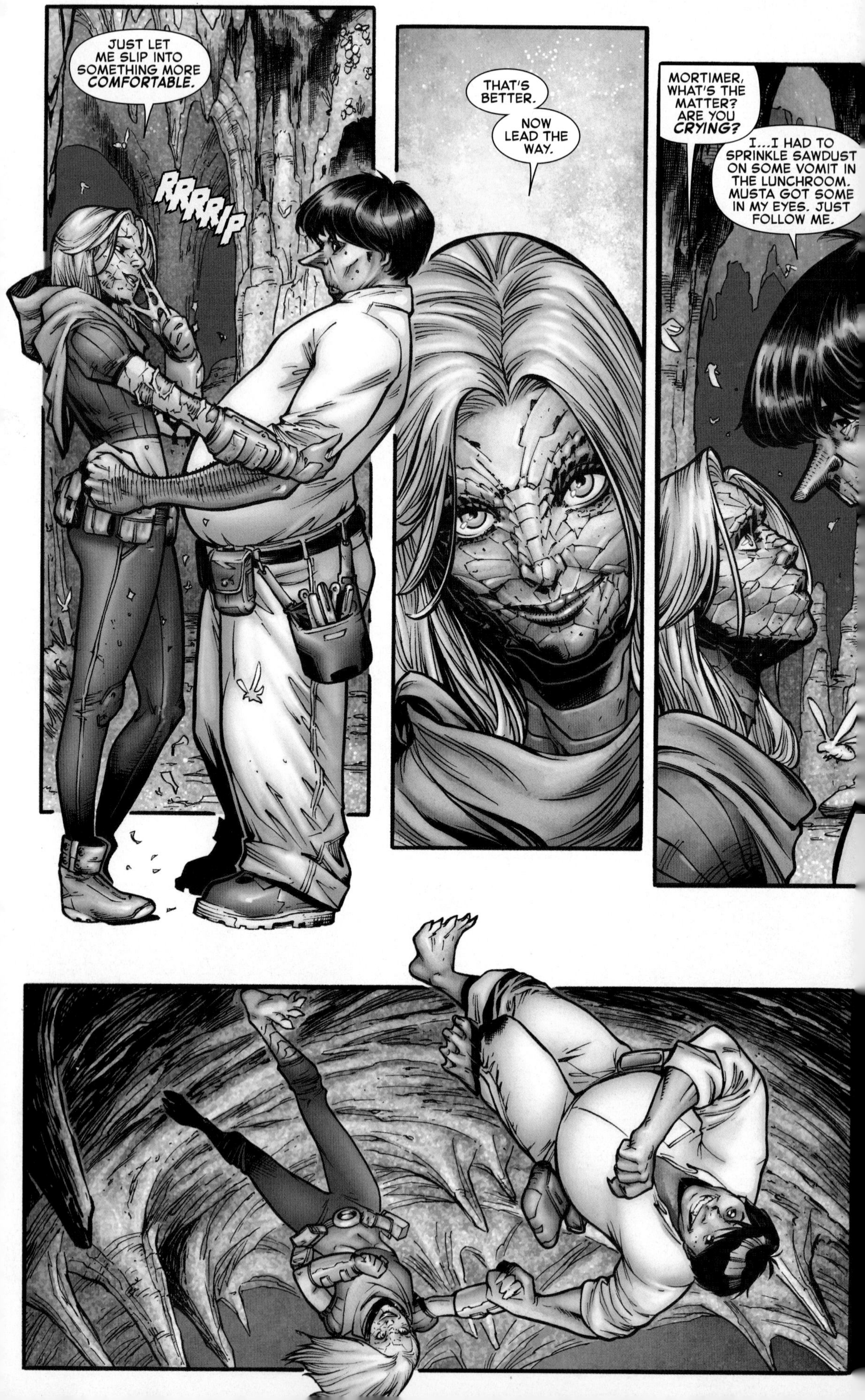
JUST LET ME SLIP INTO SOMETHING MORE COMFORTABLE.
RRRRIP
THAT'S BETTER.
NOW LEAD THE WAY.
MORTIMER, WHAT'S THE MATTER? ARE YOU CRYING?
I...I HAD TO SPRINKLE SAWDUST ON SOME VOMIT IN THE LUNCHROOM. MUSTA GOT SOME IN MY EYES. JUST FOLLOW ME.

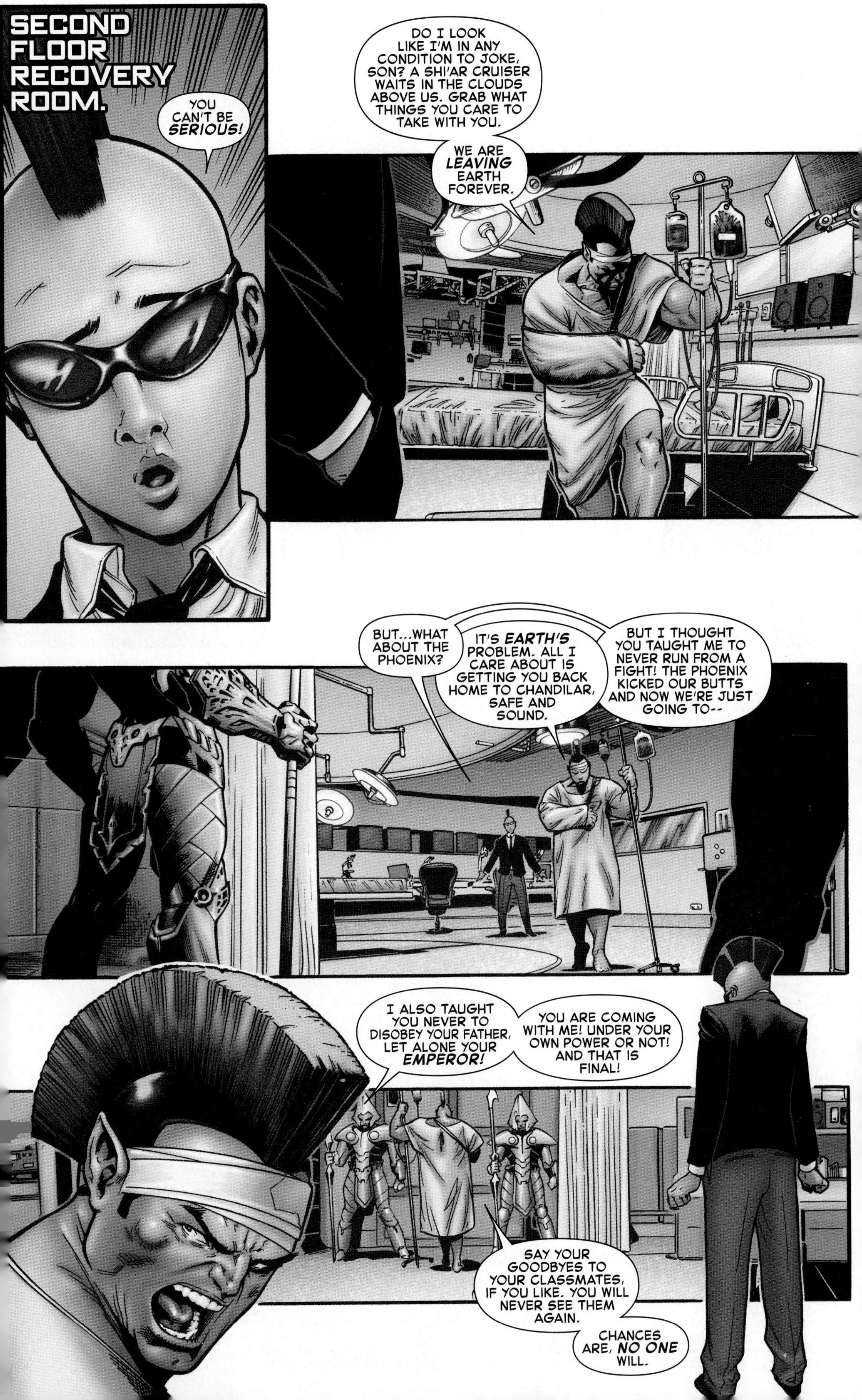
SECOND FLOOR RECOVERY ROOM.
YOU CAN'T BE SERIOUS!
DO I LOOK LIKE I'M IN ANY CONDITION TO JOKE, SON? A SHI'AR CRUISER WAITS IN THE CLOUDS ABOVE US. GRAB WHAT THINGS YOU CARE TO TAKE WITH YOU.
WE ARE LEAVING EARTH FOREVER.
BUT...WHAT ABOUT THE PHOENIX?
IT'S EARTH'S PROBLEM. ALL I CARE ABOUT IS GETTING YOU BACK HOME TO CHANDILAR, SAFE AND SOUND.
BUT I THOUGHT YOU TAUGHT ME TO NEVER RUN FROM A FIGHT! THE PHOENIX KICKED OUR BUTTS AND NOW WE'RE JUST GOING TO--
I ALSO TAUGHT YOU NEVER TO DISOBEY YOUR FATHER, LET ALONE YOUR EMPEROR!
YOU ARE COMING WITH ME! UNDER YOUR OWN POWER OR NOT! AND THAT IS FINAL!
SAY YOUR GOODBYES TO YOUR CLASSMATES, IF YOU LIKE. YOU WILL NEVER SEE THEM AGAIN.
CHANCES ARE, NO ONE WILL.

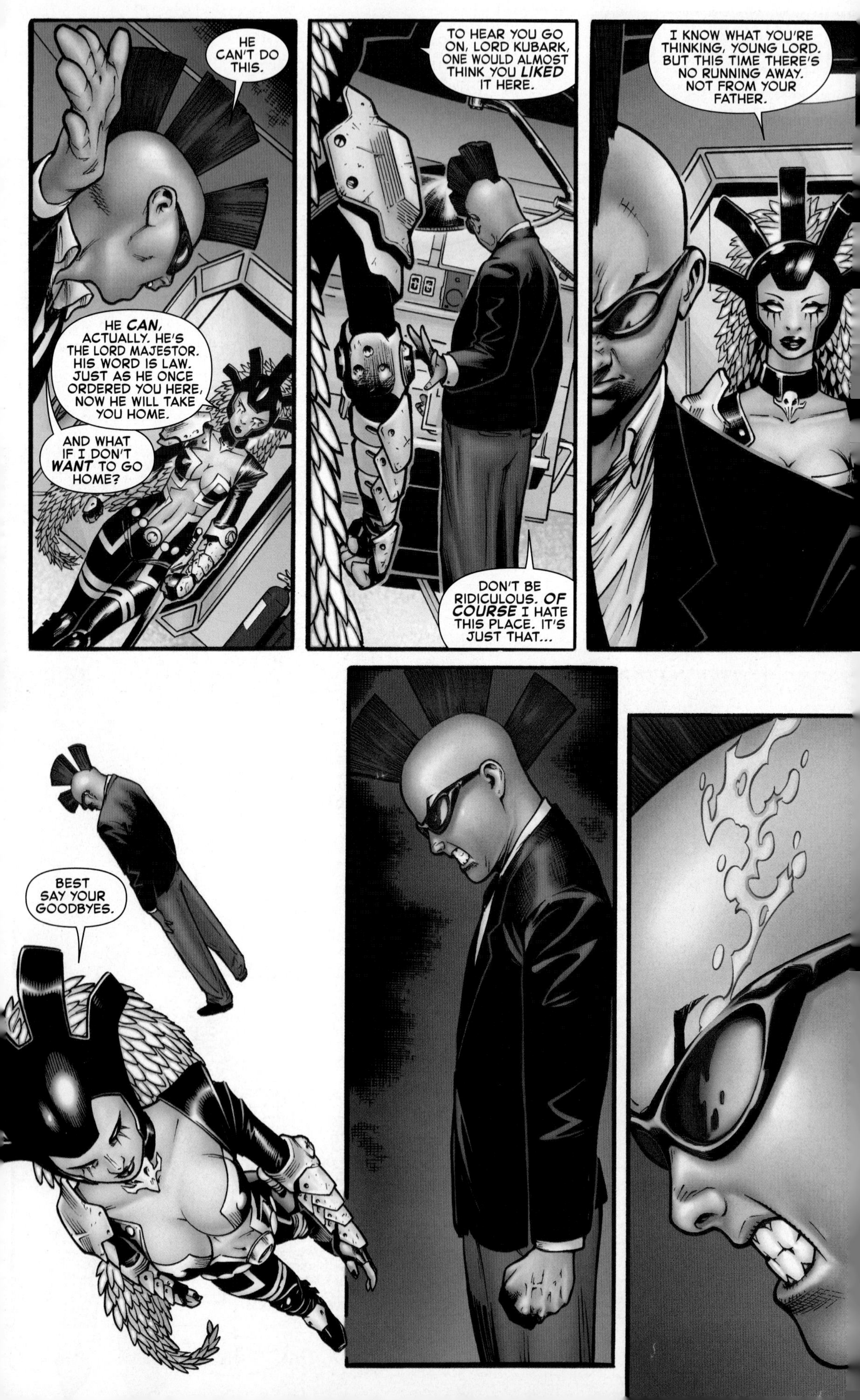
HE CAN'T DO THIS.
HE CAN, ACTUALLY. HE'S THE LORD MAJESTOR. HIS WORD IS LAW. JUST AS HE ONCE ORDERED YOU HERE, NOW HE WILL TAKE YOU HOME.
AND WHAT IF I DON'T WANT TO GO HOME?
TO HEAR YOU GO ON, LORD KUBARK, ONE WOULD ALMOST THINK YOU LIKED IT HERE.
DON'T BE RIDICULOUS. OF COURSE I HATE THIS PLACE. IT'S JUST THAT...
I KNOW WHAT YOU'RE THINKING, YOUNG LORD. BUT THIS TIME THERE'S NO RUNNING AWAY. NOT FROM YOUR FATHER.
BEST SAY YOUR GOODBYES.

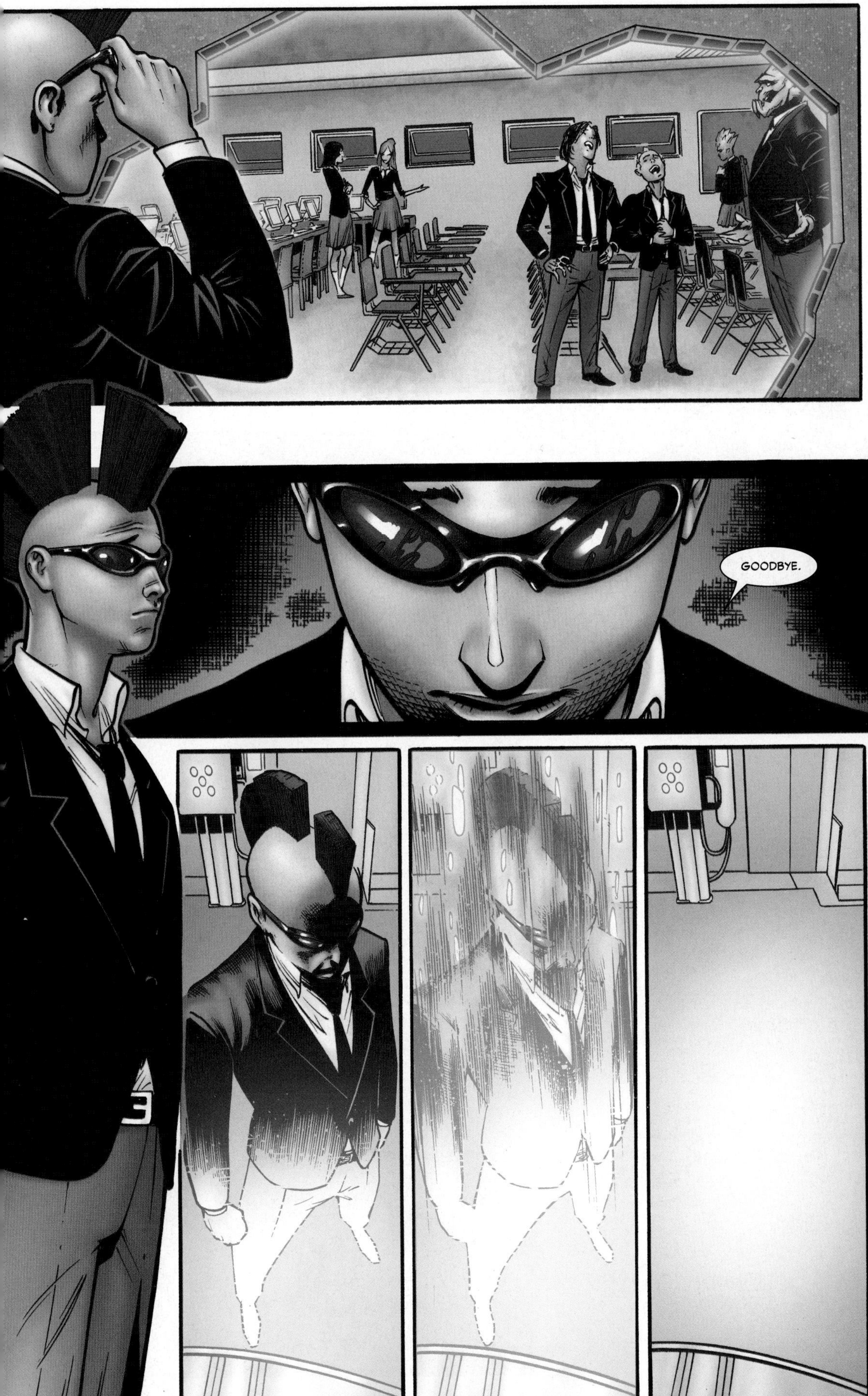
GOODBYE.

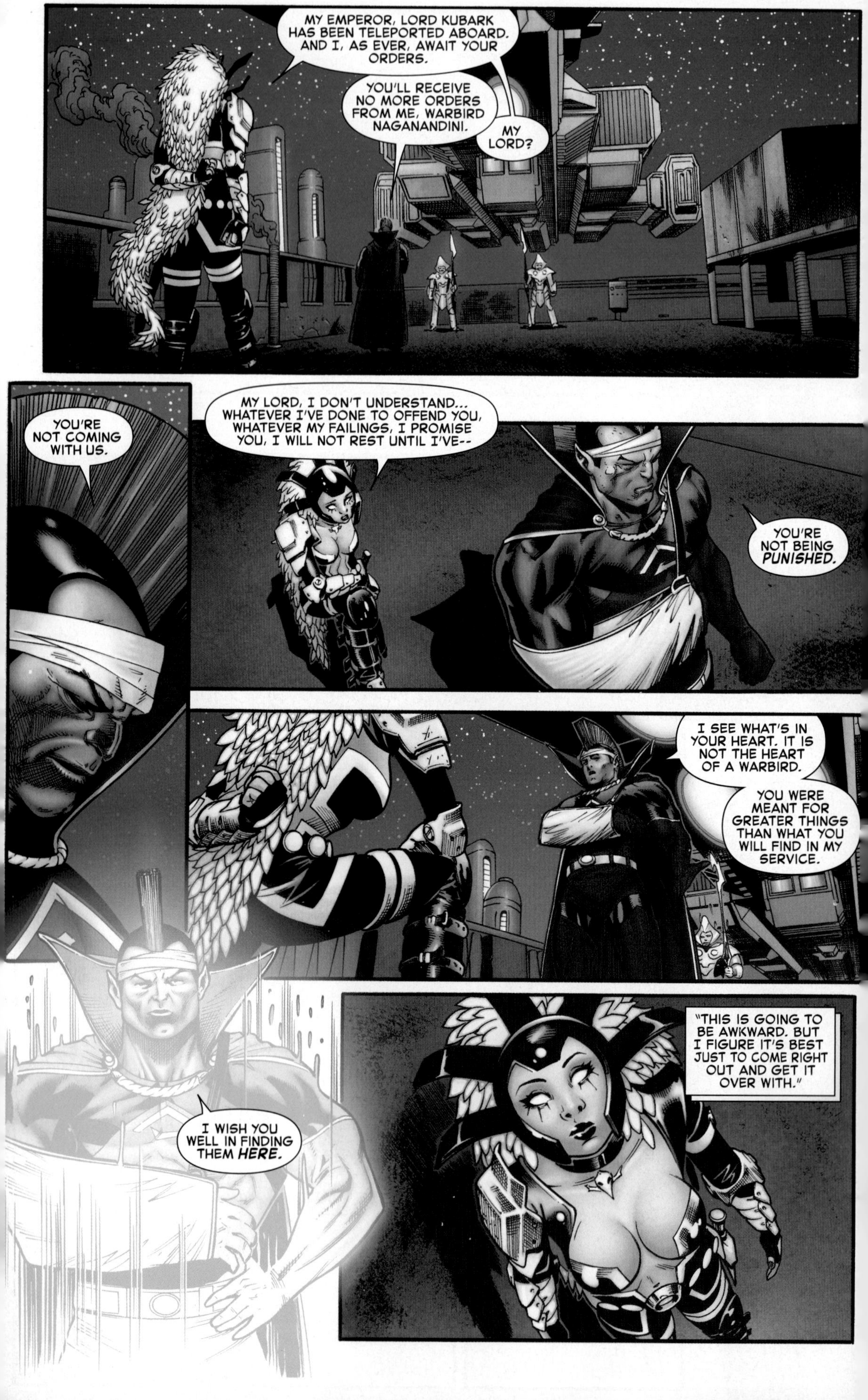
MY EMPEROR, LORD KUBARK HAS BEEN TELEPORTED ABOARD. AND I, AS EVER, AWAIT YOUR ORDERS.
YOU'LL RECEIVE NO MORE ORDERS FROM ME, WARBIRD NAGANANDINI.
MY LORD?
YOU'RE NOT COMING WITH US.
MY LORD, I DON'T UNDERSTAND... WHATEVER I'VE DONE TO OFFEND YOU, WHATEVER MY FAILINGS, I PROMISE YOU, I WILL NOT REST UNTIL I'VE--
YOU'RE NOT BEING PUNISHED.
I SEE WHAT'S IN YOUR HEART. IT IS NOT THE HEART OF A WARBIRD.
YOU WERE MEANT FOR GREATER THINGS THAN WHAT YOU WILL FIND IN MY SERVICE.
I WISH YOU WELL IN FINDING THEM HERE.
"THIS IS GOING TO BE AWKWARD. BUT I FIGURE IT'S BEST JUST TO COME RIGHT OUT AND GET IT OVER WITH."

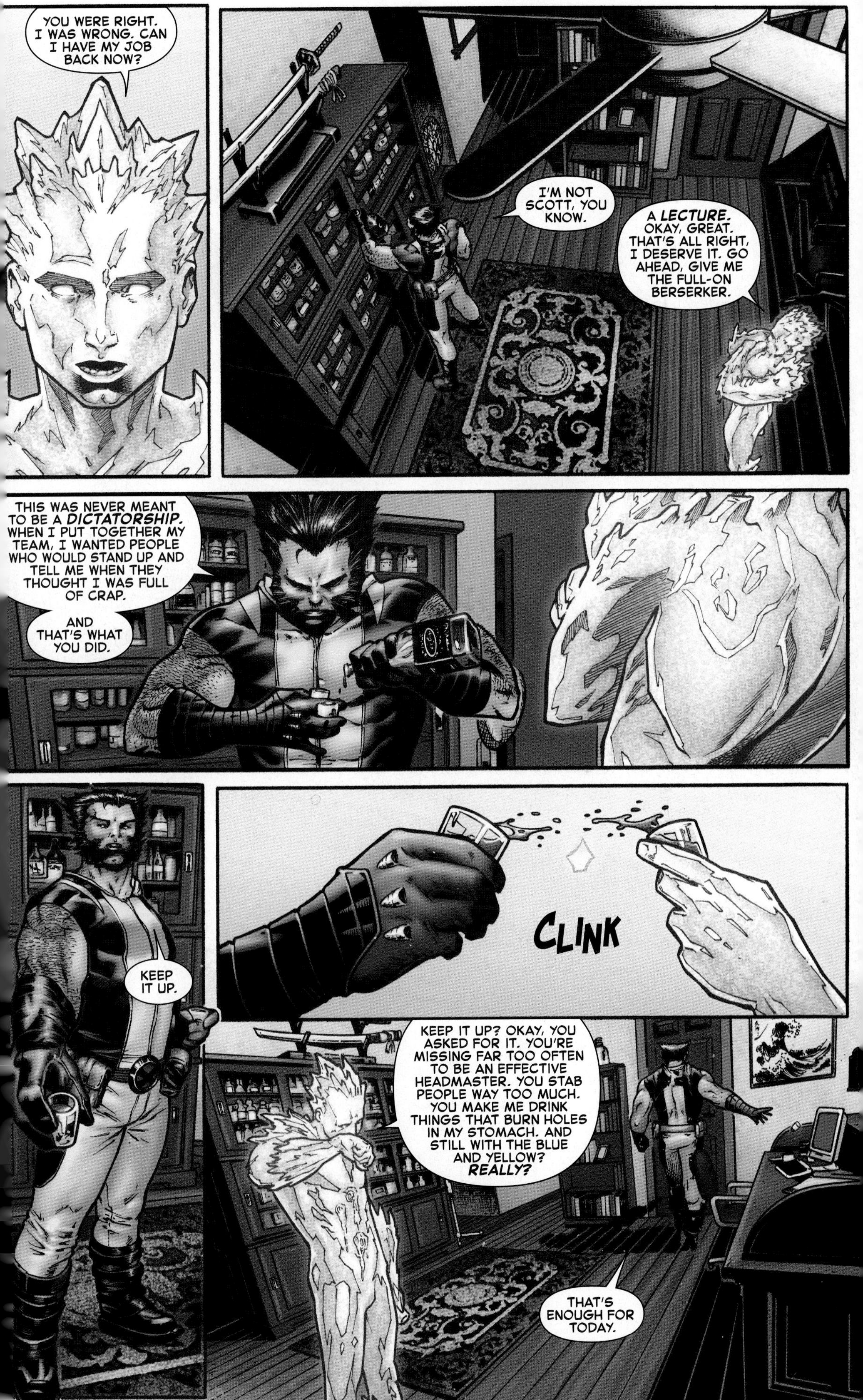
YOU WERE RIGHT. I WAS WRONG. CAN I HAVE MY JOB BACK NOW?
I'M NOT SCOTT, YOU KNOW.
A LECTURE. OKAY, GREAT. THAT'S ALL RIGHT, I DESERVE IT. GO AHEAD, GIVE ME THE FULL-ON BERSERKER.
THIS WAS NEVER MEANT TO BE A DICTATORSHIP. WHEN I PUT TOGETHER MY TEAM, I WANTED PEOPLE WHO WOULD STAND UP AND TELL ME WHEN THEY THOUGHT I WAS FULL OF CRAP.
AND THAT'S WHAT YOU DID.
KEEP IT UP.
CLINK
KEEP IT UP? OKAY, YOU ASKED FOR IT. YOU'RE MISSING FAR TOO OFTEN TO BE AN EFFECTIVE HEADMASTER. YOU STAB PEOPLE WAY TOO MUCH. YOU MAKE ME DRINK THINGS THAT BURN HOLES IN MY STOMACH. AND STILL WITH THE BLUE AND YELLOW? REALLY?
THAT'S ENOUGH FOR TODAY.

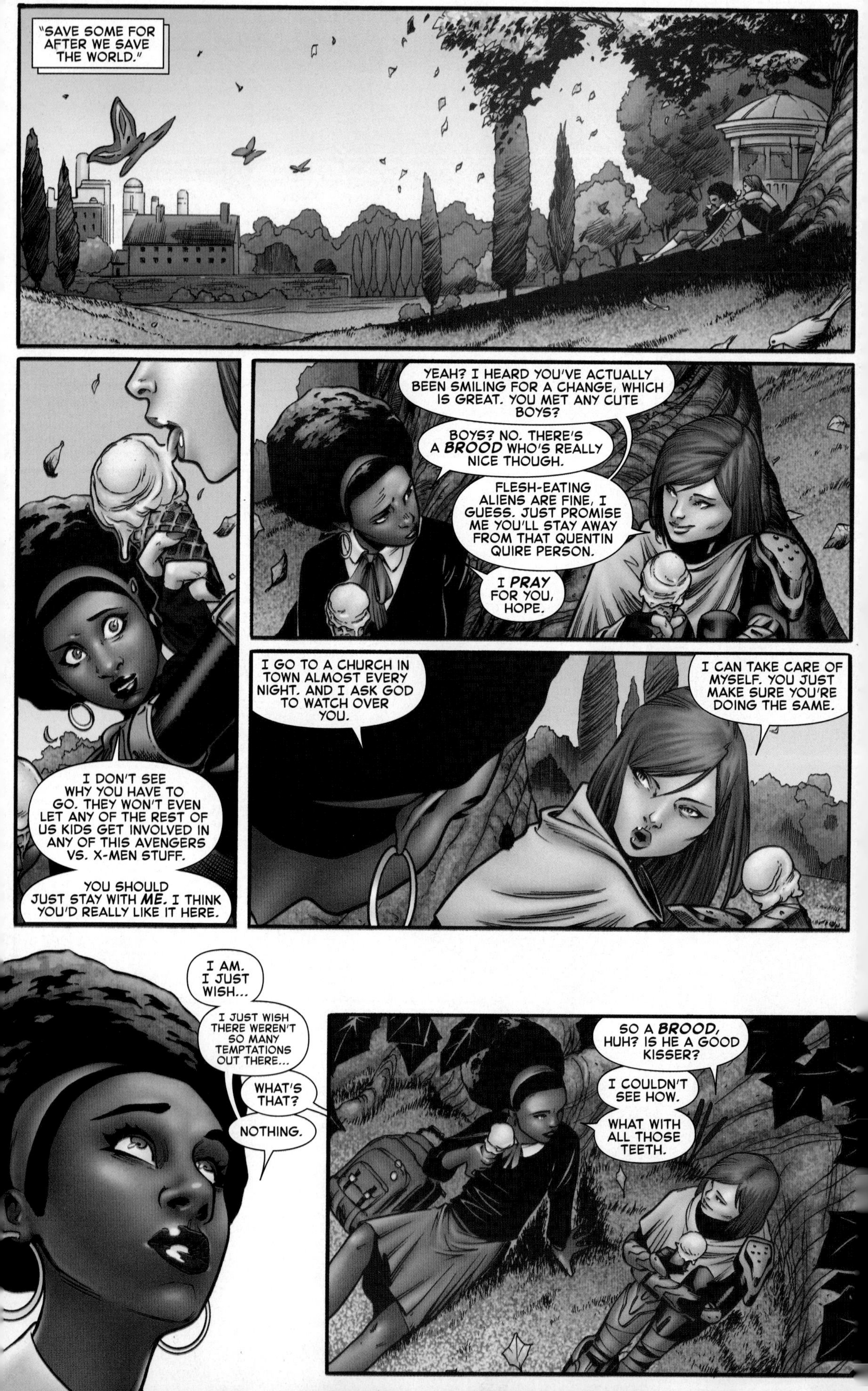
"SAVE SOME FOR AFTER WE SAVE THE WORLD."
YEAH? I HEARD YOU'VE ACTUALLY BEEN SMILING FOR A CHANGE, WHICH IS GREAT. YOU MET ANY CUTE BOYS?
BOYS? NO. THERE'S A BROOD WHO'S REALLY NICE THOUGH.
FLESH-EATING ALIENS ARE FINE, I GUESS. JUST PROMISE ME YOU'LL STAY AWAY FROM THAT QUENTIN QUIRE PERSON.
I PRAY FOR YOU, HOPE.
I GO TO A CHURCH IN TOWN ALMOST EVERY NIGHT. AND I ASK GOD TO WATCH OVER YOU.
I CAN TAKE CARE OF MYSELF. YOU JUST MAKE SURE YOU'RE DOING THE SAME.
I DON'T SEE WHY YOU HAVE TO GO. THEY WON'T EVEN LET ANY OF THE REST OF US KIDS GET INVOLVED IN ANY OF THIS AVENGERS VS. X-MEN STUFF.
YOU SHOULD JUST STAY WITH ME. I THINK YOU'D REALLY LIKE IT HERE.
I AM. I JUST WISH...
I JUST WISH THERE WEREN'T SO MANY TEMPTATIONS OUT THERE...
WHAT'S THAT?
NOTHING.
SO A BROOD, HUH? IS HE A GOOD KISSER?
I COULDN'T SEE HOW.
WHAT WITH ALL THOSE TEETH.

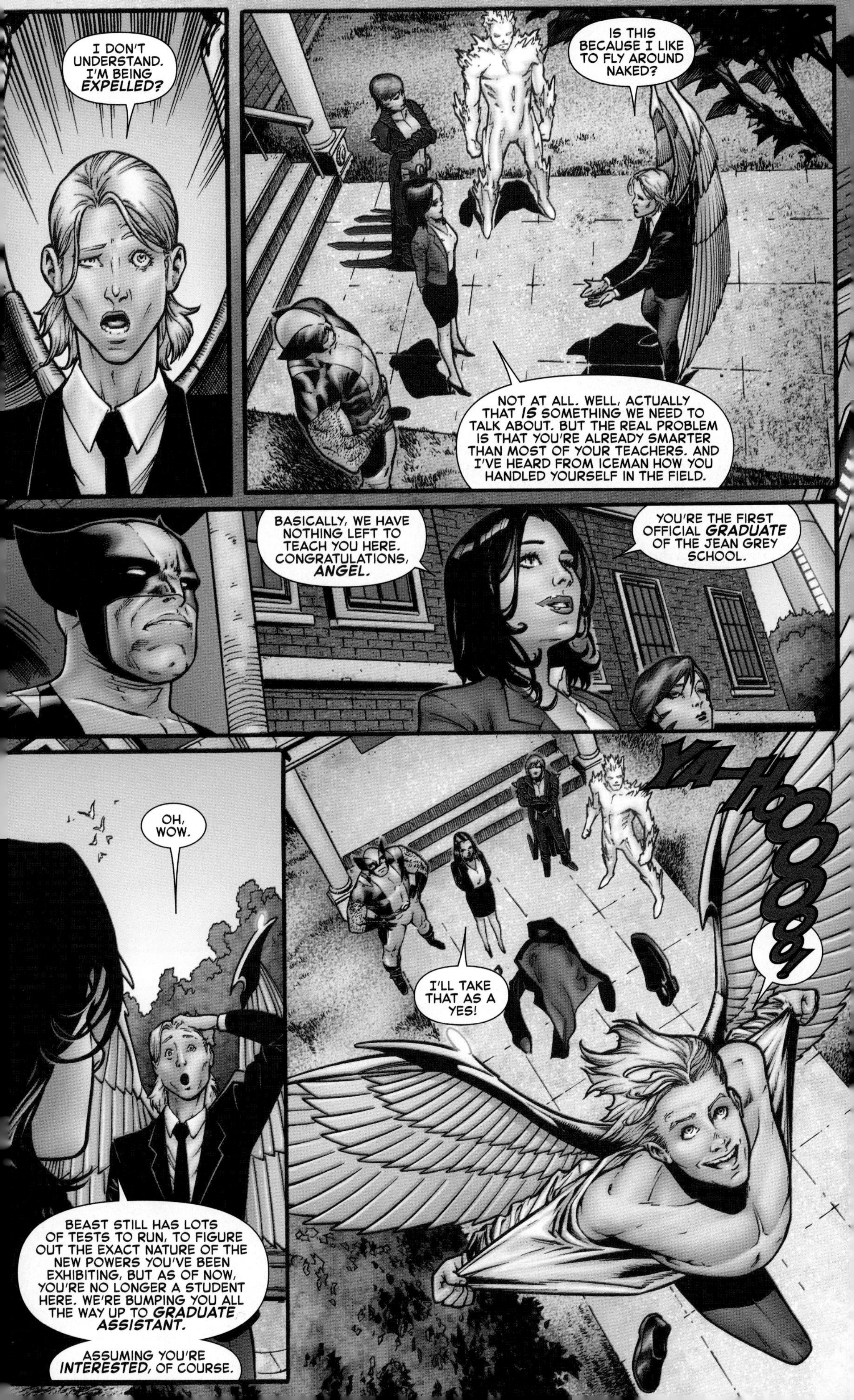
I DON'T UNDERSTAND. I'M BEING EXPELLED?
IS THIS BECAUSE I LIKE TO FLY AROUND NAKED?
NOT AT ALL. WELL, ACTUALLY THAT IS SOMETHING WE NEED TO TALK ABOUT. BUT THE REAL PROBLEM IS THAT YOU'RE ALREADY SMARTER THAN MOST OF YOUR TEACHERS. AND I'VE HEARD FROM ICEMAN HOW YOU HANDLED YOURSELF IN THE FIELD.
BASICALLY, WE HAVE NOTHING LEFT TO TEACH YOU HERE. CONGRATULATIONS, ANGEL.
YOU'RE THE FIRST OFFICIAL GRADUATE OF THE JEAN GREY SCHOOL.
OH, WOW.
BEAST STILL HAS LOTS OF TESTS TO RUN, TO FIGURE OUT THE EXACT NATURE OF THE NEW POWERS YOU'VE BEEN EXHIBITING, BUT AS OF NOW, YOU'RE NO LONGER A STUDENT HERE. WE'RE BUMPING YOU ALL THE WAY UP TO GRADUATE ASSISTANT.
ASSUMING YOU'RE INTERESTED, OF COURSE.
YA-HOOOOOO!
I'LL TAKE THAT AS A YES!

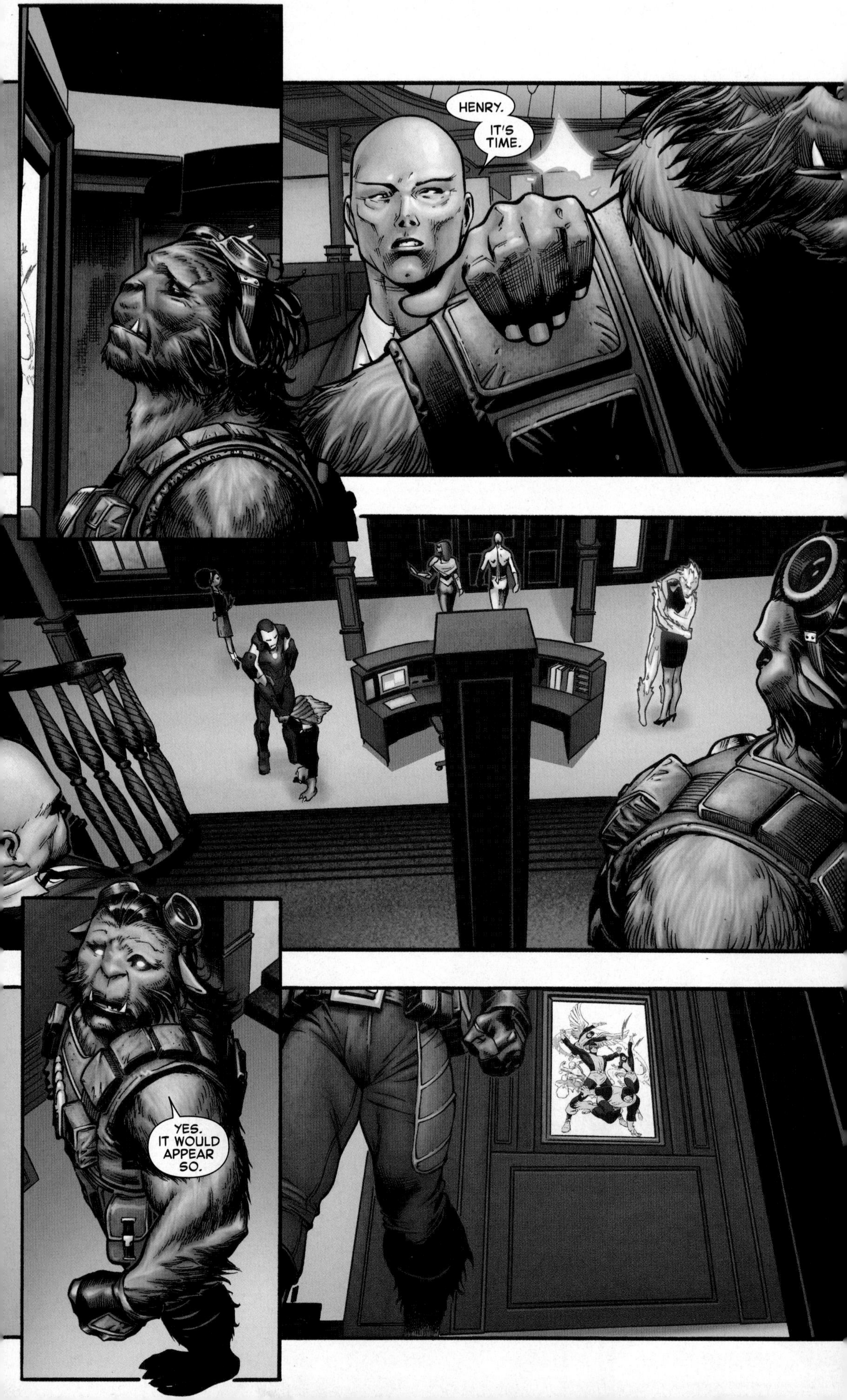
HENRY.
IT'S TIME.
YES. IT WOULD APPEAR SO.

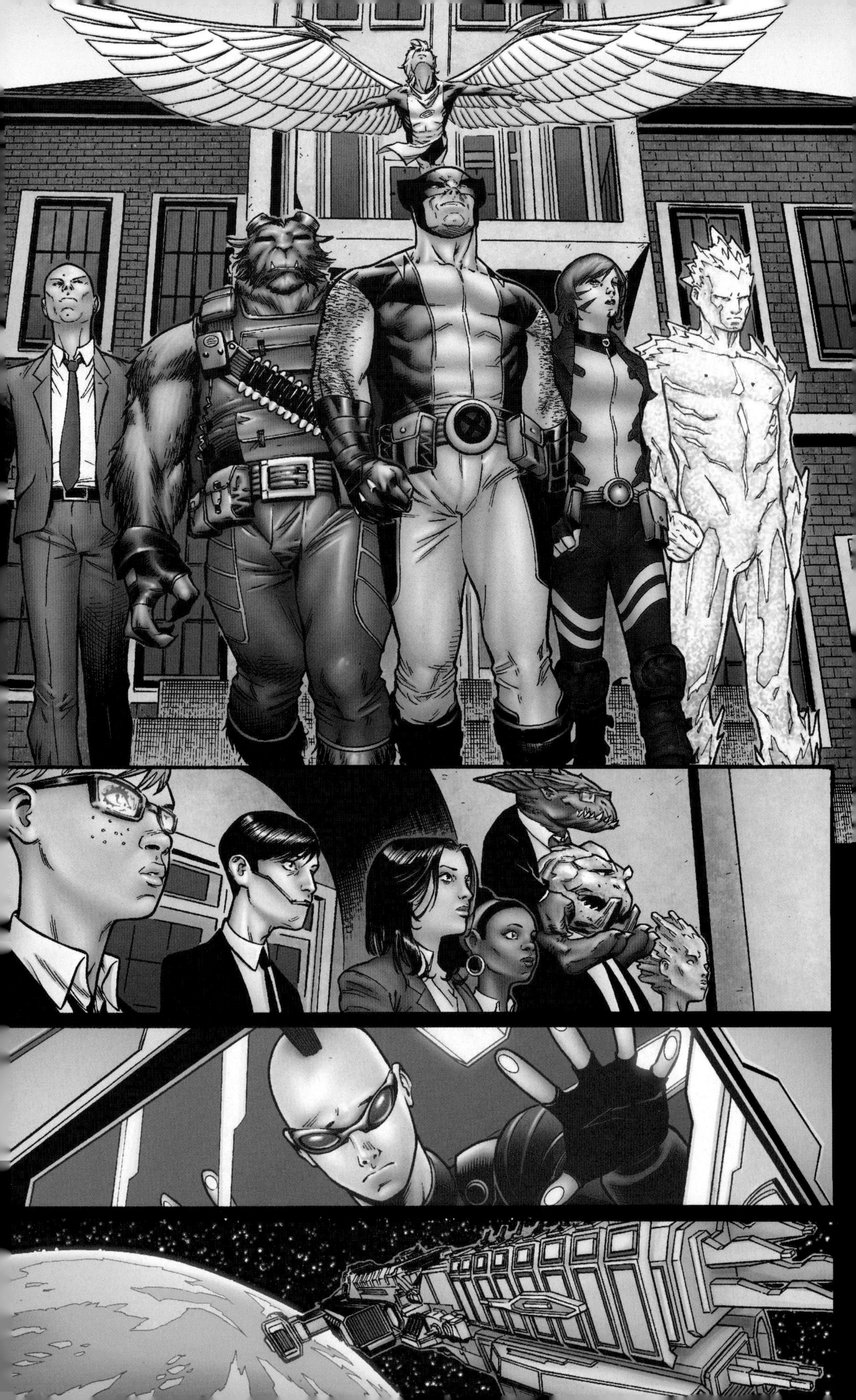

16 "THE FIRES OF HELL A-GLOWING"

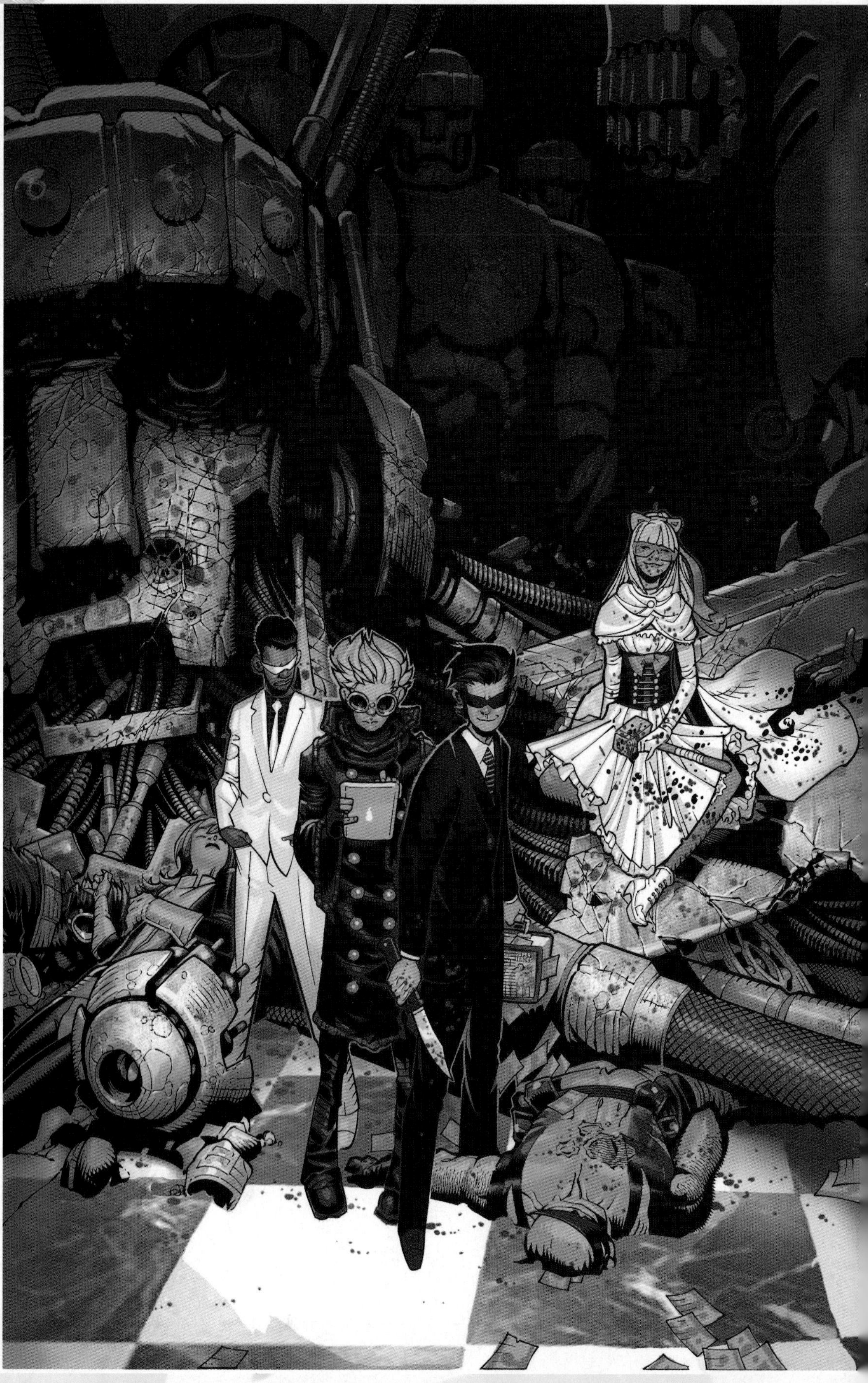

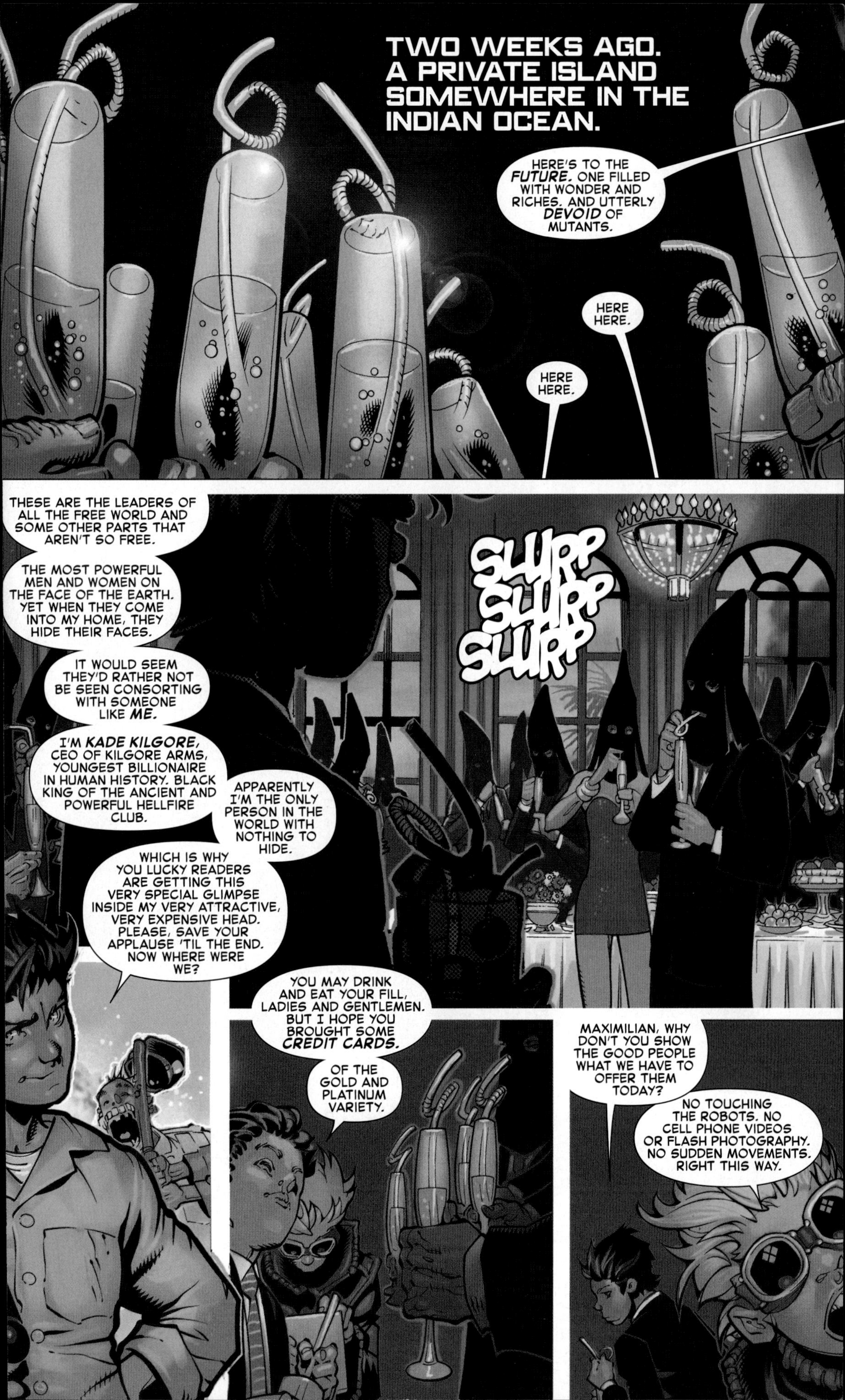

TWO WEEKS AGO. A PRIVATE ISLAND SOMEWHERE IN THE INDIAN OCEAN.
HERE'S TO THE FUTURE. ONE FILLED WITH WONDER AND RICHES. AND UTTERLY DEVOID OF MUTANTS.
HERE HERE.
HERE HERE.
THESE ARE THE LEADERS OF ALL THE FREE WORLD AND SOME OTHER PARTS THAT AREN'T SO FREE.
THE MOST POWERFUL MEN AND WOMEN ON THE FACE OF THE EARTH. YET WHEN THEY COME INTO MY HOME, THEY HIDE THEIR FACES.
IT WOULD SEEM THEY'D RATHER NOT BE SEEN CONSORTING WITH SOMEONE LIKE ME.
SLURP SLURP SLURP
I'M KADE KILGORE, CEO OF KILGORE ARMS, YOUNGEST BILLIONAIRE IN HUMAN HISTORY. BLACK KING OF THE ANCIENT AND POWERFUL HELLFIRE CLUB.
APPARENTLY I'M THE ONLY PERSON IN THE WORLD WITH NOTHING TO HIDE.
WHICH IS WHY YOU LUCKY READERS ARE GETTING THIS VERY SPECIAL GLIMPSE INSIDE MY VERY ATTRACTIVE, VERY EXPENSIVE HEAD. PLEASE, SAVE YOUR APPLAUSE 'TIL THE END. NOW WHERE WERE WE?
YOU MAY DRINK AND EAT YOUR FILL, LADIES AND GENTLEMEN. BUT I HOPE YOU BROUGHT SOME CREDIT CARDS.
OF THE GOLD AND PLATINUM VARIETY.
MAXIMILIAN, WHY DON'T YOU SHOW THE GOOD PEOPLE WHAT WE HAVE TO OFFER THEM TODAY?
NO TOUCHING THE ROBOTS. NO CELL PHONE VIDEOS OR FLASH PHOTOGRAPHY. NO SUDDEN MOVEMENTS. RIGHT THIS WAY.

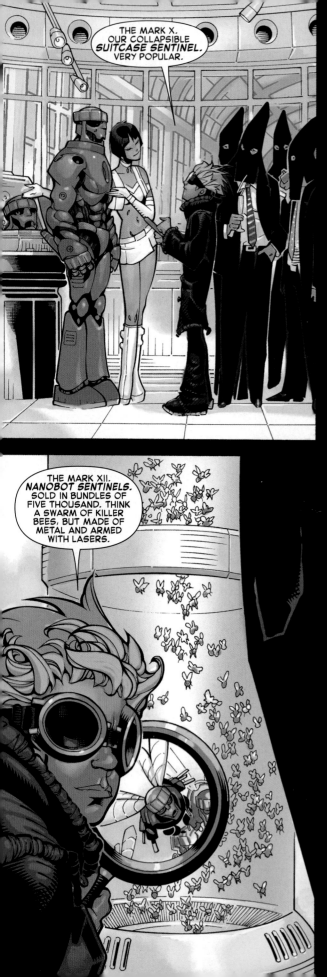

THE MARK X. OUR COLLAPSIBLE **SUITCASE SENTINEL.** VERY POPULAR.

THE MARK XI. TRANSFORMABLE **ALL-TERRAIN** MODELS. FOR MURDER BY LAND, AIR OR SEA.

THE MARK XII. **NANOBOT SENTINELS.** SOLD IN BUNDLES OF FIVE THOUSAND. THINK A SWARM OF KILLER BEES, BUT MADE OF METAL AND ARMED WITH LASERS.

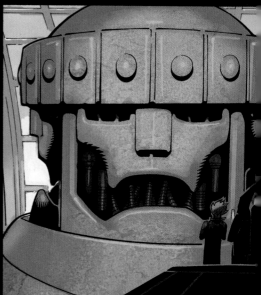

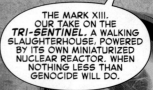

THE MARK XIII. OUR TAKE ON THE **TRI-SENTINEL.** A WALKING SLAUGHTERHOUSE, POWERED BY ITS OWN MINIATURIZED NUCLEAR REACTOR. WHEN NOTHING LESS THAN GENOCIDE WILL DO.

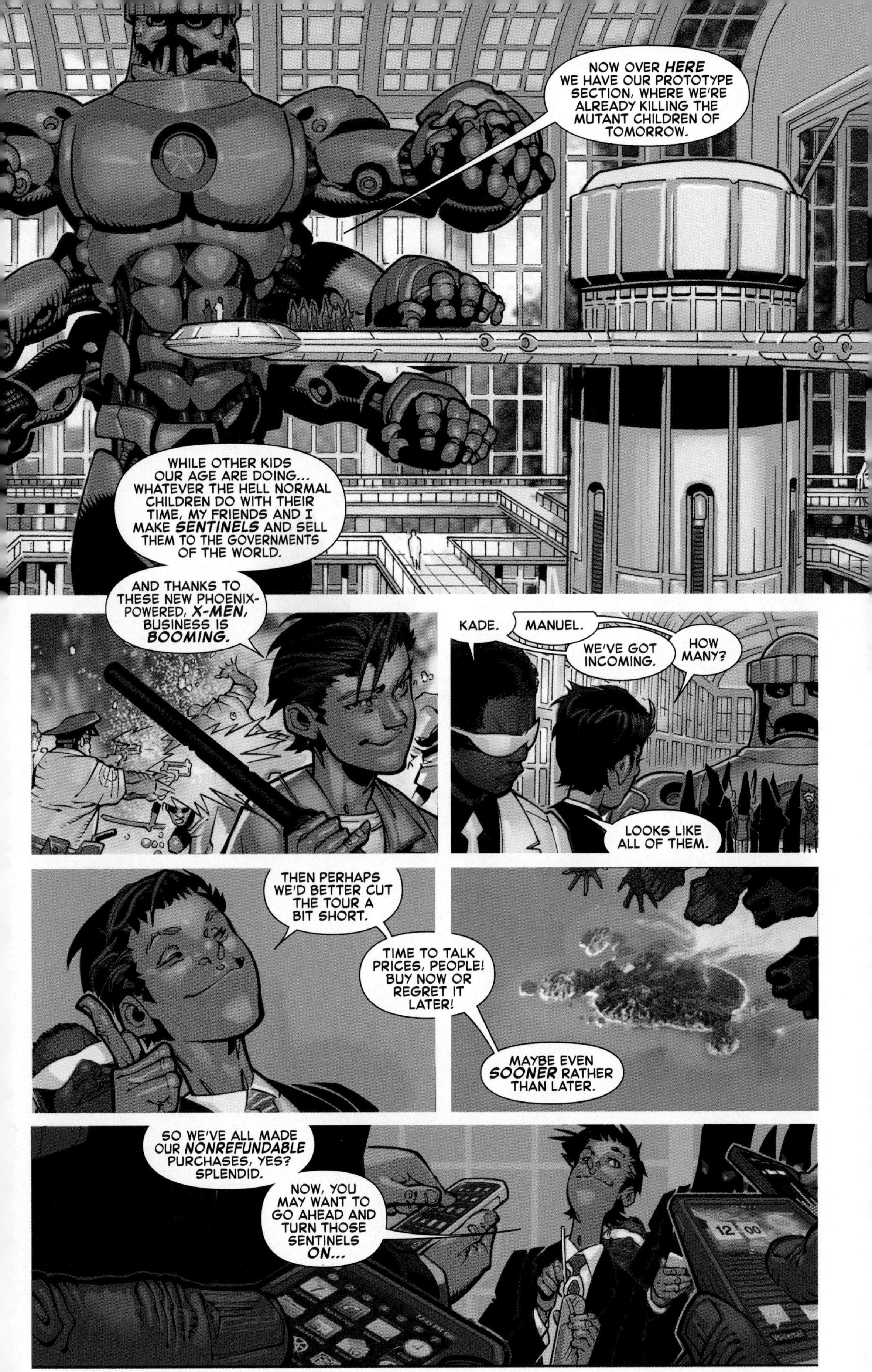
NOW OVER HERE WE HAVE OUR PROTOTYPE SECTION, WHERE WE'RE ALREADY KILLING THE MUTANT CHILDREN OF TOMORROW.
WHILE OTHER KIDS OUR AGE ARE DOING... WHATEVER THE HELL NORMAL CHILDREN DO WITH THEIR TIME, MY FRIENDS AND I MAKE SENTINELS AND SELL THEM TO THE GOVERNMENTS OF THE WORLD.
AND THANKS TO THESE NEW PHOENIX-POWERED, X-MEN, BUSINESS IS BOOMING.
KADE.
MANUEL.
WE'VE GOT INCOMING.
HOW MANY?
LOOKS LIKE ALL OF THEM.
THEN PERHAPS WE'D BETTER CUT THE TOUR A BIT SHORT.
TIME TO TALK PRICES, PEOPLE! BUY NOW OR REGRET IT LATER!
MAYBE EVEN SOONER RATHER THAN LATER.
SO WE'VE ALL MADE OUR NONREFUNDABLE PURCHASES, YES? SPLENDID.
NOW, YOU MAY WANT TO GO AHEAD AND TURN THOSE SENTINELS ON...

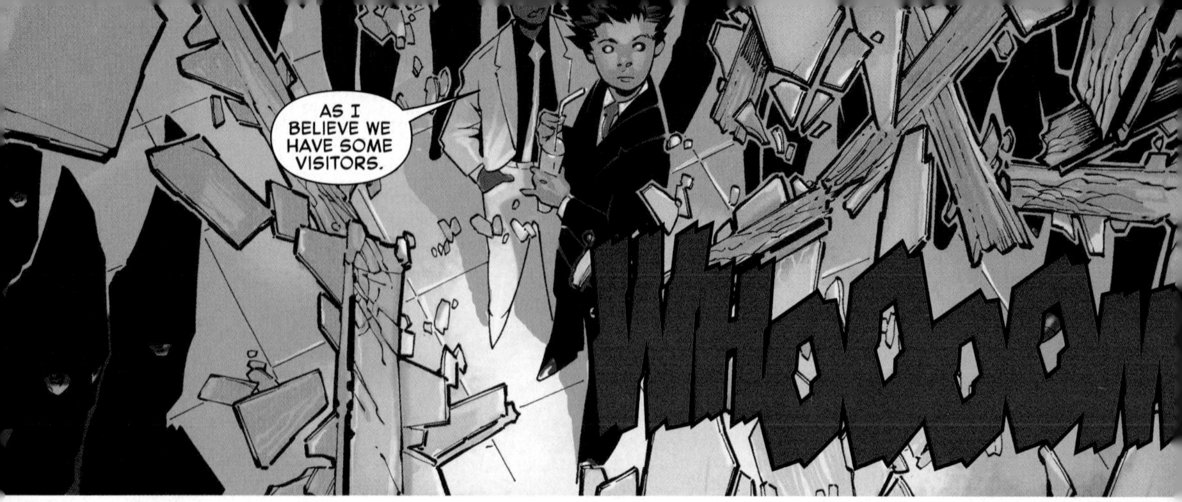
AS I BELIEVE WE HAVE SOME VISITORS.
WHOOOOM

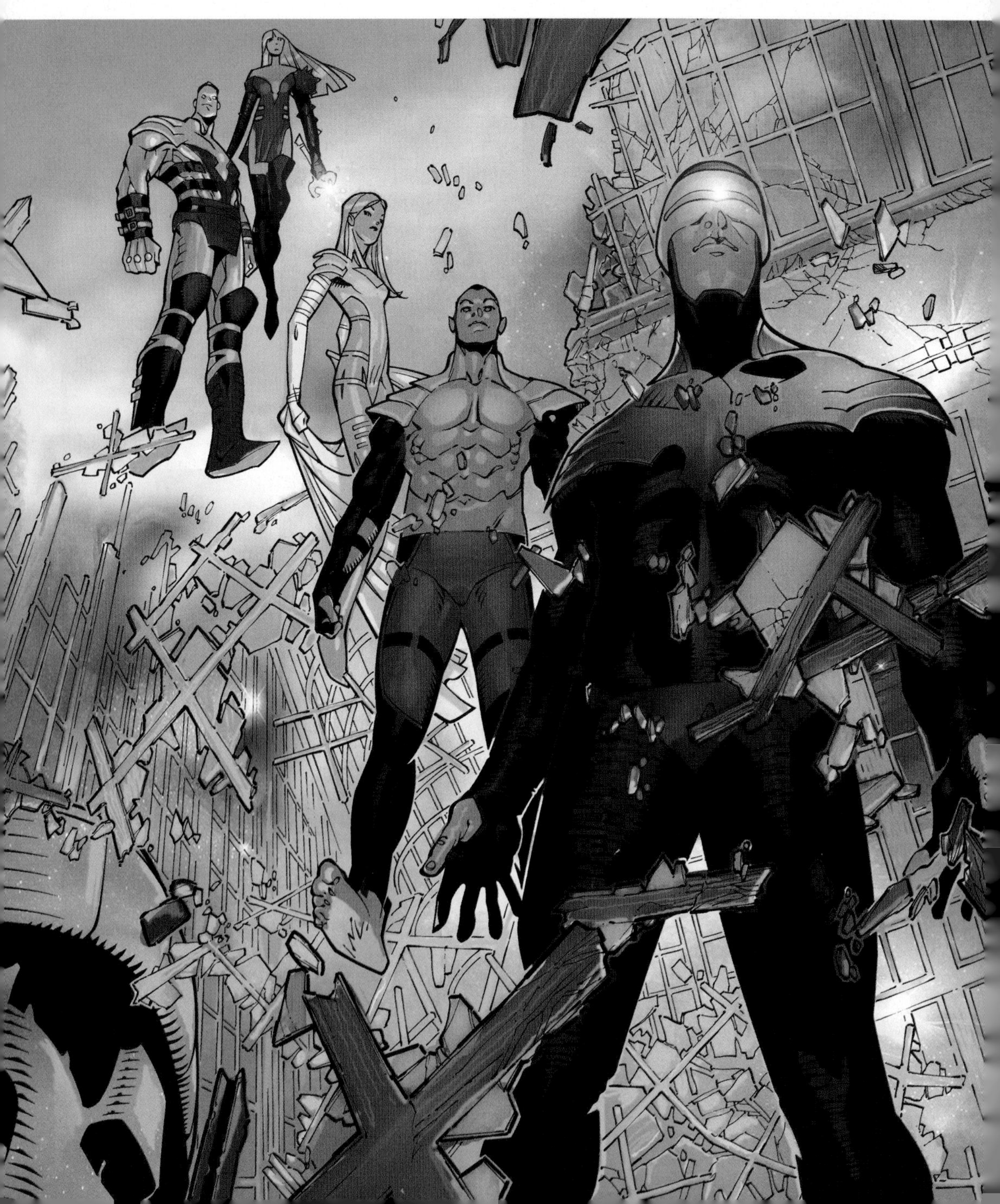

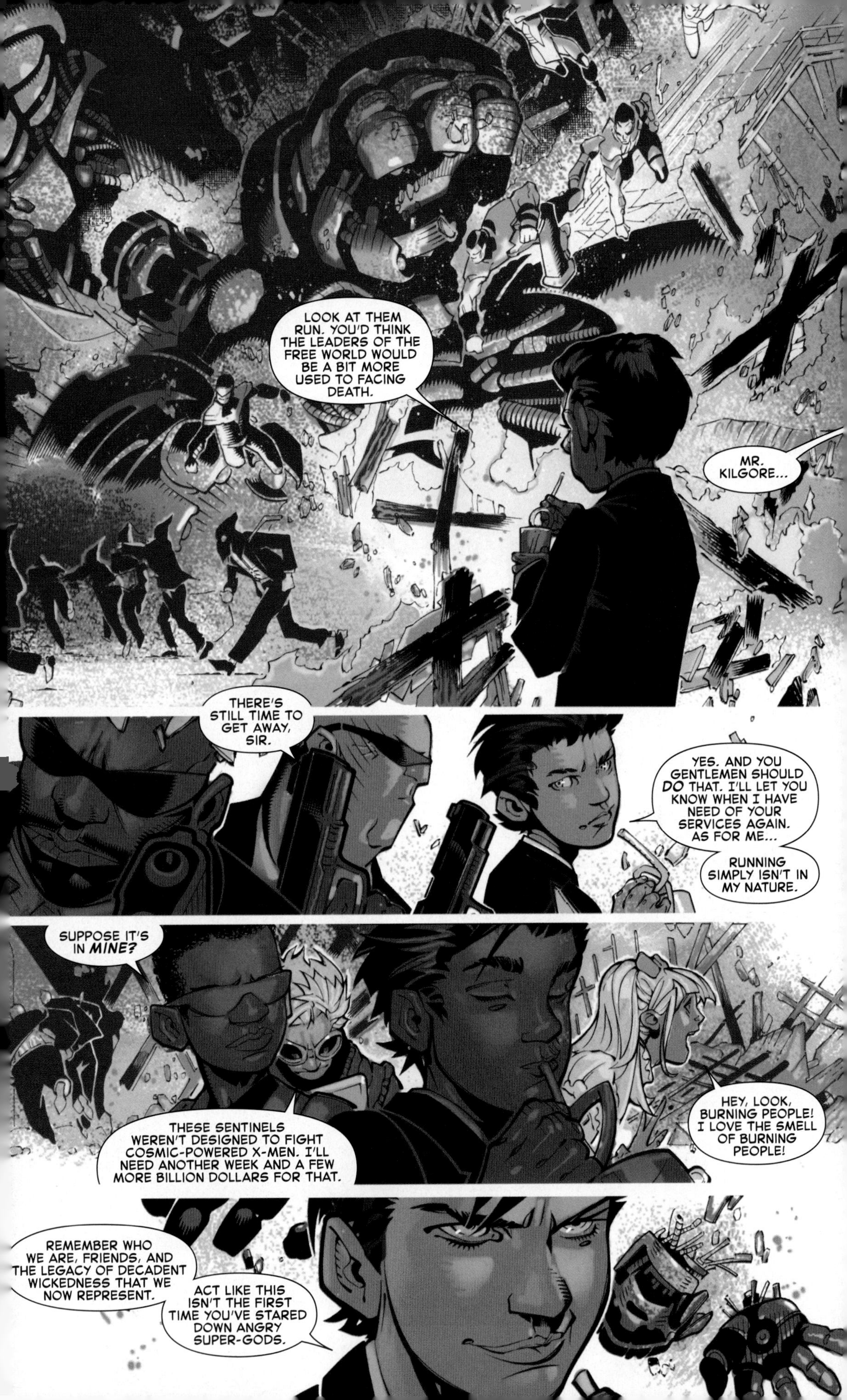
LOOK AT THEM RUN. YOU'D THINK THE LEADERS OF THE FREE WORLD WOULD BE A BIT MORE USED TO FACING DEATH.
MR. KILGORE...
THERE'S STILL TIME TO GET AWAY, SIR.
YES. AND YOU GENTLEMEN SHOULD DO THAT. I'LL LET YOU KNOW WHEN I HAVE NEED OF YOUR SERVICES AGAIN. AS FOR ME...
RUNNING SIMPLY ISN'T IN MY NATURE.
SUPPOSE IT'S IN MINE?
THESE SENTINELS WEREN'T DESIGNED TO FIGHT COSMIC-POWERED X-MEN. I'LL NEED ANOTHER WEEK AND A FEW MORE BILLION DOLLARS FOR THAT.
HEY, LOOK, BURNING PEOPLE! I LOVE THE SMELL OF BURNING PEOPLE!
REMEMBER WHO WE ARE, FRIENDS, AND THE LEGACY OF DECADENT WICKEDNESS THAT WE NOW REPRESENT.
ACT LIKE THIS ISN'T THE FIRST TIME YOU'VE STARED DOWN ANGRY SUPER-GODS.

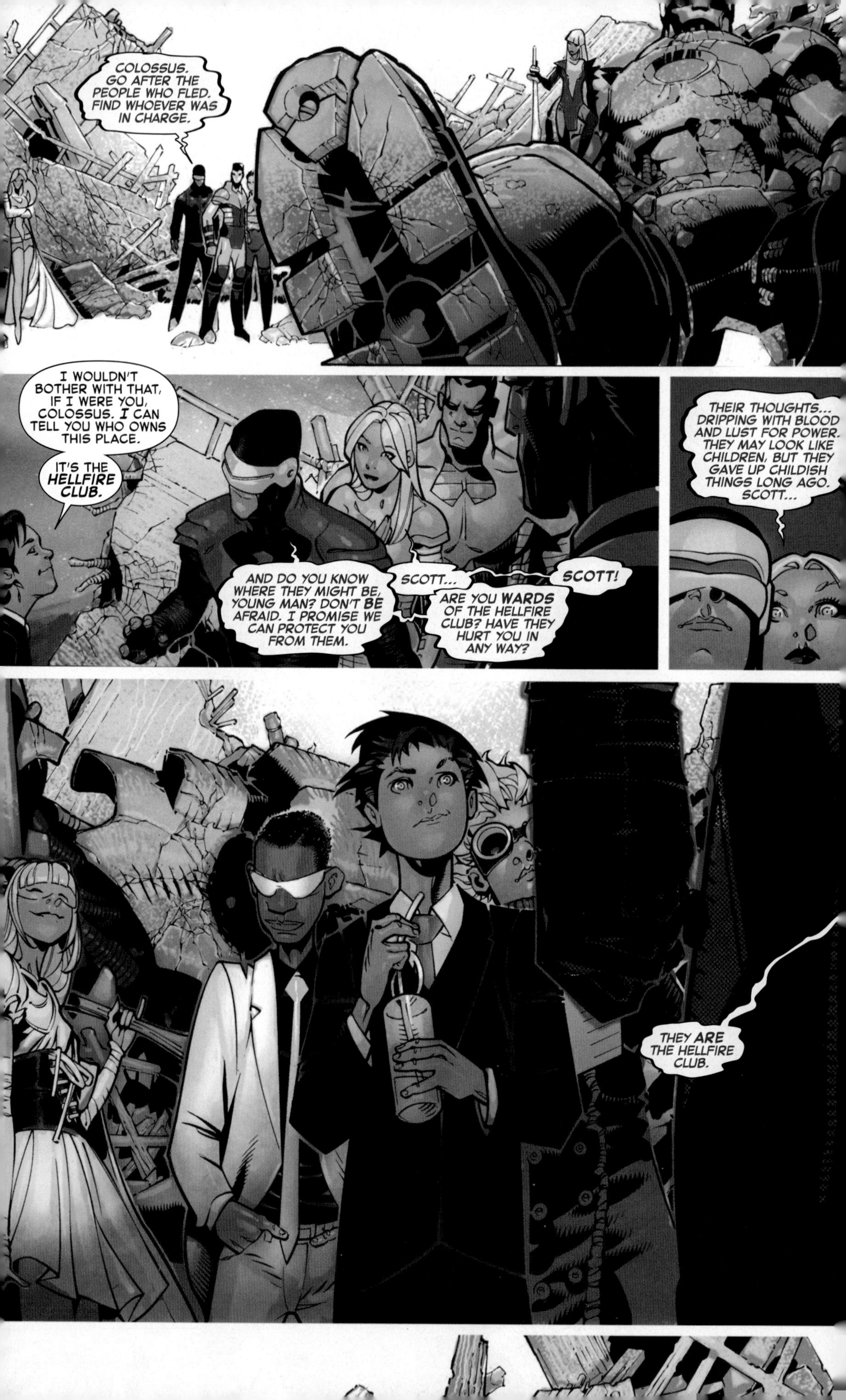
COLOSSUS. GO AFTER THE PEOPLE WHO FLED. FIND WHOEVER WAS IN CHARGE.
I WOULDN'T BOTHER WITH THAT, IF I WERE YOU, COLOSSUS. *I* CAN TELL YOU WHO OWNS THIS PLACE.
IT'S THE *HELLFIRE CLUB.*
AND DO YOU KNOW WHERE THEY MIGHT BE, YOUNG MAN? DON'T **BE** AFRAID. I PROMISE WE CAN PROTECT YOU FROM THEM.
SCOTT...
ARE YOU **WARDS** OF THE HELLFIRE CLUB? HAVE THEY HURT YOU IN ANY WAY?
SCOTT!
THEIR THOUGHTS... DRIPPING WITH BLOOD AND LUST FOR POWER. THEY MAY LOOK LIKE CHILDREN, BUT THEY GAVE UP CHILDISH THINGS LONG AGO. SCOTT...
THEY **ARE** THE HELLFIRE CLUB.

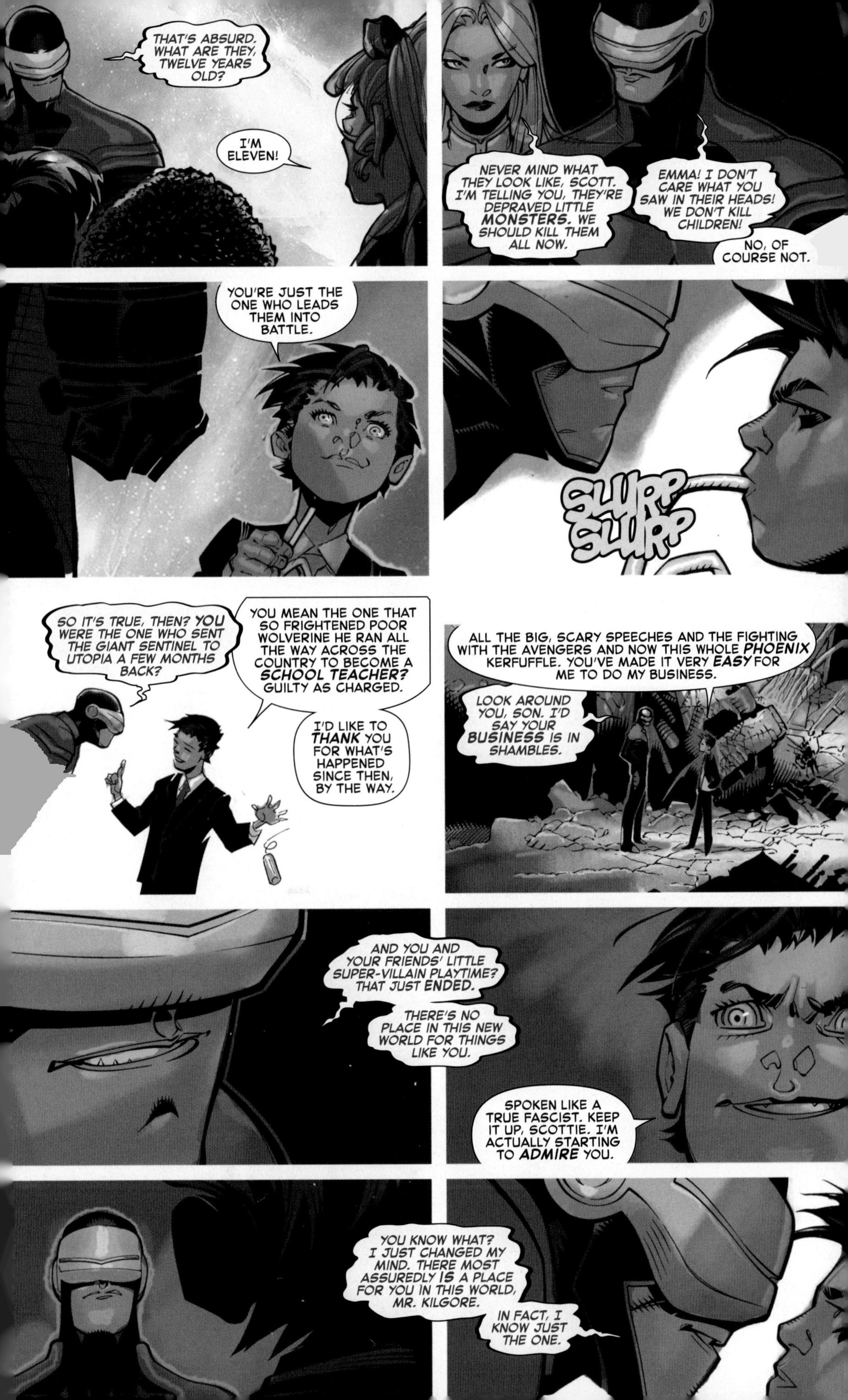
THAT'S ABSURD. WHAT ARE THEY, TWELVE YEARS OLD?
I'M ELEVEN!
NEVER MIND WHAT THEY LOOK LIKE, SCOTT. I'M TELLING YOU, THEY'RE DEPRAVED LITTLE MONSTERS. WE SHOULD KILL THEM ALL NOW.
EMMA! I DON'T CARE WHAT YOU SAW IN THEIR HEADS! WE DON'T KILL CHILDREN!
NO, OF COURSE NOT.
YOU'RE JUST THE ONE WHO LEADS THEM INTO BATTLE.
SLURP SLURP
SO IT'S TRUE, THEN? YOU WERE THE ONE WHO SENT THE GIANT SENTINEL TO UTOPIA A FEW MONTHS BACK?
YOU MEAN THE ONE THAT SO FRIGHTENED POOR WOLVERINE HE RAN ALL THE WAY ACROSS THE COUNTRY TO BECOME A SCHOOL TEACHER? GUILTY AS CHARGED.
I'D LIKE TO THANK YOU FOR WHAT'S HAPPENED SINCE THEN, BY THE WAY.
ALL THE BIG, SCARY SPEECHES AND THE FIGHTING WITH THE AVENGERS AND NOW THIS WHOLE PHOENIX KERFUFFLE. YOU'VE MADE IT VERY EASY FOR ME TO DO MY BUSINESS.
LOOK AROUND YOU, SON. I'D SAY YOUR BUSINESS IS IN SHAMBLES.
AND YOU AND YOUR FRIENDS' LITTLE SUPER-VILLAIN PLAYTIME? THAT JUST ENDED.
THERE'S NO PLACE IN THIS NEW WORLD FOR THINGS LIKE YOU.
SPOKEN LIKE A TRUE FASCIST. KEEP IT UP, SCOTTIE. I'M ACTUALLY STARTING TO ADMIRE YOU.
YOU KNOW WHAT? I JUST CHANGED MY MIND. THERE MOST ASSUREDLY IS A PLACE FOR YOU IN THIS WORLD, MR. KILGORE.
IN FACT, I KNOW JUST THE ONE.

YOUNGEST INMATE EVER ADMITTED TO RYKERS ISLAND. ADD THAT TO THE LIST OF ACCOMPLISHMENTS.

"WHAT'S THAT THEY SAY ABOUT YOUR FIRST DAY IN PRISON? YOU HAVE TO FIND THE BIGGEST, TOUGHEST GUY YOU CAN...

"AND SHOW HIM WHAT YOU'RE MADE OF.

"ANTHONY TAMAZZOTTI. THEY CALL HIM *TONY TAPIOCA* BECAUSE HIS VICTIMS LOOK LIKE *PUDDING* BY THE TIME HE'S DONE WITH THEM.

"THEY HAVE NO IDEA HOW MANY PEOPLE HE'S KILLED. THEY'RE STILL SORTING THROUGH THE BLOODY SOUP IN HIS BATHTUB.

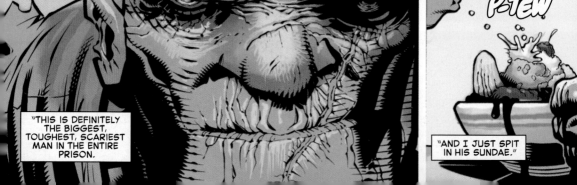

"THIS IS DEFINITELY THE BIGGEST, TOUGHEST, SCARIEST MAN IN THE ENTIRE PRISON.

P-TEW

"AND I JUST SPIT IN HIS SUNDAE."

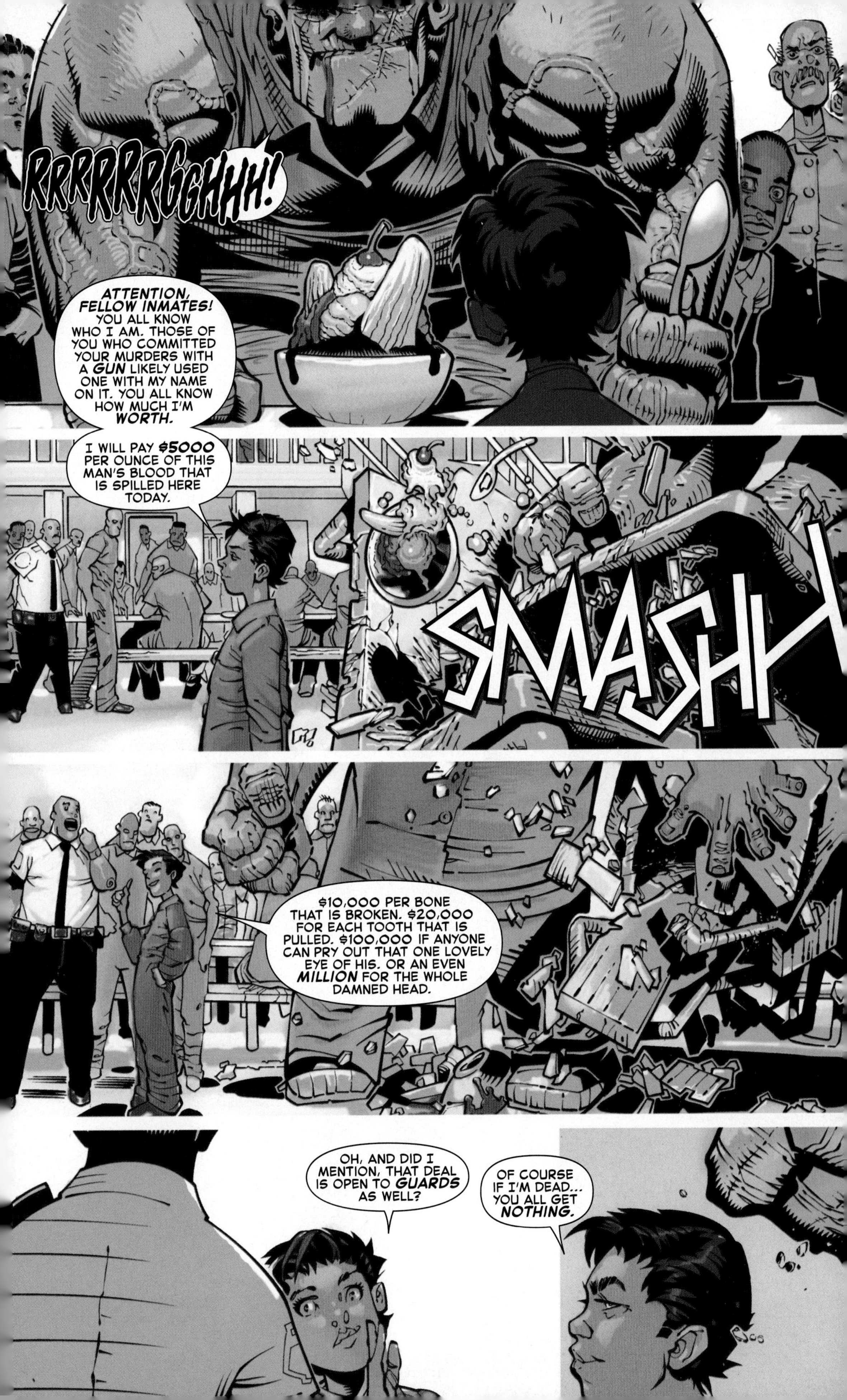
RRRRRRGGHHH!
ATTENTION, FELLOW INMATES! YOU ALL KNOW WHO I AM. THOSE OF YOU WHO COMMITTED YOUR MURDERS WITH A GUN LIKELY USED ONE WITH MY NAME ON IT. YOU ALL KNOW HOW MUCH I'M WORTH.
I WILL PAY $5000 PER OUNCE OF THIS MAN'S BLOOD THAT IS SPILLED HERE TODAY.
SMASH
$10,000 PER BONE THAT IS BROKEN. $20,000 FOR EACH TOOTH THAT IS PULLED. $100,000 IF ANYONE CAN PRY OUT THAT ONE LOVELY EYE OF HIS. OR AN EVEN MILLION FOR THE WHOLE DAMNED HEAD.
OH, AND DID I MENTION, THAT DEAL IS OPEN TO GUARDS AS WELL?
OF COURSE IF I'M DEAD... YOU ALL GET NOTHING.

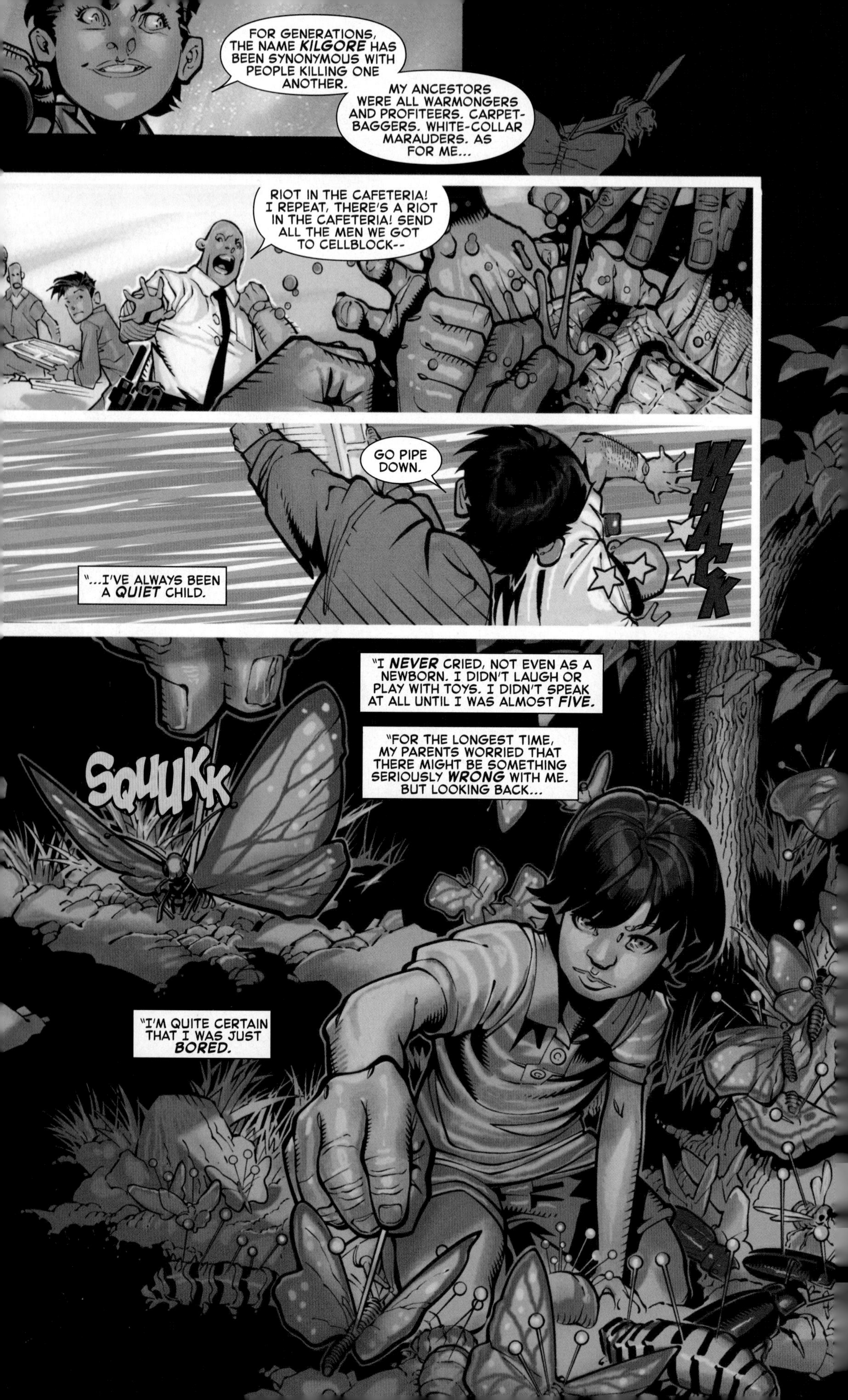
FOR GENERATIONS, THE NAME *KILGORE* HAS BEEN SYNONYMOUS WITH PEOPLE KILLING ONE ANOTHER.
MY ANCESTORS WERE ALL WARMONGERS AND PROFITEERS. CARPET-BAGGERS. WHITE-COLLAR MARAUDERS. AS FOR ME...
RIOT IN THE CAFETERIA! I REPEAT, THERE'S A RIOT IN THE CAFETERIA! SEND ALL THE MEN WE GOT TO CELLBLOCK--
GO PIPE DOWN.
WHACK
"...I'VE ALWAYS BEEN A *QUIET* CHILD.
"I *NEVER* CRIED, NOT EVEN AS A NEWBORN. I DIDN'T LAUGH OR PLAY WITH TOYS. I DIDN'T SPEAK AT ALL UNTIL I WAS ALMOST *FIVE.*
"FOR THE LONGEST TIME, MY PARENTS WORRIED THAT THERE MIGHT BE SOMETHING SERIOUSLY *WRONG* WITH ME. BUT LOOKING BACK...
SQUUKK
"I'M QUITE CERTAIN THAT I WAS JUST *BORED.*

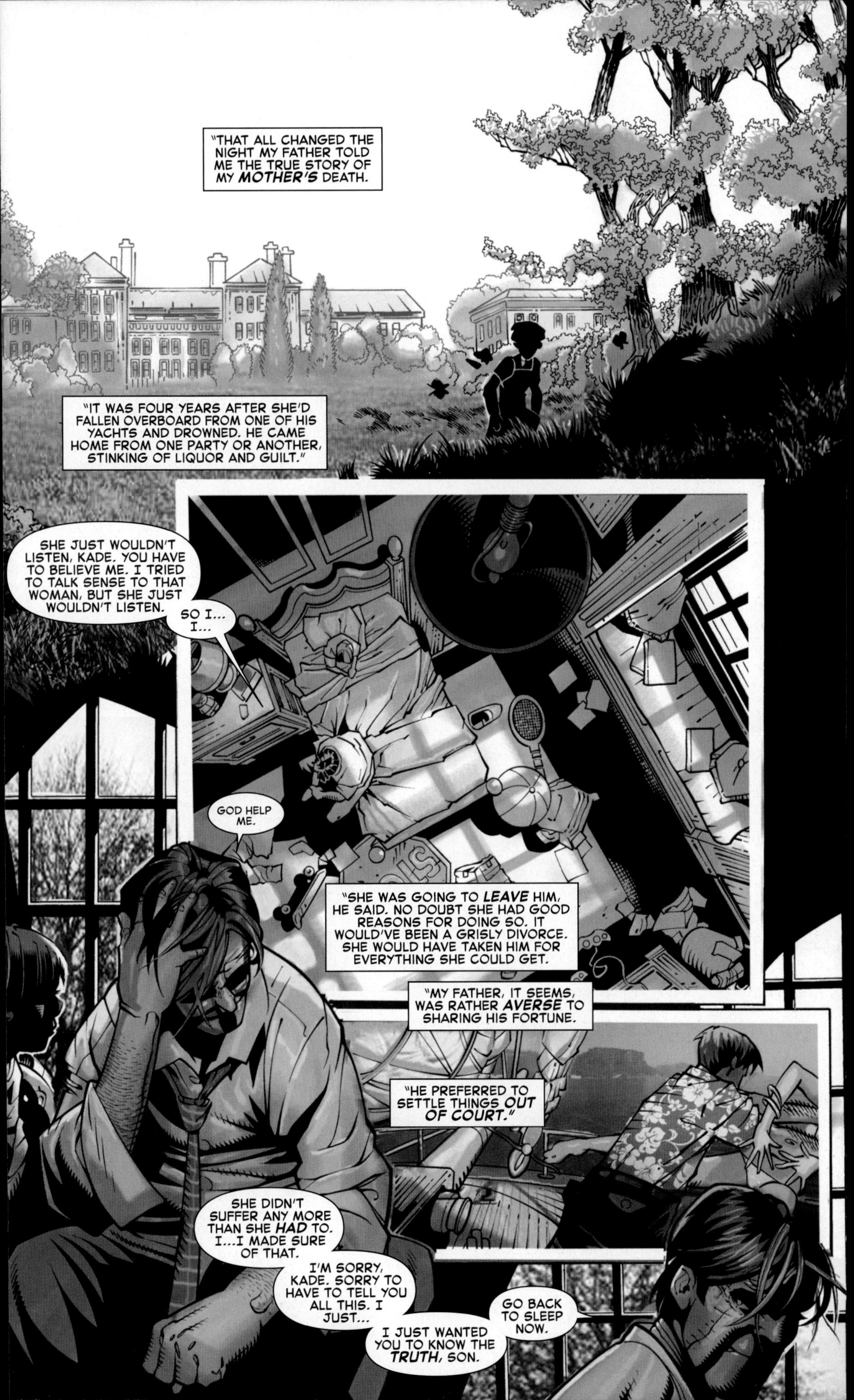
"THAT ALL CHANGED THE NIGHT MY FATHER TOLD ME THE TRUE STORY OF MY MOTHER'S DEATH.
"IT WAS FOUR YEARS AFTER SHE'D FALLEN OVERBOARD FROM ONE OF HIS YACHTS AND DROWNED. HE CAME HOME FROM ONE PARTY OR ANOTHER, STINKING OF LIQUOR AND GUILT."
SHE JUST WOULDN'T LISTEN, KADE. YOU HAVE TO BELIEVE ME. I TRIED TO TALK SENSE TO THAT WOMAN, BUT SHE JUST WOULDN'T LISTEN.
SO I... I...
GOD HELP ME.
"SHE WAS GOING TO LEAVE HIM, HE SAID. NO DOUBT SHE HAD GOOD REASONS FOR DOING SO. IT WOULD'VE BEEN A GRISLY DIVORCE. SHE WOULD HAVE TAKEN HIM FOR EVERYTHING SHE COULD GET.
"MY FATHER, IT SEEMS, WAS RATHER AVERSE TO SHARING HIS FORTUNE.
"HE PREFERRED TO SETTLE THINGS OUT OF COURT."
SHE DIDN'T SUFFER ANY MORE THAN SHE HAD TO. I...I MADE SURE OF THAT.
I'M SORRY, KADE. SORRY TO HAVE TO TELL YOU ALL THIS. I JUST...
I JUST WANTED YOU TO KNOW THE TRUTH, SON.
GO BACK TO SLEEP NOW.

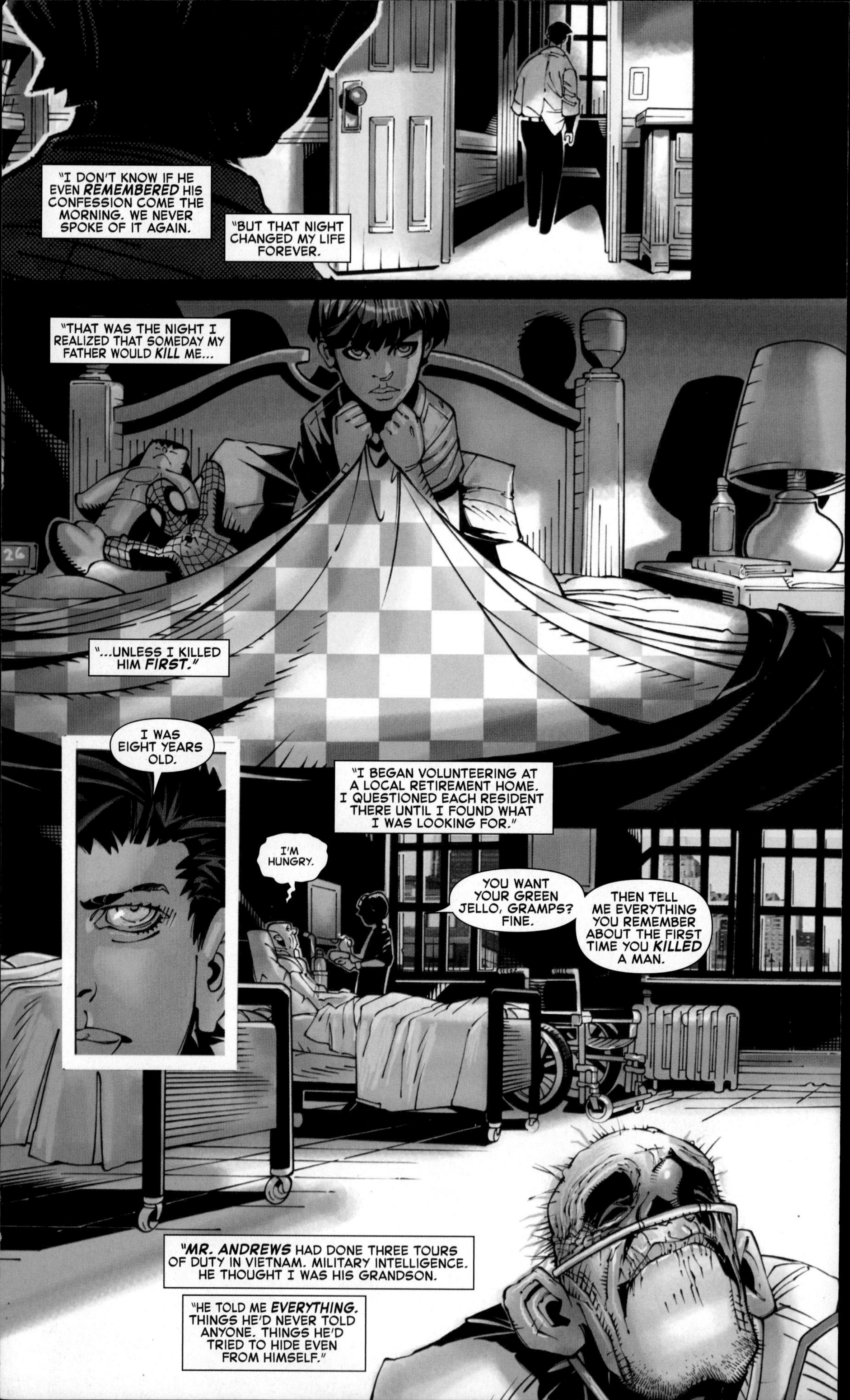
"I DON'T KNOW IF HE EVEN REMEMBERED HIS CONFESSION COME THE MORNING. WE NEVER SPOKE OF IT AGAIN.
"BUT THAT NIGHT CHANGED MY LIFE FOREVER.
"THAT WAS THE NIGHT I REALIZED THAT SOMEDAY MY FATHER WOULD KILL ME...
"...UNLESS I KILLED HIM FIRST."
I WAS EIGHT YEARS OLD.
"I BEGAN VOLUNTEERING AT A LOCAL RETIREMENT HOME. I QUESTIONED EACH RESIDENT THERE UNTIL I FOUND WHAT I WAS LOOKING FOR."
I'M HUNGRY.
YOU WANT YOUR GREEN JELLO, GRAMPS? FINE.
THEN TELL ME EVERYTHING YOU REMEMBER ABOUT THE FIRST TIME YOU KILLED A MAN.
"MR. ANDREWS HAD DONE THREE TOURS OF DUTY IN VIETNAM. MILITARY INTELLIGENCE. HE THOUGHT I WAS HIS GRANDSON.
"HE TOLD ME EVERYTHING. THINGS HE'D NEVER TOLD ANYONE. THINGS HE'D TRIED TO HIDE EVEN FROM HIMSELF."

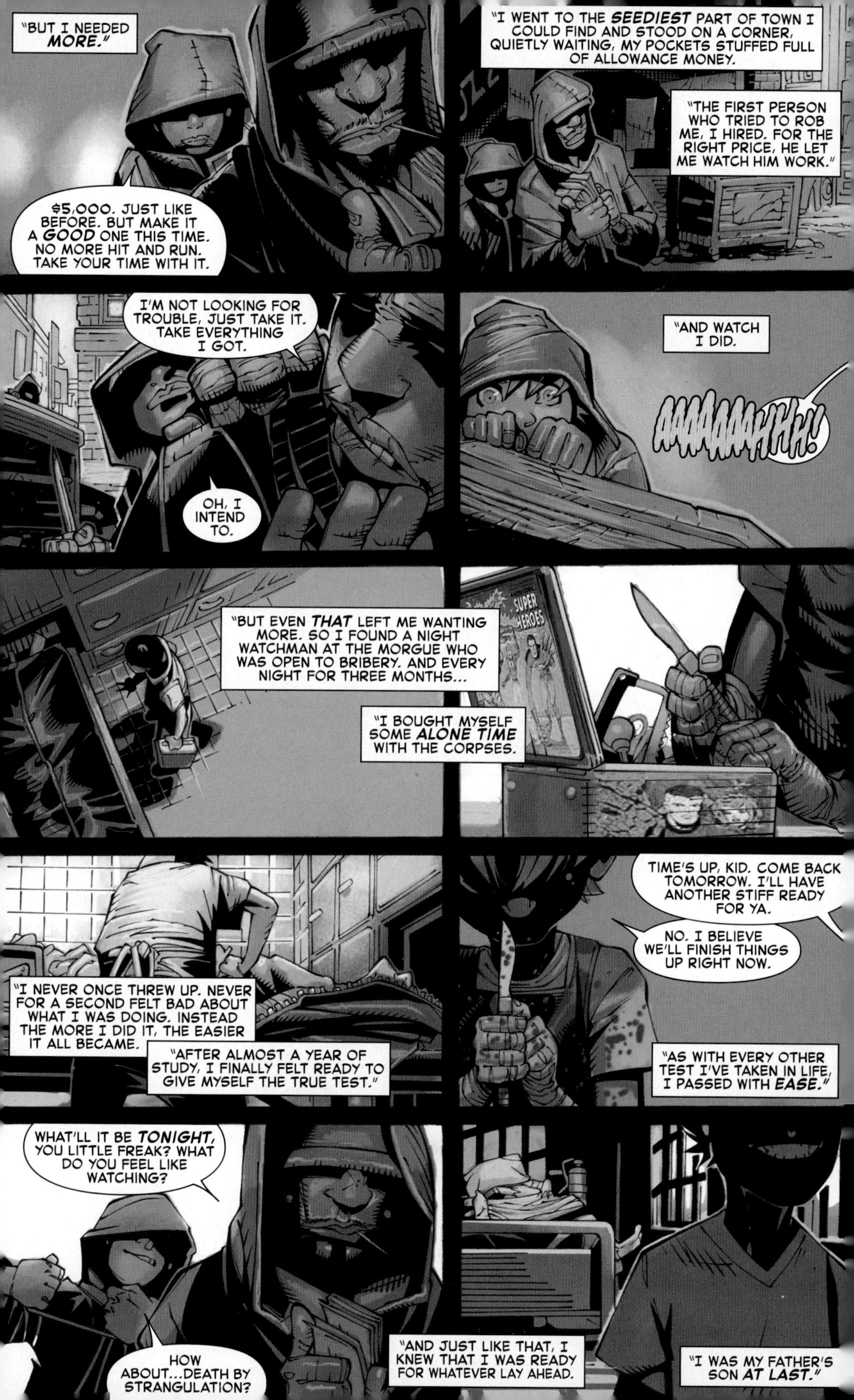
"BUT I NEEDED MORE."
$5,000. JUST LIKE BEFORE. BUT MAKE IT A GOOD ONE THIS TIME. NO MORE HIT AND RUN. TAKE YOUR TIME WITH IT.
"I WENT TO THE SEEDIEST PART OF TOWN I COULD FIND AND STOOD ON A CORNER, QUIETLY WAITING, MY POCKETS STUFFED FULL OF ALLOWANCE MONEY.
"THE FIRST PERSON WHO TRIED TO ROB ME, I HIRED. FOR THE RIGHT PRICE, HE LET ME WATCH HIM WORK."
I'M NOT LOOKING FOR TROUBLE, JUST TAKE IT. TAKE EVERYTHING I GOT.
OH, I INTEND TO.
"AND WATCH I DID.
AAAAAAAAHHH!
"BUT EVEN THAT LEFT ME WANTING MORE. SO I FOUND A NIGHT WATCHMAN AT THE MORGUE WHO WAS OPEN TO BRIBERY. AND EVERY NIGHT FOR THREE MONTHS...
"I BOUGHT MYSELF SOME ALONE TIME WITH THE CORPSES.
SUPER HEROES
"I NEVER ONCE THREW UP. NEVER FOR A SECOND FELT BAD ABOUT WHAT I WAS DOING. INSTEAD THE MORE I DID IT, THE EASIER IT ALL BECAME.
"AFTER ALMOST A YEAR OF STUDY, I FINALLY FELT READY TO GIVE MYSELF THE TRUE TEST."
TIME'S UP, KID. COME BACK TOMORROW. I'LL HAVE ANOTHER STIFF READY FOR YA.
NO. I BELIEVE WE'LL FINISH THINGS UP RIGHT NOW.
"AS WITH EVERY OTHER TEST I'VE TAKEN IN LIFE, I PASSED WITH EASE."
WHAT'LL IT BE TONIGHT, YOU LITTLE FREAK? WHAT DO YOU FEEL LIKE WATCHING?
HOW ABOUT...DEATH BY STRANGULATION?
"AND JUST LIKE THAT, I KNEW THAT I WAS READY FOR WHATEVER LAY AHEAD.
"I WAS MY FATHER'S SON AT LAST."

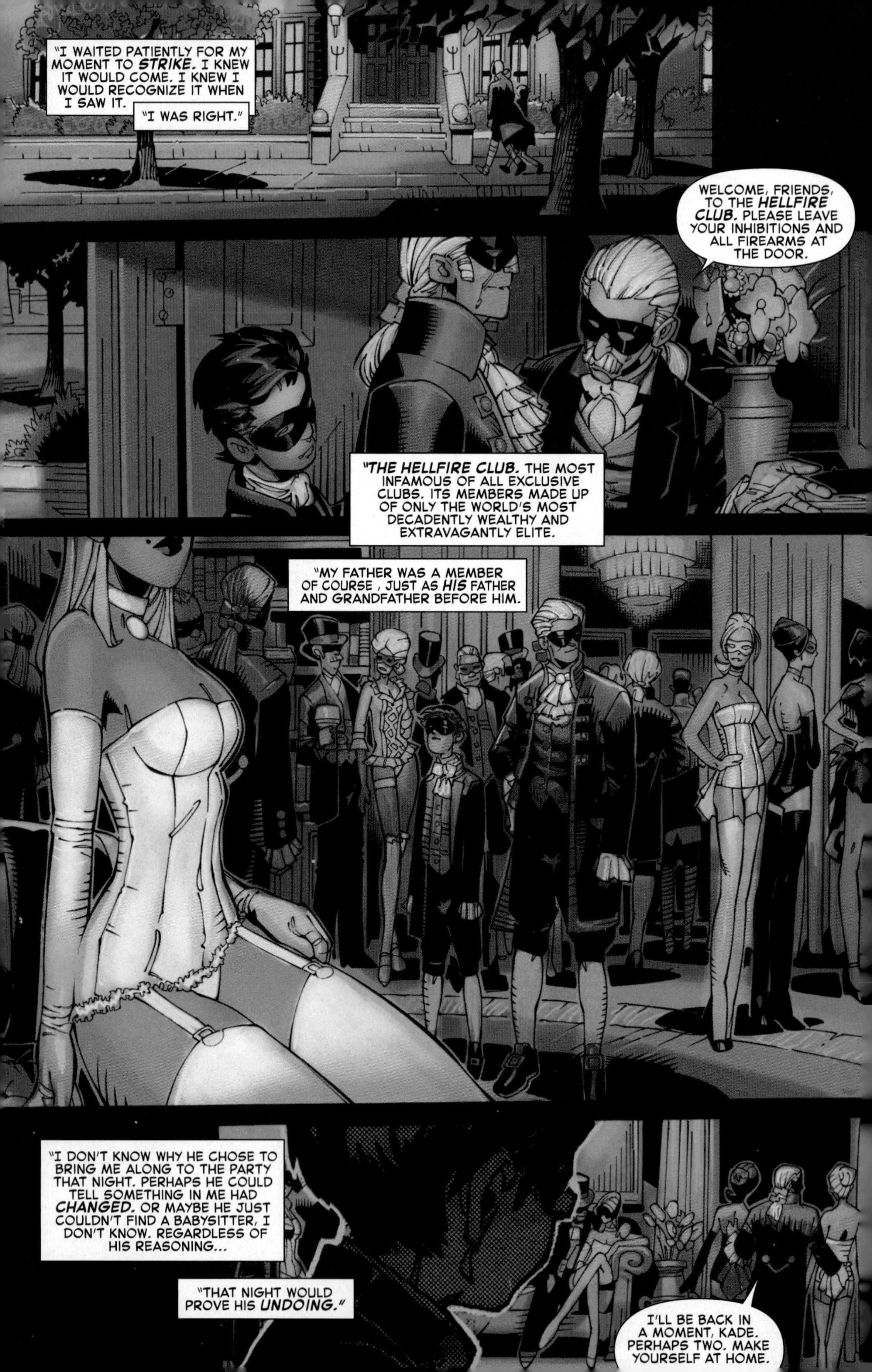
"I WAITED PATIENTLY FOR MY MOMENT TO STRIKE. I KNEW IT WOULD COME. I KNEW I WOULD RECOGNIZE IT WHEN I SAW IT.
"I WAS RIGHT."
WELCOME, FRIENDS, TO THE HELLFIRE CLUB. PLEASE LEAVE YOUR INHIBITIONS AND ALL FIREARMS AT THE DOOR.
"THE HELLFIRE CLUB. THE MOST INFAMOUS OF ALL EXCLUSIVE CLUBS. ITS MEMBERS MADE UP OF ONLY THE WORLD'S MOST DECADENTLY WEALTHY AND EXTRAVAGANTLY ELITE.
"MY FATHER WAS A MEMBER OF COURSE , JUST AS HIS FATHER AND GRANDFATHER BEFORE HIM.
"I DON'T KNOW WHY HE CHOSE TO BRING ME ALONG TO THE PARTY THAT NIGHT. PERHAPS HE COULD TELL SOMETHING IN ME HAD CHANGED. OR MAYBE HE JUST COULDN'T FIND A BABYSITTER, I DON'T KNOW. REGARDLESS OF HIS REASONING...
"THAT NIGHT WOULD PROVE HIS UNDOING."
I'LL BE BACK IN A MOMENT, KADE. PERHAPS TWO. MAKE YOURSELF AT HOME.

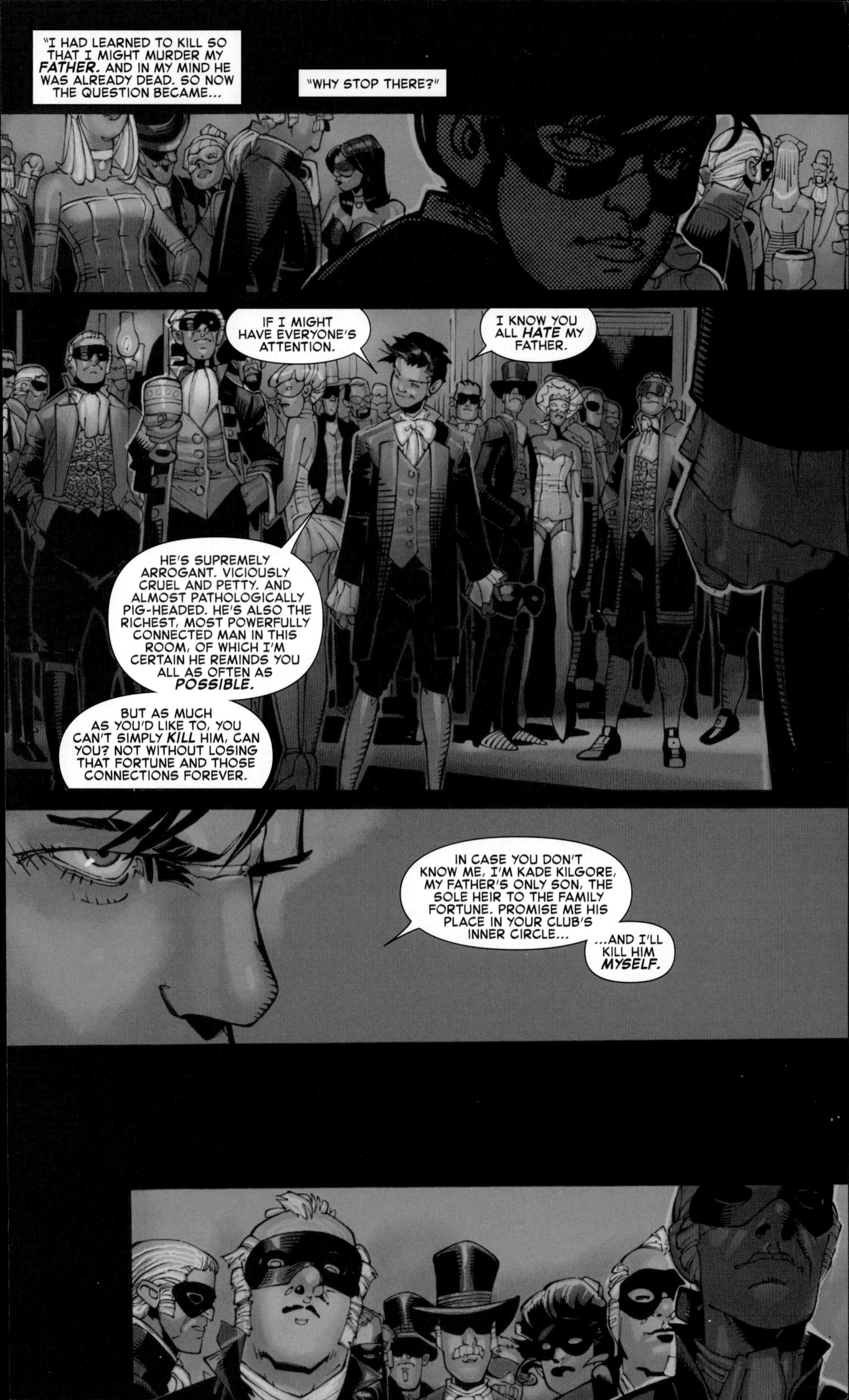
"I HAD LEARNED TO KILL SO THAT I MIGHT MURDER MY FATHER. AND IN MY MIND HE WAS ALREADY DEAD. SO NOW THE QUESTION BECAME...
"WHY STOP THERE?"
IF I MIGHT HAVE EVERYONE'S ATTENTION.
I KNOW YOU ALL HATE MY FATHER.
HE'S SUPREMELY ARROGANT. VICIOUSLY CRUEL AND PETTY. AND ALMOST PATHOLOGICALLY PIG-HEADED. HE'S ALSO THE RICHEST, MOST POWERFULLY CONNECTED MAN IN THIS ROOM, OF WHICH I'M CERTAIN HE REMINDS YOU ALL AS OFTEN AS POSSIBLE.
BUT AS MUCH AS YOU'D LIKE TO, YOU CAN'T SIMPLY KILL HIM, CAN YOU? NOT WITHOUT LOSING THAT FORTUNE AND THOSE CONNECTIONS FOREVER.
IN CASE YOU DON'T KNOW ME, I'M KADE KILGORE, MY FATHER'S ONLY SON, THE SOLE HEIR TO THE FAMILY FORTUNE. PROMISE ME HIS PLACE IN YOUR CLUB'S INNER CIRCLE...
...AND I'LL KILL HIM MYSELF.

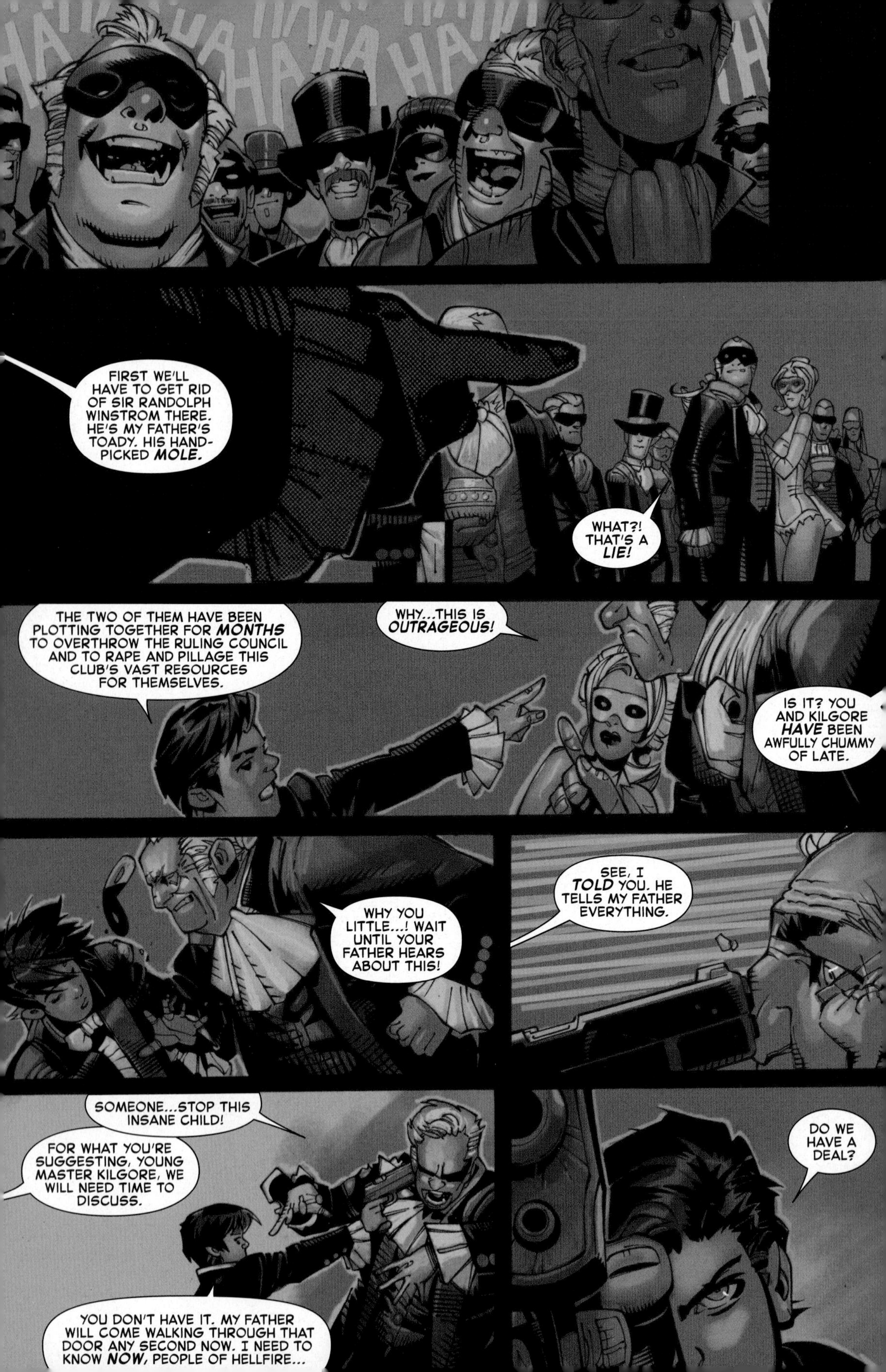
HA HA HA HA HA
FIRST WE'LL HAVE TO GET RID OF SIR RANDOLPH WINSTROM THERE. HE'S MY FATHER'S TOADY. HIS HAND-PICKED MOLE.
WHAT?! THAT'S A LIE!
THE TWO OF THEM HAVE BEEN PLOTTING TOGETHER FOR MONTHS TO OVERTHROW THE RULING COUNCIL AND TO RAPE AND PILLAGE THIS CLUB'S VAST RESOURCES FOR THEMSELVES.
WHY...THIS IS OUTRAGEOUS!
IS IT? YOU AND KILGORE HAVE BEEN AWFULLY CHUMMY OF LATE.
WHY YOU LITTLE...! WAIT UNTIL YOUR FATHER HEARS ABOUT THIS!
SEE, I TOLD YOU. HE TELLS MY FATHER EVERYTHING.
SOMEONE...STOP THIS INSANE CHILD!
FOR WHAT YOU'RE SUGGESTING, YOUNG MASTER KILGORE, WE WILL NEED TIME TO DISCUSS.
YOU DON'T HAVE IT. MY FATHER WILL COME WALKING THROUGH THAT DOOR ANY SECOND NOW. I NEED TO KNOW NOW, PEOPLE OF HELLFIRE...
DO WE HAVE A DEAL?

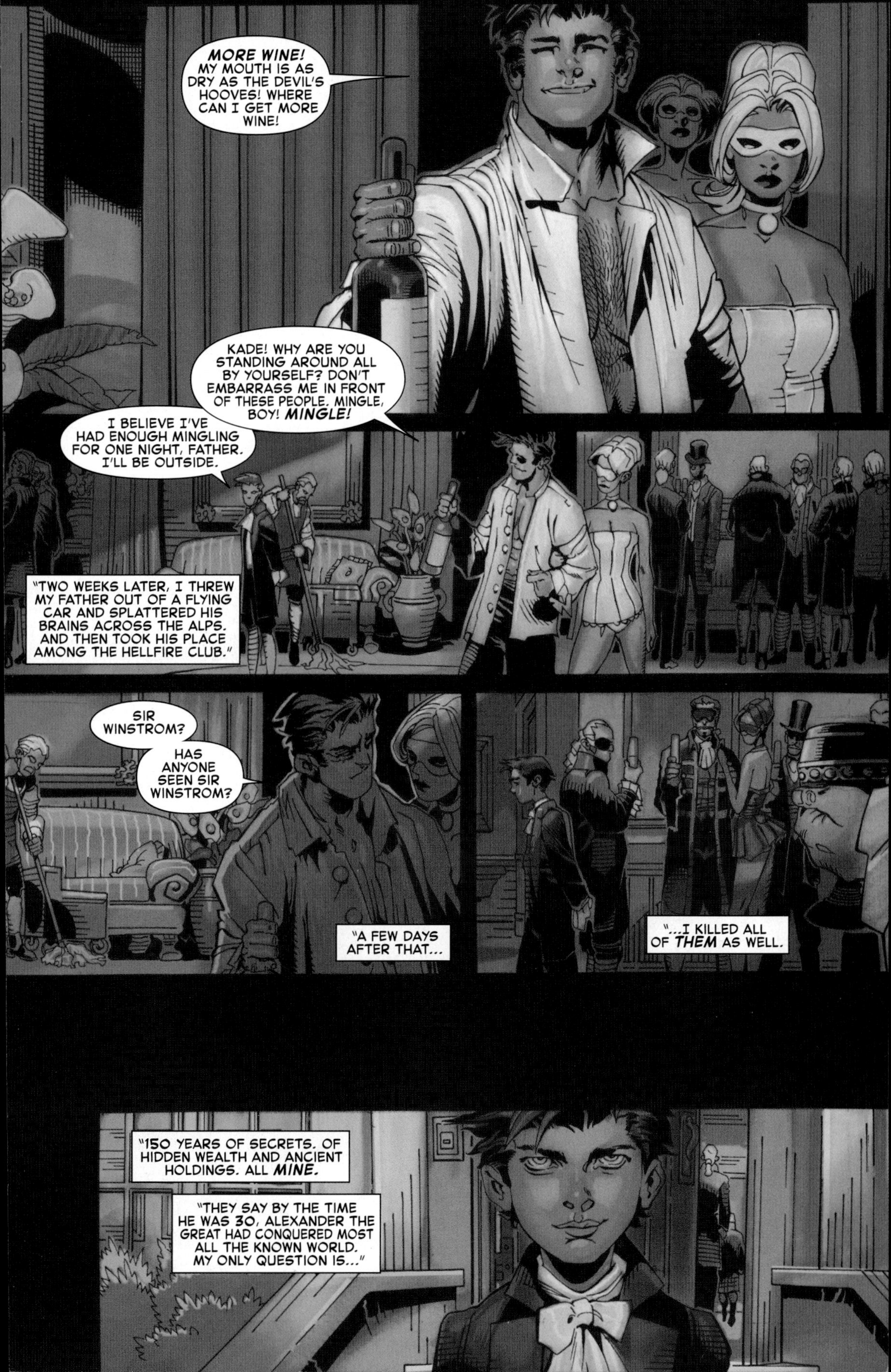
MORE WINE! MY MOUTH IS AS DRY AS THE DEVIL'S HOOVES! WHERE CAN I GET MORE WINE!
KADE! WHY ARE YOU STANDING AROUND ALL BY YOURSELF? DON'T EMBARRASS ME IN FRONT OF THESE PEOPLE. MINGLE, BOY! MINGLE!
I BELIEVE I'VE HAD ENOUGH MINGLING FOR ONE NIGHT, FATHER. I'LL BE OUTSIDE.
"TWO WEEKS LATER, I THREW MY FATHER OUT OF A FLYING CAR AND SPLATTERED HIS BRAINS ACROSS THE ALPS. AND THEN TOOK HIS PLACE AMONG THE HELLFIRE CLUB."
SIR WINSTROM?
HAS ANYONE SEEN SIR WINSTROM?
"A FEW DAYS AFTER THAT...
"...I KILLED ALL OF THEM AS WELL.
"150 YEARS OF SECRETS. OF HIDDEN WEALTH AND ANCIENT HOLDINGS. ALL MINE.
"THEY SAY BY THE TIME HE WAS 30, ALEXANDER THE GREAT HAD CONQUERED MOST ALL THE KNOWN WORLD. MY ONLY QUESTION IS..."

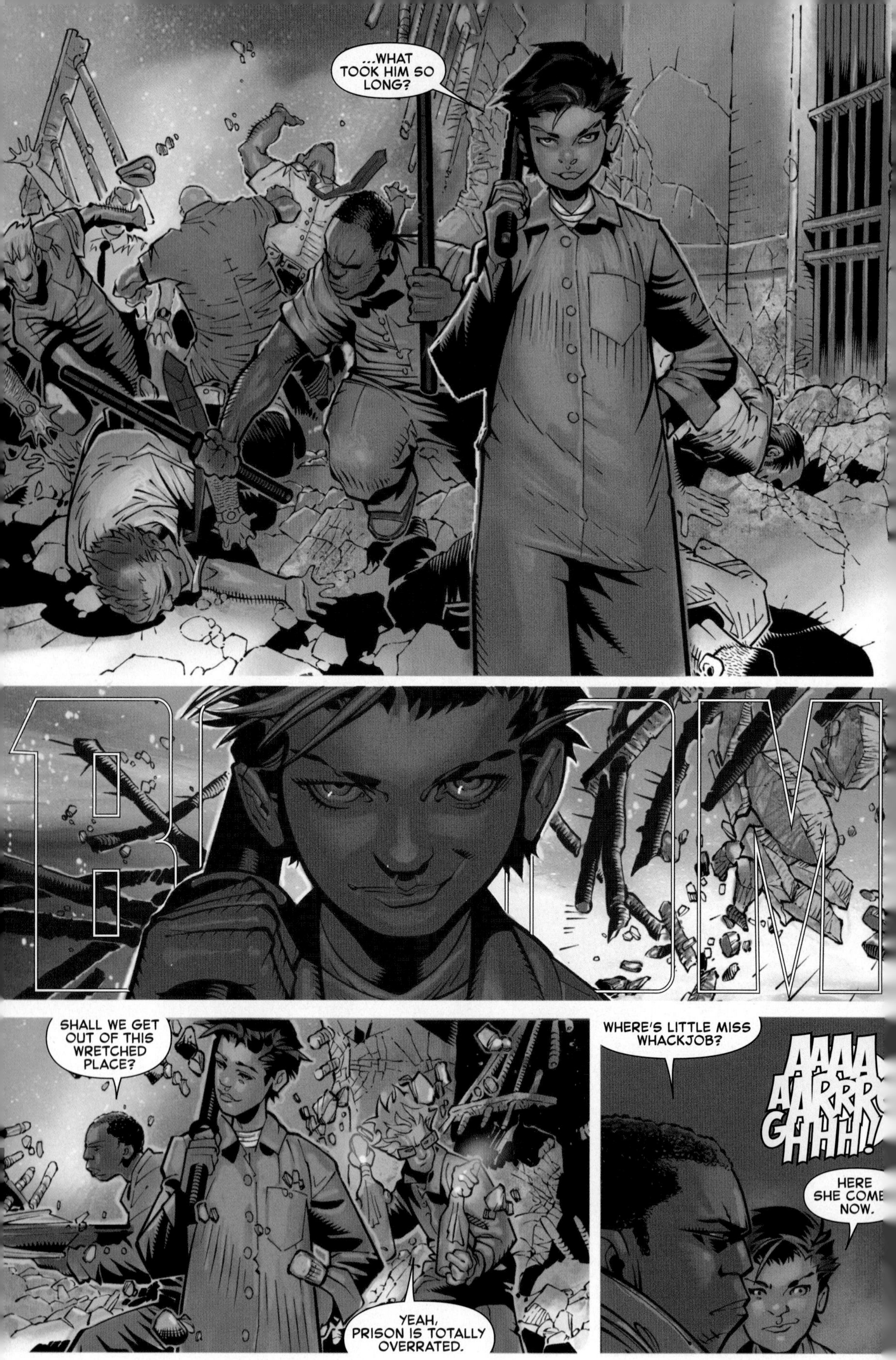
...WHAT TOOK HIM SO LONG?
SHALL WE GET OUT OF THIS WRETCHED PLACE?
YEAH, PRISON IS TOTALLY OVERRATED.
WHERE'S LITTLE MISS WHACKJOB?
AAAAARRRGHHH!
HERE SHE COME NOW.

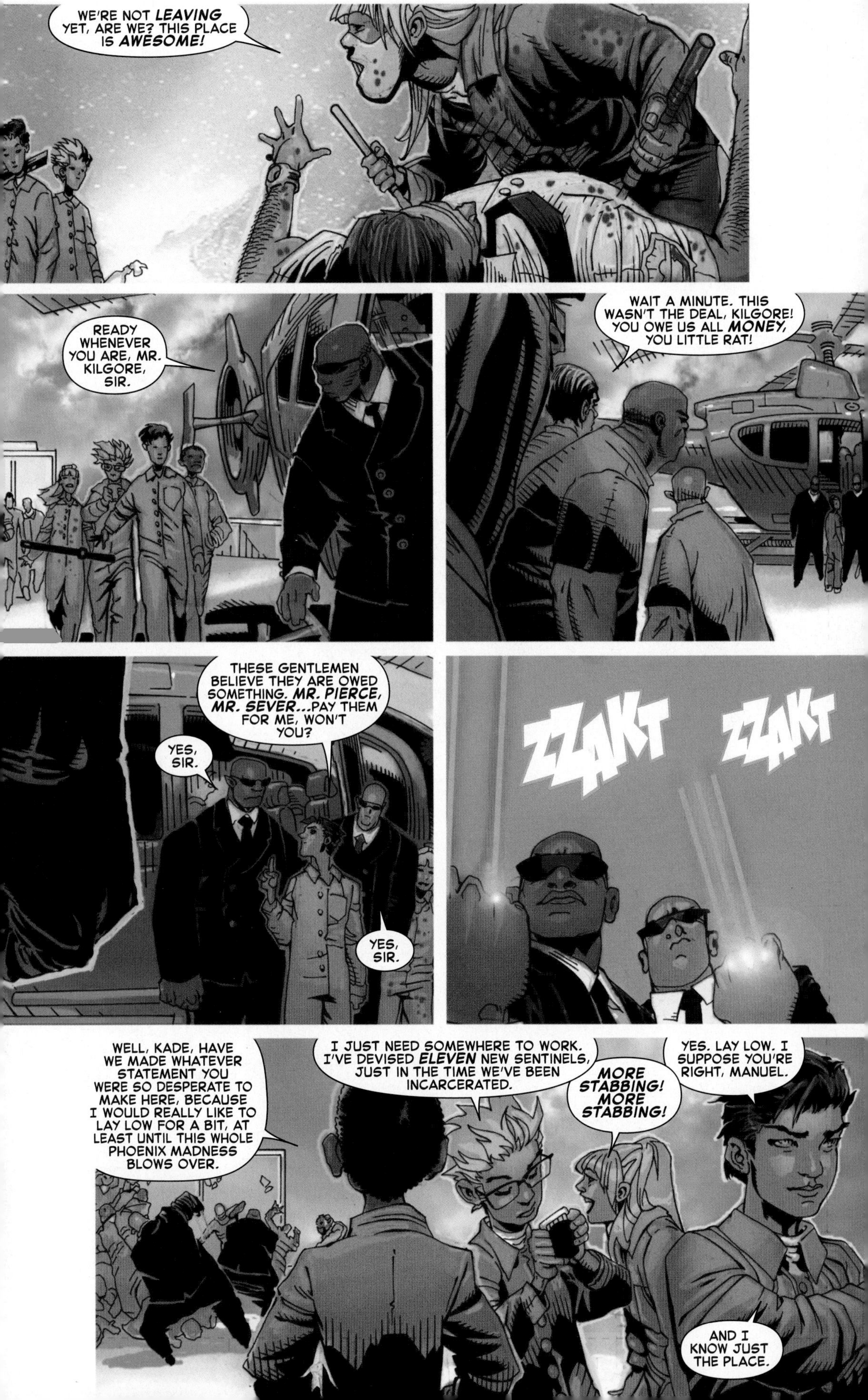
WE'RE NOT LEAVING YET, ARE WE? THIS PLACE IS AWESOME!
READY WHENEVER YOU ARE, MR. KILGORE, SIR.
WAIT A MINUTE. THIS WASN'T THE DEAL, KILGORE! YOU OWE US ALL MONEY, YOU LITTLE RAT!
THESE GENTLEMEN BELIEVE THEY ARE OWED SOMETHING. MR. PIERCE, MR. SEVER...PAY THEM FOR ME, WON'T YOU?
YES, SIR.
YES, SIR.
ZZAKT ZZAKT
WELL, KADE, HAVE WE MADE WHATEVER STATEMENT YOU WERE SO DESPERATE TO MAKE HERE, BECAUSE I WOULD REALLY LIKE TO LAY LOW FOR A BIT, AT LEAST UNTIL THIS WHOLE PHOENIX MADNESS BLOWS OVER.
I JUST NEED SOMEWHERE TO WORK. I'VE DEVISED ELEVEN NEW SENTINELS, JUST IN THE TIME WE'VE BEEN INCARCERATED.
MORE STABBING! MORE STABBING!
YES. LAY LOW. I SUPPOSE YOU'RE RIGHT, MANUEL.
AND I KNOW JUST THE PLACE.

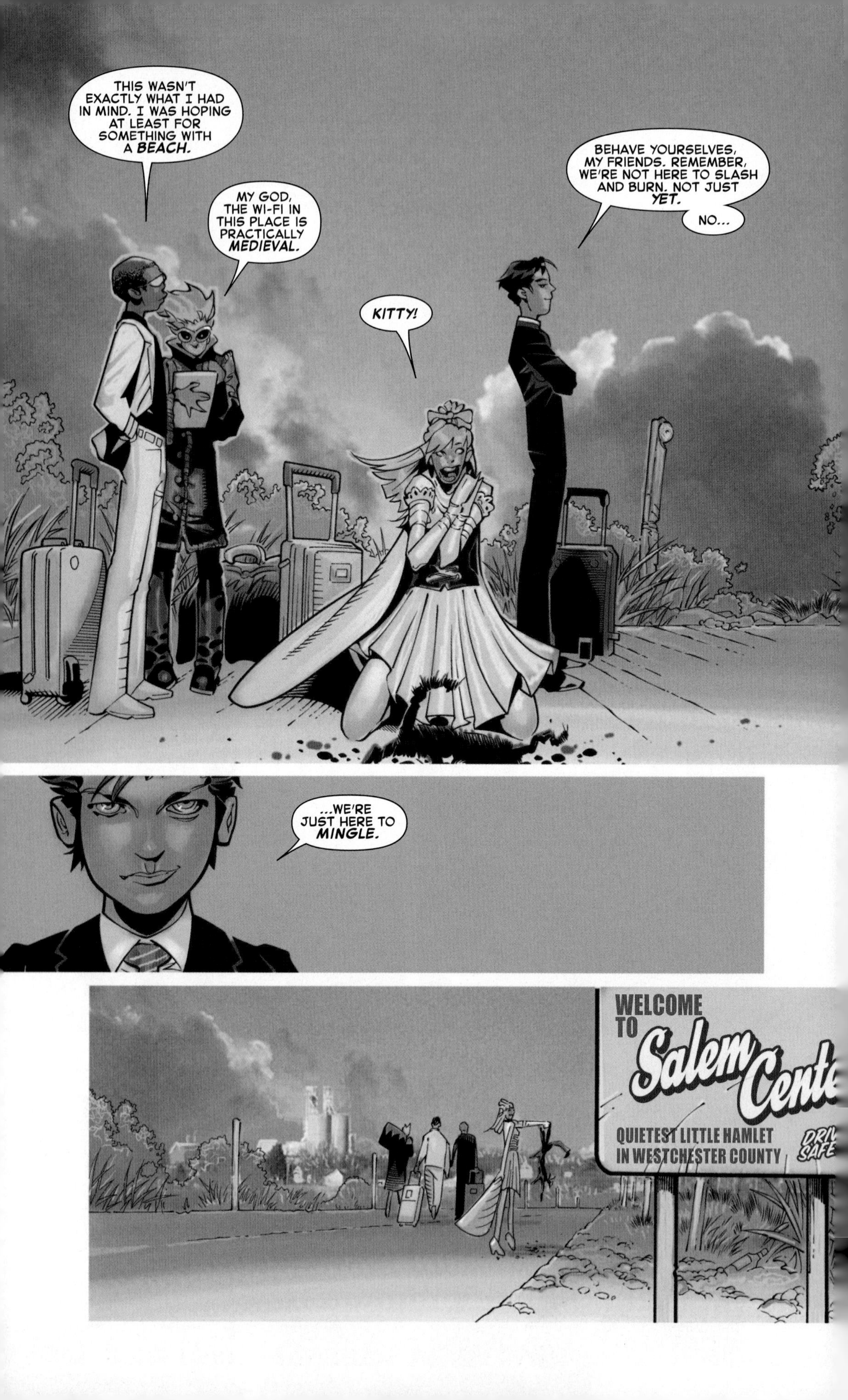
THIS WASN'T EXACTLY WHAT I HAD IN MIND. I WAS HOPING AT LEAST FOR SOMETHING WITH A BEACH.
MY GOD, THE WI-FI IN THIS PLACE IS PRACTICALLY MEDIEVAL.
KITTY!
BEHAVE YOURSELVES, MY FRIENDS. REMEMBER, WE'RE NOT HERE TO SLASH AND BURN. NOT JUST YET.
NO...
...WE'RE JUST HERE TO MINGLE.
WELCOME TO
Salem Cente
QUIETEST LITTLE HAMLET IN WESTCHESTER COUNTY
DRIV SAFE

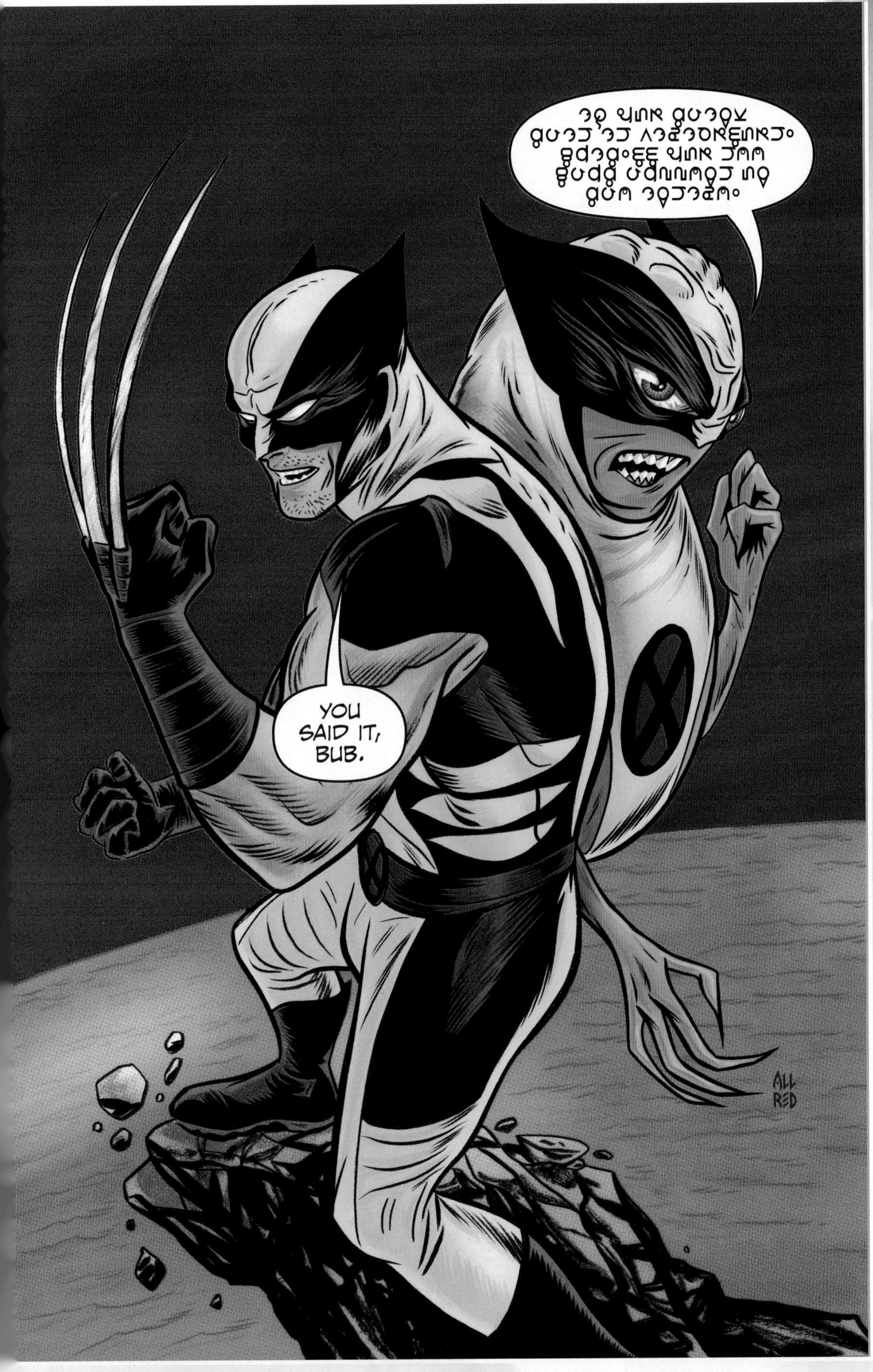
YOU SAID IT, BUB.
ALL RED

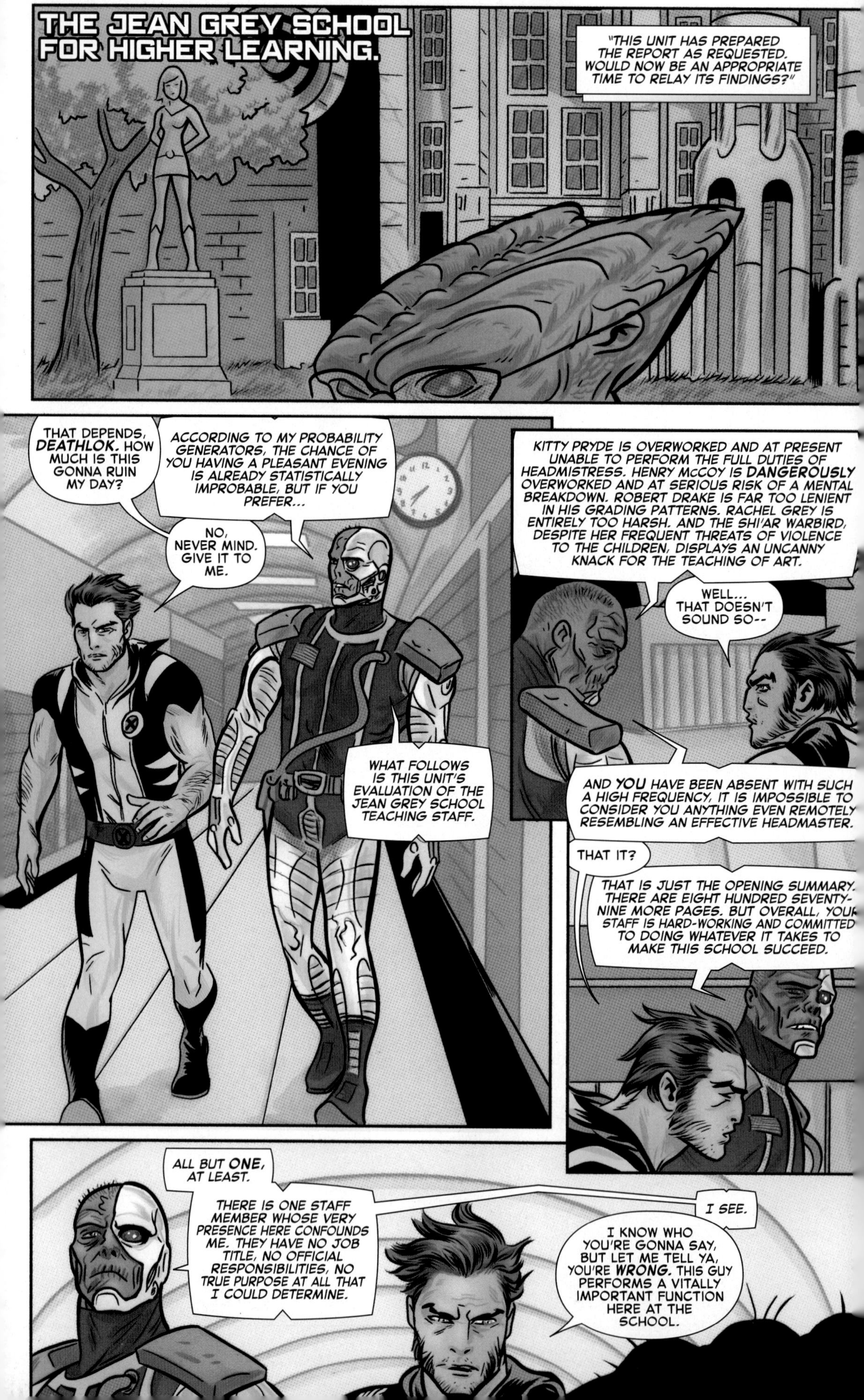
THE JEAN GREY SCHOOL FOR HIGHER LEARNING.
"THIS UNIT HAS PREPARED THE REPORT AS REQUESTED. WOULD NOW BE AN APPROPRIATE TIME TO RELAY ITS FINDINGS?"
THAT DEPENDS, DEATHLOK. HOW MUCH IS THIS GONNA RUIN MY DAY?
ACCORDING TO MY PROBABILITY GENERATORS, THE CHANCE OF YOU HAVING A PLEASANT EVENING IS ALREADY STATISTICALLY IMPROBABLE, BUT IF YOU PREFER...
NO, NEVER MIND. GIVE IT TO ME.
WHAT FOLLOWS IS THIS UNIT'S EVALUATION OF THE JEAN GREY SCHOOL TEACHING STAFF.
KITTY PRYDE IS OVERWORKED AND AT PRESENT UNABLE TO PERFORM THE FULL DUTIES OF HEADMISTRESS. HENRY McCOY IS DANGEROUSLY OVERWORKED AND AT SERIOUS RISK OF A MENTAL BREAKDOWN. ROBERT DRAKE IS FAR TOO LENIENT IN HIS GRADING PATTERNS. RACHEL GREY IS ENTIRELY TOO HARSH. AND THE SHI'AR WARBIRD, DESPITE HER FREQUENT THREATS OF VIOLENCE TO THE CHILDREN, DISPLAYS AN UNCANNY KNACK FOR THE TEACHING OF ART.
WELL... THAT DOESN'T SOUND SO--
AND YOU HAVE BEEN ABSENT WITH SUCH A HIGH FREQUENCY, IT IS IMPOSSIBLE TO CONSIDER YOU ANYTHING EVEN REMOTELY RESEMBLING AN EFFECTIVE HEADMASTER.
THAT IT?
THAT IS JUST THE OPENING SUMMARY. THERE ARE EIGHT HUNDRED SEVENTY-NINE MORE PAGES. BUT OVERALL, YOUR STAFF IS HARD-WORKING AND COMMITTED TO DOING WHATEVER IT TAKES TO MAKE THIS SCHOOL SUCCEED.
ALL BUT ONE, AT LEAST.
THERE IS ONE STAFF MEMBER WHOSE VERY PRESENCE HERE CONFOUNDS ME. THEY HAVE NO JOB TITLE, NO OFFICIAL RESPONSIBILITIES, NO TRUE PURPOSE AT ALL THAT I COULD DETERMINE.
I SEE.
I KNOW WHO YOU'RE GONNA SAY, BUT LET ME TELL YA, YOU'RE WRONG. THIS GUY PERFORMS A VITALLY IMPORTANT FUNCTION HERE AT THE SCHOOL.

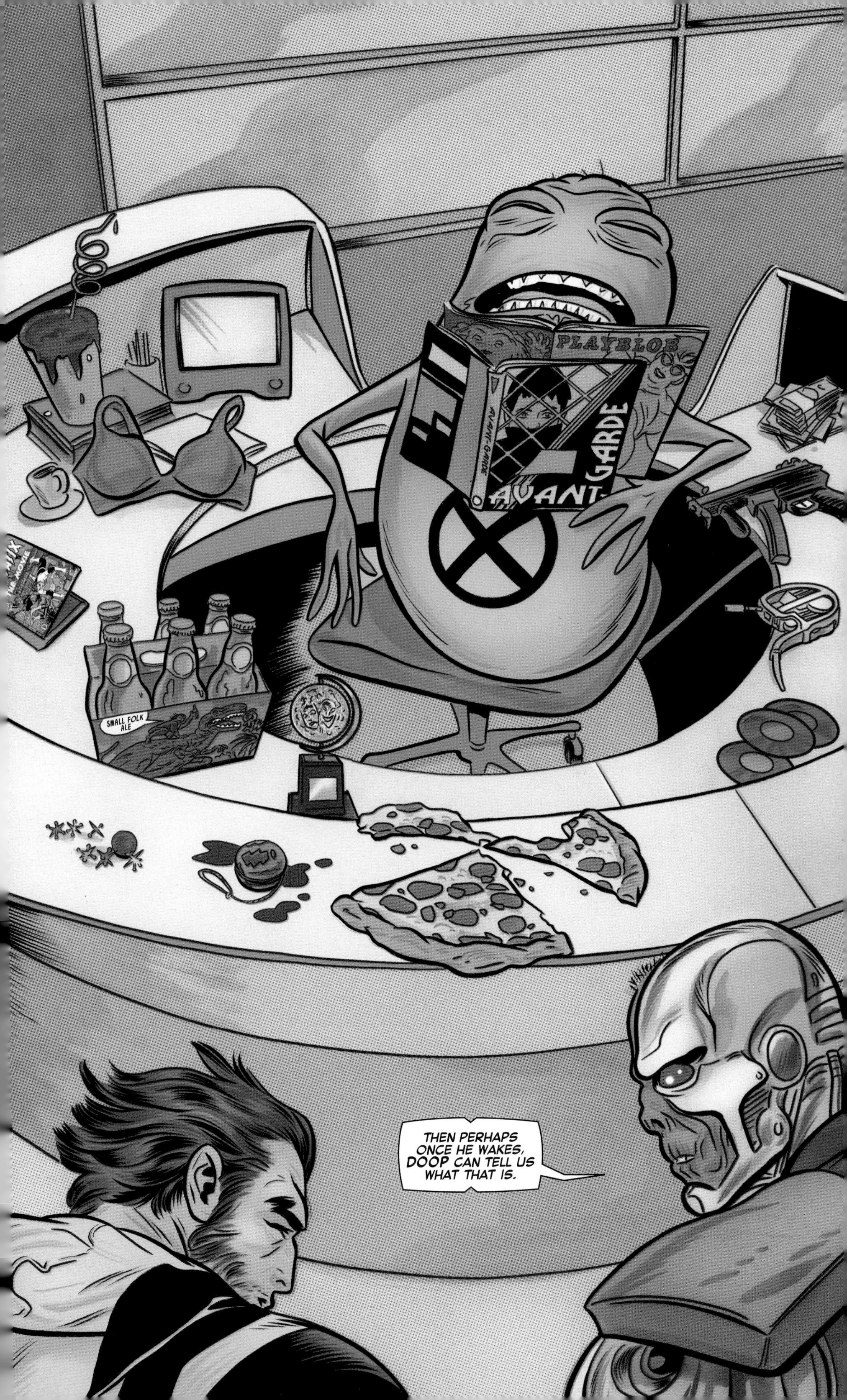
PLAYBLOB
AVANT-GARDE
SMALL FOLK ALE
THEN PERHAPS ONCE HE WAKES, DOOP CAN TELL US WHAT THAT IS.

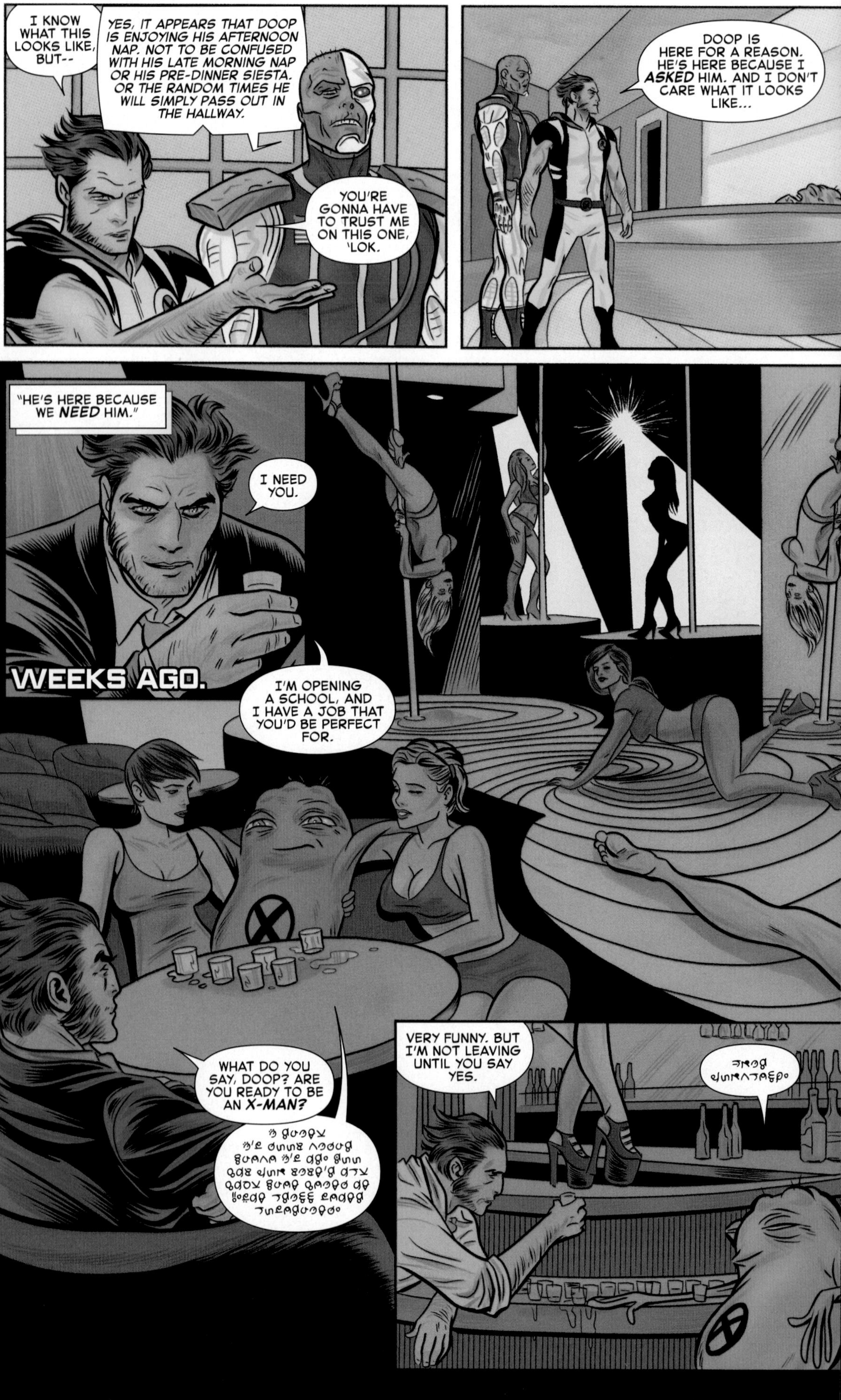
I KNOW WHAT THIS LOOKS LIKE, BUT--
YES, IT APPEARS THAT DOOP IS ENJOYING HIS AFTERNOON NAP. NOT TO BE CONFUSED WITH HIS LATE MORNING NAP OR HIS PRE-DINNER SIESTA. OR THE RANDOM TIMES HE WILL SIMPLY PASS OUT IN THE HALLWAY.
YOU'RE GONNA HAVE TO TRUST ME ON THIS ONE, 'LOK.
DOOP IS HERE FOR A REASON. HE'S HERE BECAUSE I ASKED HIM. AND I DON'T CARE WHAT IT LOOKS LIKE...
"HE'S HERE BECAUSE WE NEED HIM."
I NEED YOU.
WEEKS AGO.
I'M OPENING A SCHOOL, AND I HAVE A JOB THAT YOU'D BE PERFECT FOR.
WHAT DO YOU SAY, DOOP? ARE YOU READY TO BE AN X-MAN?
VERY FUNNY. BUT I'M NOT LEAVING UNTIL YOU SAY YES.

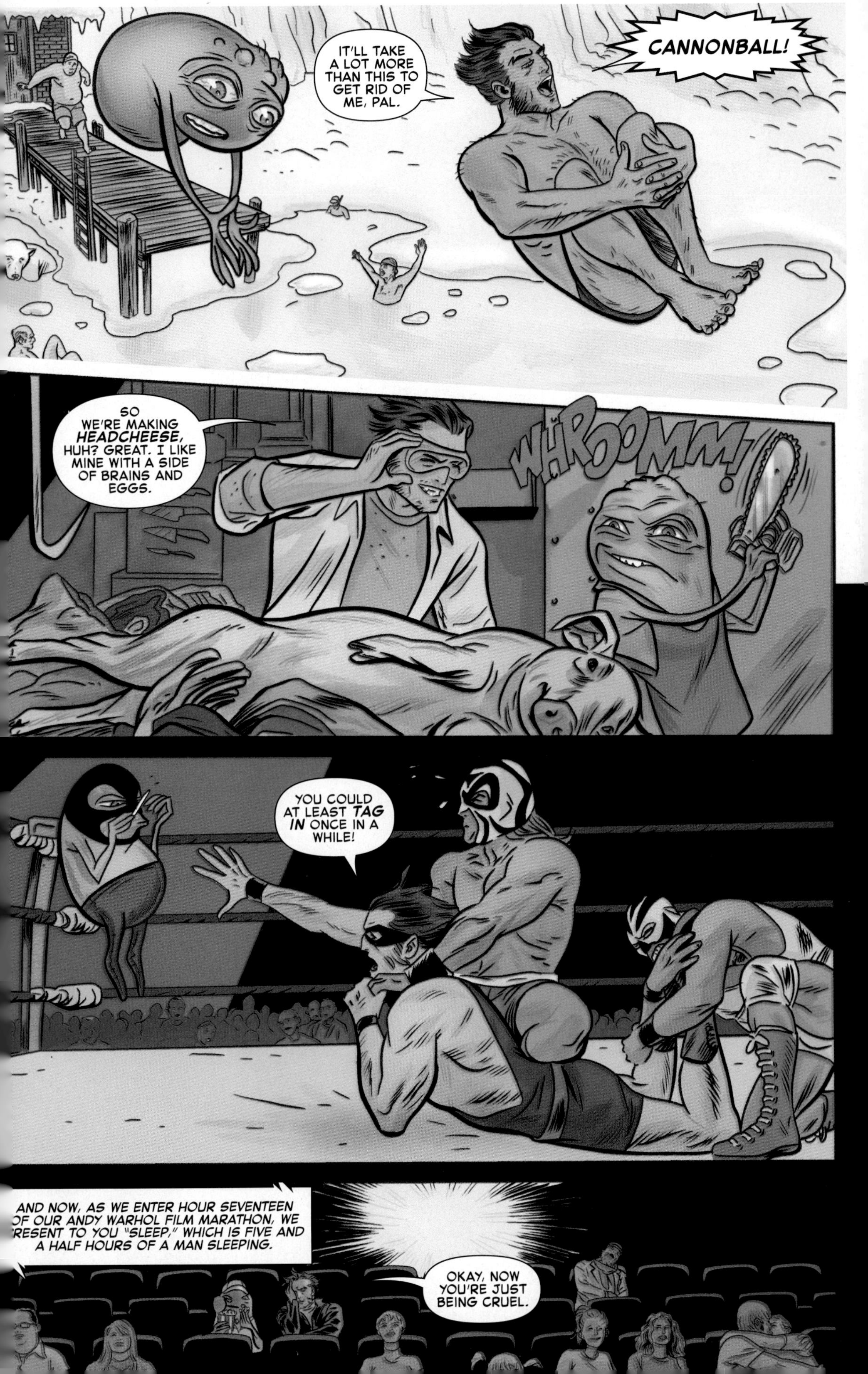
IT'LL TAKE A LOT MORE THAN THIS TO GET RID OF ME, PAL.
CANNONBALL!
SO WE'RE MAKING HEADCHEESE, HUH? GREAT. I LIKE MINE WITH A SIDE OF BRAINS AND EGGS.
WHROOMM!
YOU COULD AT LEAST TAG IN ONCE IN A WHILE!
AND NOW, AS WE ENTER HOUR SEVENTEEN OF OUR ANDY WARHOL FILM MARATHON, WE PRESENT TO YOU "SLEEP," WHICH IS FIVE AND A HALF HOURS OF A MAN SLEEPING.
OKAY, NOW YOU'RE JUST BEING CRUEL.

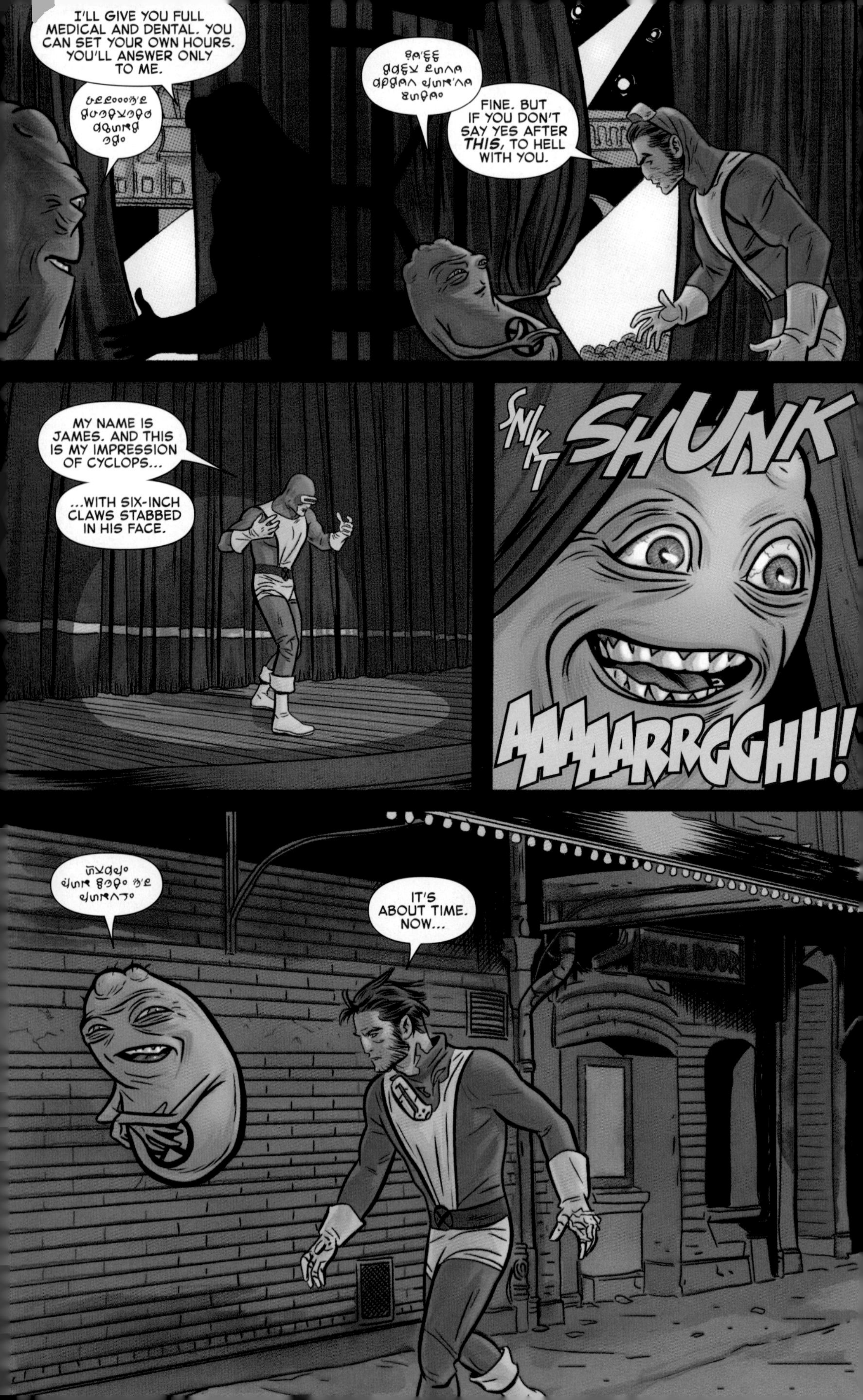
I'LL GIVE YOU FULL MEDICAL AND DENTAL. YOU CAN SET YOUR OWN HOURS. YOU'LL ANSWER ONLY TO ME.
FINE. BUT IF YOU DON'T SAY YES AFTER THIS, TO HELL WITH YOU.
MY NAME IS JAMES. AND THIS IS MY IMPRESSION OF CYCLOPS...
...WITH SIX-INCH CLAWS STABBED IN HIS FACE.
SNIKT
SHUNK
AAAAARRGGHH!
IT'S ABOUT TIME. NOW...
STAGE DOOR

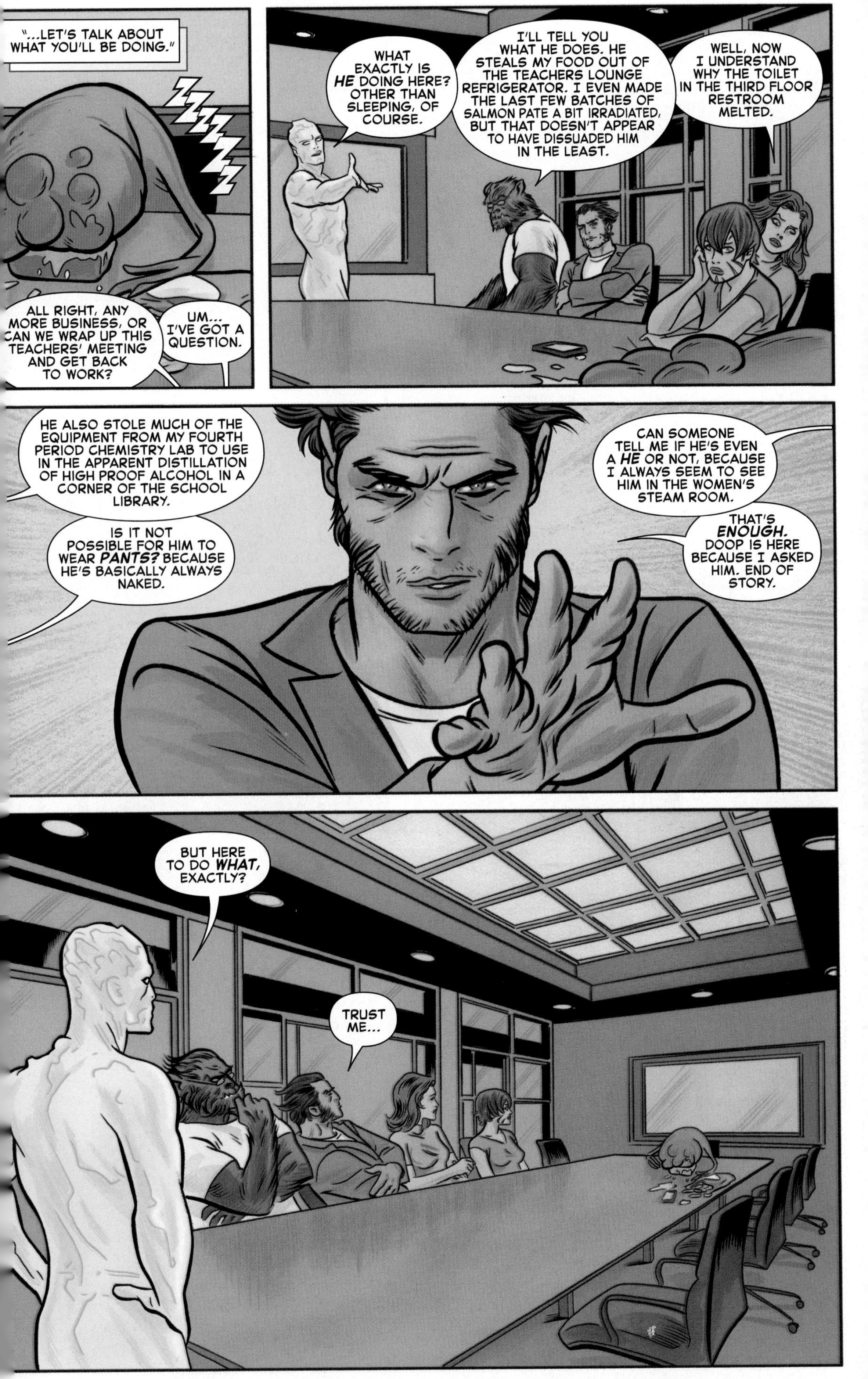
"...LET'S TALK ABOUT WHAT YOU'LL BE DOING."
ZZZZZ
ALL RIGHT, ANY MORE BUSINESS, OR CAN WE WRAP UP THIS TEACHERS' MEETING AND GET BACK TO WORK?
UM... I'VE GOT A QUESTION.
WHAT EXACTLY IS *HE* DOING HERE? OTHER THAN SLEEPING, OF COURSE.
I'LL TELL YOU WHAT HE DOES. HE STEALS MY FOOD OUT OF THE TEACHERS LOUNGE REFRIGERATOR. I EVEN MADE THE LAST FEW BATCHES OF SALMON PATE A BIT IRRADIATED, BUT THAT DOESN'T APPEAR TO HAVE DISSUADED HIM IN THE LEAST.
WELL, NOW I UNDERSTAND WHY THE TOILET IN THE THIRD FLOOR RESTROOM MELTED.
HE ALSO STOLE MUCH OF THE EQUIPMENT FROM MY FOURTH PERIOD CHEMISTRY LAB TO USE IN THE APPARENT DISTILLATION OF HIGH PROOF ALCOHOL IN A CORNER OF THE SCHOOL LIBRARY.
IS IT NOT POSSIBLE FOR HIM TO WEAR *PANTS?* BECAUSE HE'S BASICALLY ALWAYS NAKED.
CAN SOMEONE TELL ME IF HE'S EVEN A *HE* OR NOT, BECAUSE I ALWAYS SEEM TO SEE HIM IN THE WOMEN'S STEAM ROOM.
THAT'S *ENOUGH.* DOOP IS HERE BECAUSE I ASKED HIM. END OF STORY.
BUT HERE TO DO *WHAT,* EXACTLY?
TRUST ME...

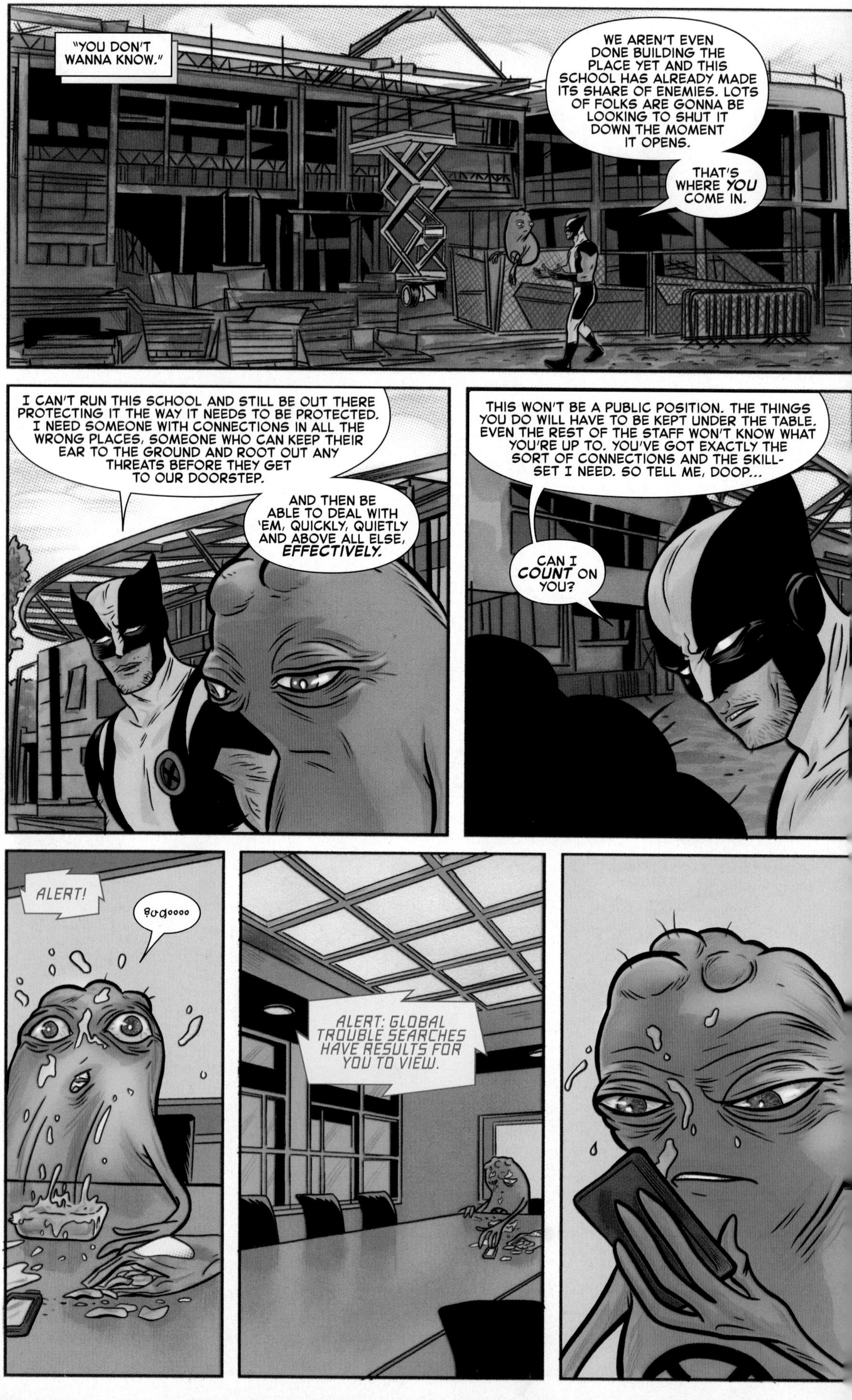

"YOU DON'T WANNA KNOW."
WE AREN'T EVEN DONE BUILDING THE PLACE YET AND THIS SCHOOL HAS ALREADY MADE ITS SHARE OF ENEMIES. LOTS OF FOLKS ARE GONNA BE LOOKING TO SHUT IT DOWN THE MOMENT IT OPENS.
THAT'S WHERE *YOU* COME IN.
I CAN'T RUN THIS SCHOOL AND STILL BE OUT THERE PROTECTING IT THE WAY IT NEEDS TO BE PROTECTED. I NEED SOMEONE WITH CONNECTIONS IN ALL THE WRONG PLACES, SOMEONE WHO CAN KEEP THEIR EAR TO THE GROUND AND ROOT OUT ANY THREATS BEFORE THEY GET TO OUR DOORSTEP.
AND THEN BE ABLE TO DEAL WITH 'EM, QUICKLY, QUIETLY AND ABOVE ALL ELSE, ***EFFECTIVELY.***
THIS WON'T BE A PUBLIC POSITION. THE THINGS YOU DO WILL HAVE TO BE KEPT UNDER THE TABLE. EVEN THE REST OF THE STAFF WON'T KNOW WHAT YOU'RE UP TO. YOU'VE GOT EXACTLY THE SORT OF CONNECTIONS AND THE SKILL-SET I NEED. SO TELL ME, DOOP...
CAN I ***COUNT*** ON YOU?
ALERT!
ALERT: GLOBAL TROUBLE SEARCHES HAVE RESULTS FOR YOU TO VIEW.

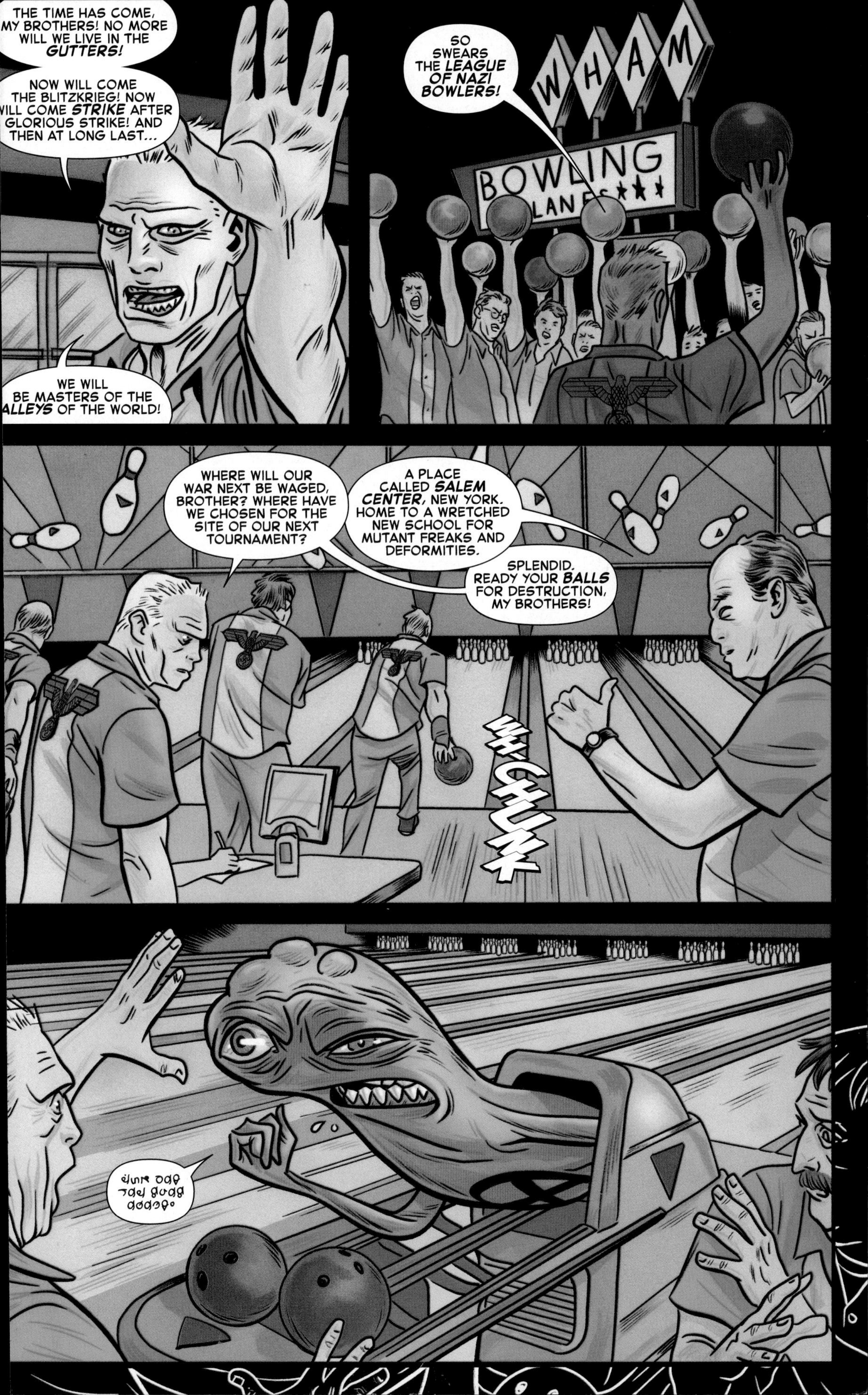
THE TIME HAS COME, MY BROTHERS! NO MORE WILL WE LIVE IN THE GUTTERS!
NOW WILL COME THE BLITZKRIEG! NOW WILL COME STRIKE AFTER GLORIOUS STRIKE! AND THEN AT LONG LAST...
WE WILL BE MASTERS OF THE ALLEYS OF THE WORLD!
SO SWEARS THE LEAGUE OF NAZI BOWLERS!
WHAM
BOWLING LANES
WHERE WILL OUR WAR NEXT BE WAGED, BROTHER? WHERE HAVE WE CHOSEN FOR THE SITE OF OUR NEXT TOURNAMENT?
A PLACE CALLED SALEM CENTER, NEW YORK. HOME TO A WRETCHED NEW SCHOOL FOR MUTANT FREAKS AND DEFORMITIES.
SPLENDID. READY YOUR BALLS FOR DESTRUCTION, MY BROTHERS!
WH-CHUNK

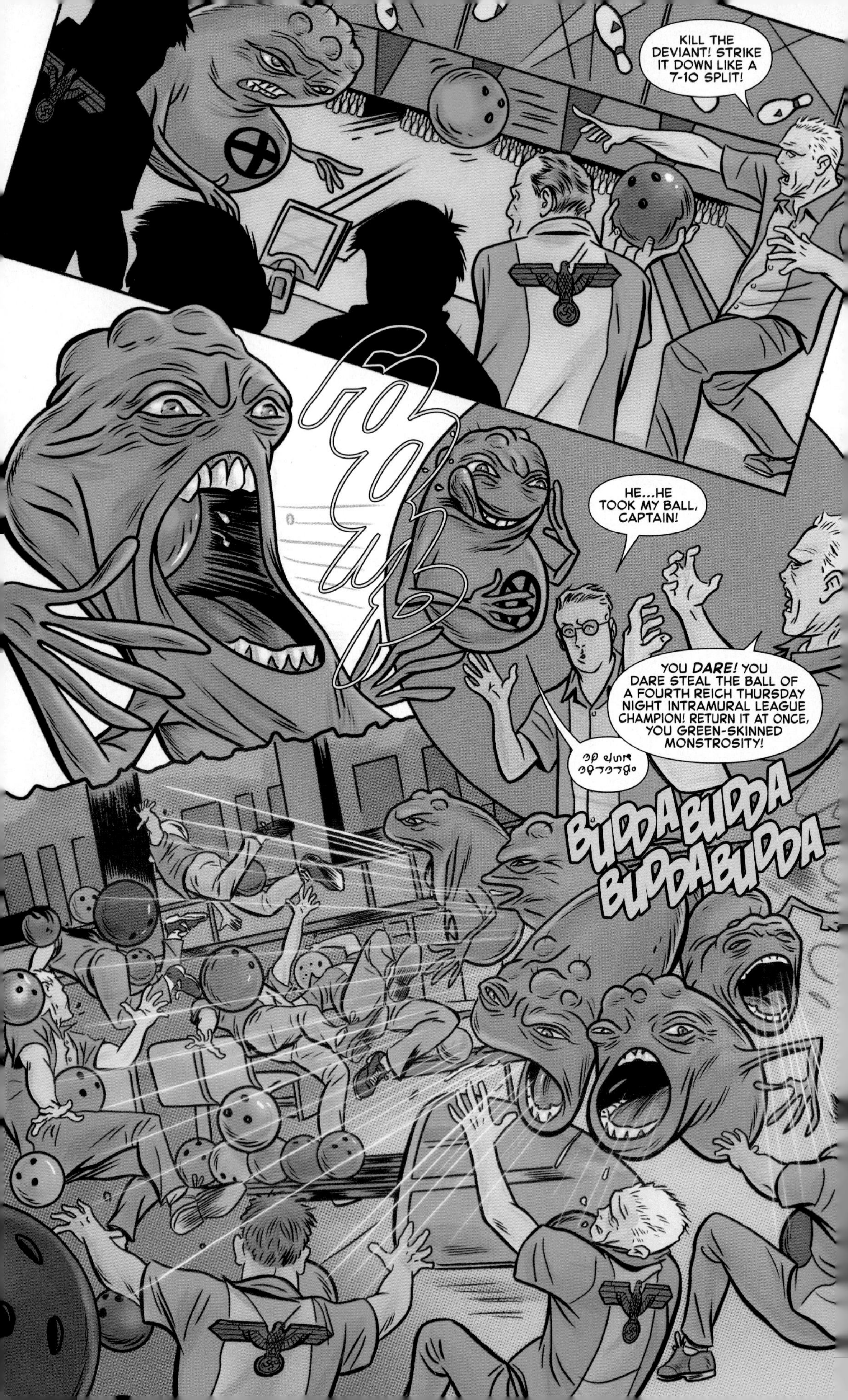
KILL THE DEVIANT! STRIKE IT DOWN LIKE A 7-10 SPLIT!
HE...HE TOOK MY BALL, CAPTAIN!
YOU *DARE!* YOU DARE STEAL THE BALL OF A FOURTH REICH THURSDAY NIGHT INTRAMURAL LEAGUE CHAMPION! RETURN IT AT ONCE, YOU GREEN-SKINNED MONSTROSITY!
BUDDABUDDA BUDDABUDDA

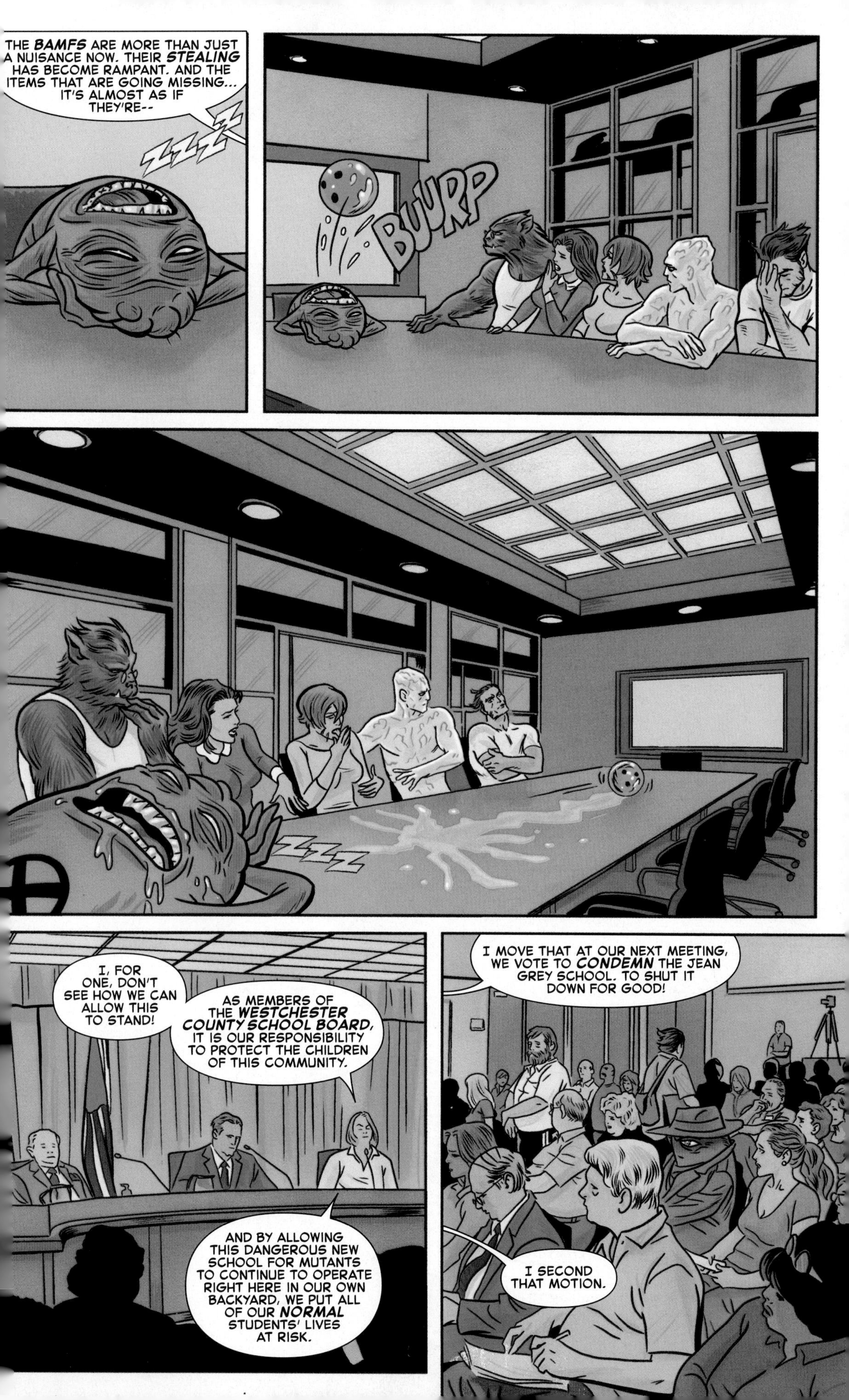
THE BAMFS ARE MORE THAN JUST A NUISANCE NOW. THEIR STEALING HAS BECOME RAMPANT. AND THE ITEMS THAT ARE GOING MISSING... IT'S ALMOST AS IF THEY'RE--
ZZZZ
ZZZZ
BUURP
ZZZZ
I, FOR ONE, DON'T SEE HOW WE CAN ALLOW THIS TO STAND!
AS MEMBERS OF THE WESTCHESTER COUNTY SCHOOL BOARD, IT IS OUR RESPONSIBILITY TO PROTECT THE CHILDREN OF THIS COMMUNITY.
AND BY ALLOWING THIS DANGEROUS NEW SCHOOL FOR MUTANTS TO CONTINUE TO OPERATE RIGHT HERE IN OUR OWN BACKYARD, WE PUT ALL OF OUR NORMAL STUDENTS' LIVES AT RISK.
I MOVE THAT AT OUR NEXT MEETING, WE VOTE TO CONDEMN THE JEAN GREY SCHOOL. TO SHUT IT DOWN FOR GOOD!
I SECOND THAT MOTION.

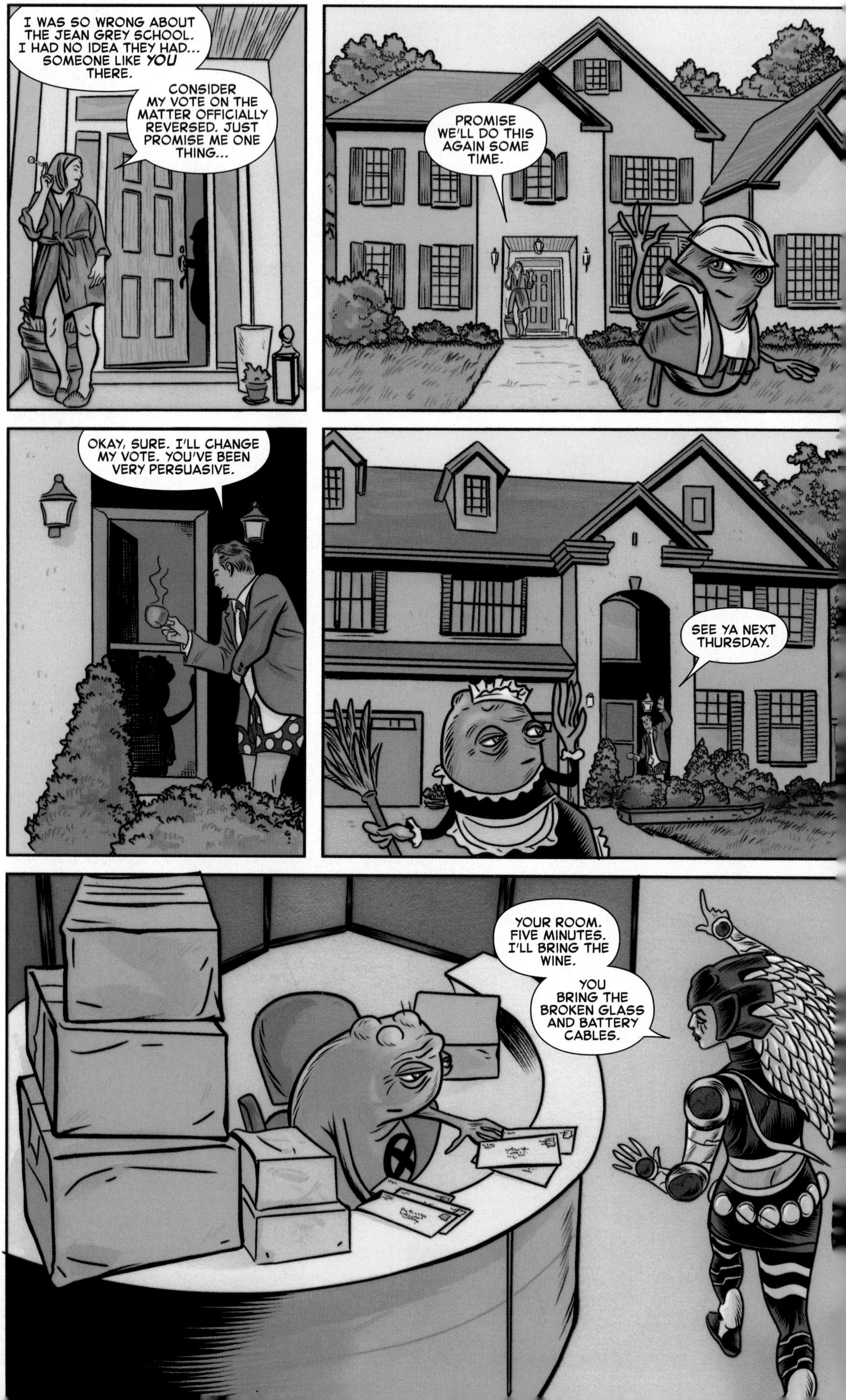
I WAS SO WRONG ABOUT THE JEAN GREY SCHOOL. I HAD NO IDEA THEY HAD... SOMEONE LIKE YOU THERE.
CONSIDER MY VOTE ON THE MATTER OFFICIALLY REVERSED. JUST PROMISE ME ONE THING...
PROMISE WE'LL DO THIS AGAIN SOME TIME.
OKAY, SURE. I'LL CHANGE MY VOTE. YOU'VE BEEN VERY PERSUASIVE.
SEE YA NEXT THURSDAY.
YOUR ROOM. FIVE MINUTES. I'LL BRING THE WINE.
YOU BRING THE BROKEN GLASS AND BATTERY CABLES.

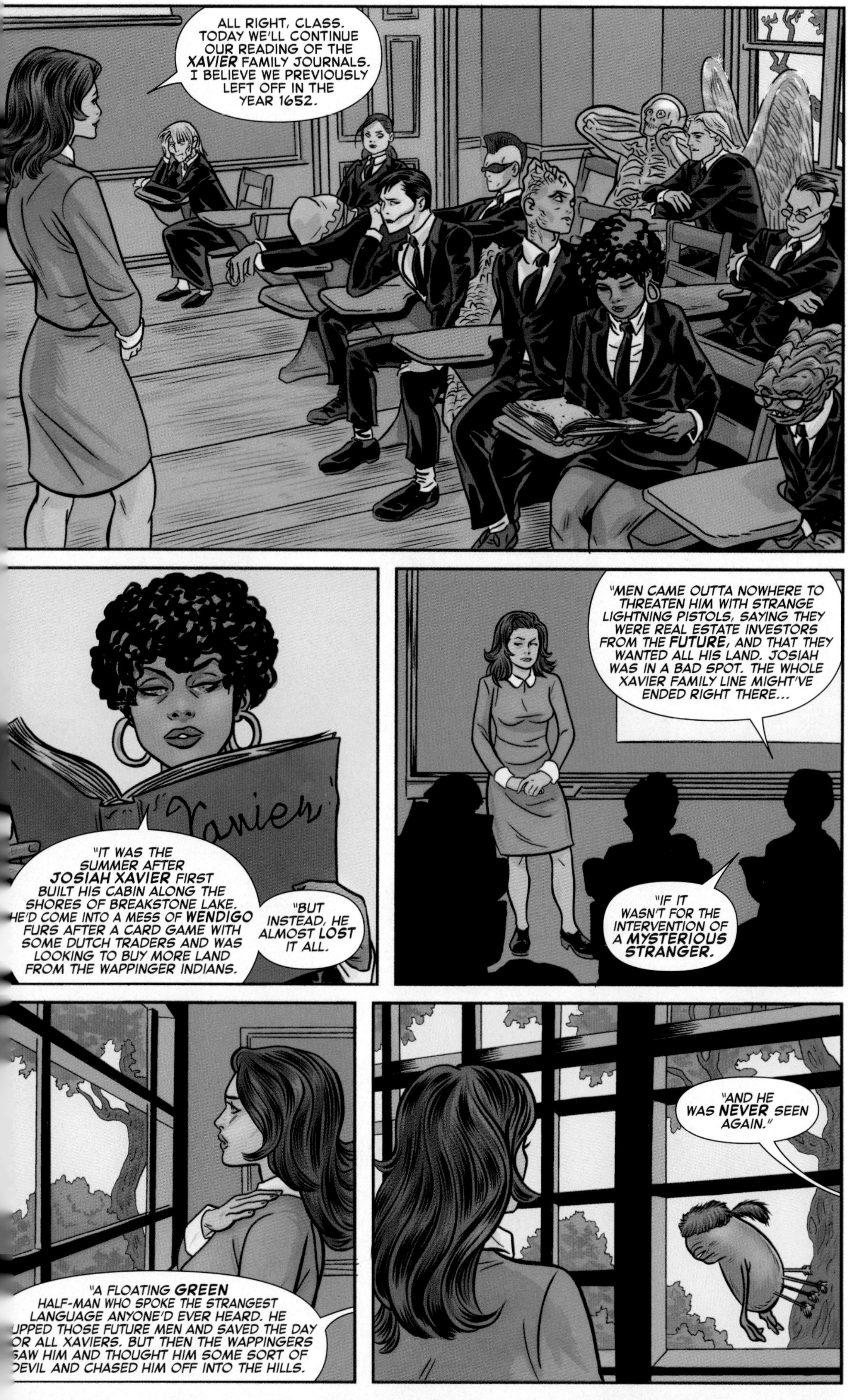
ALL RIGHT, CLASS. TODAY WE'LL CONTINUE OUR READING OF THE XAVIER FAMILY JOURNALS. I BELIEVE WE PREVIOUSLY LEFT OFF IN THE YEAR 1652.
Xavier
"IT WAS THE SUMMER AFTER JOSIAH XAVIER FIRST BUILT HIS CABIN ALONG THE SHORES OF BREAKSTONE LAKE. HE'D COME INTO A MESS OF WENDIGO FURS AFTER A CARD GAME WITH SOME DUTCH TRADERS AND WAS LOOKING TO BUY MORE LAND FROM THE WAPPINGER INDIANS.
"BUT INSTEAD, HE ALMOST LOST IT ALL.
"MEN CAME OUTTA NOWHERE TO THREATEN HIM WITH STRANGE LIGHTNING PISTOLS, SAYING THEY WERE REAL ESTATE INVESTORS FROM THE FUTURE, AND THAT THEY WANTED ALL HIS LAND. JOSIAH WAS IN A BAD SPOT. THE WHOLE XAVIER FAMILY LINE MIGHT'VE ENDED RIGHT THERE...
"IF IT WASN'T FOR THE INTERVENTION OF A MYSTERIOUS STRANGER.
"A FLOATING GREEN HALF-MAN WHO SPOKE THE STRANGEST LANGUAGE ANYONE'D EVER HEARD. HE UPPED THOSE FUTURE MEN AND SAVED THE DAY FOR ALL XAVIERS. BUT THEN THE WAPPINGERS SAW HIM AND THOUGHT HIM SOME SORT OF DEVIL AND CHASED HIM OFF INTO THE HILLS.
"AND HE WAS NEVER SEEN AGAIN."

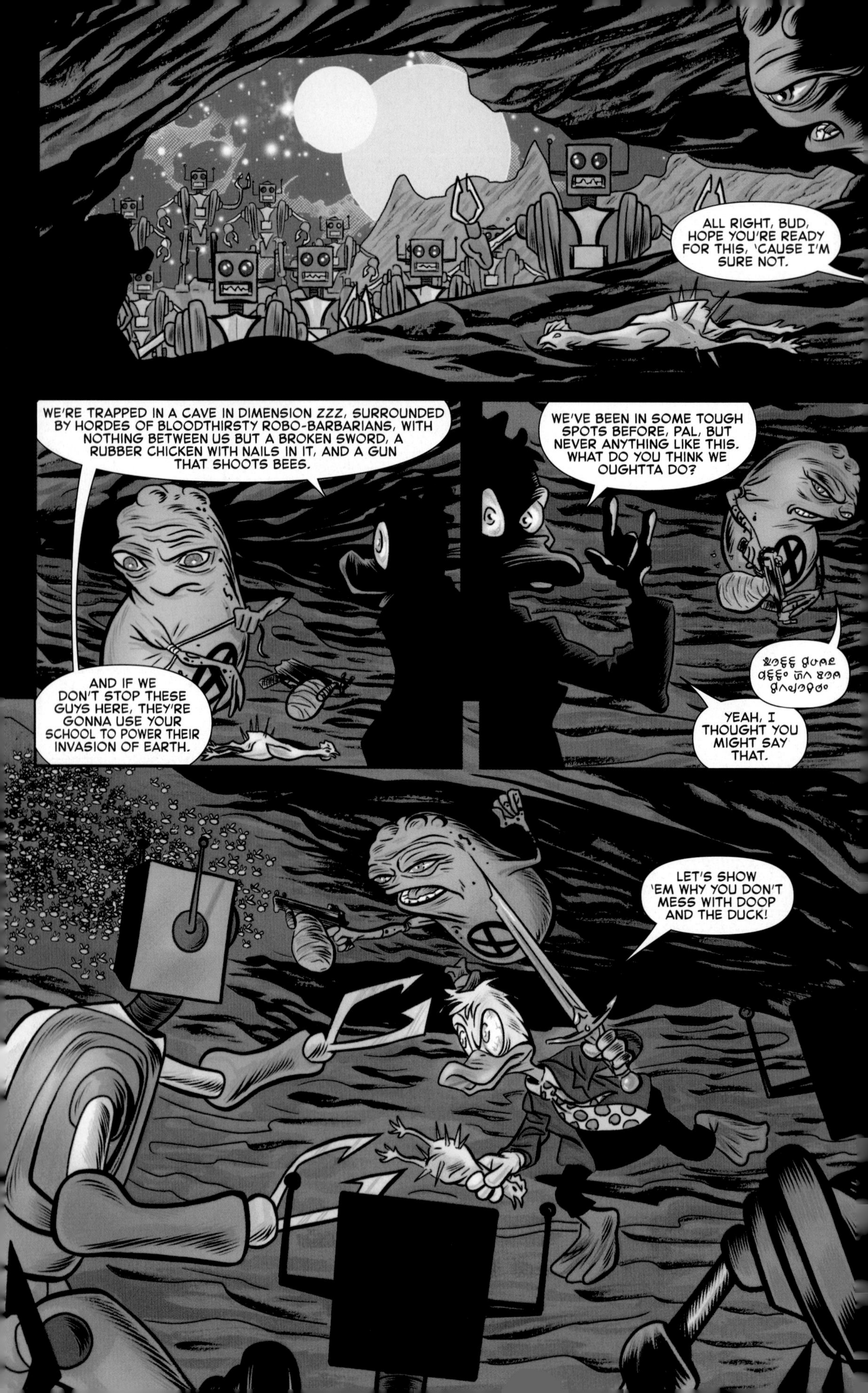
ALL RIGHT, BUD, HOPE YOU'RE READY FOR THIS, 'CAUSE I'M SURE NOT.
WE'RE TRAPPED IN A CAVE IN DIMENSION ZZZ, SURROUNDED BY HORDES OF BLOODTHIRSTY ROBO-BARBARIANS, WITH NOTHING BETWEEN US BUT A BROKEN SWORD, A RUBBER CHICKEN WITH NAILS IN IT, AND A GUN THAT SHOOTS BEES.
AND IF WE DON'T STOP THESE GUYS HERE, THEY'RE GONNA USE YOUR SCHOOL TO POWER THEIR INVASION OF EARTH.
WE'VE BEEN IN SOME TOUGH SPOTS BEFORE, PAL, BUT NEVER ANYTHING LIKE THIS. WHAT DO YOU THINK WE OUGHTTA DO?
YEAH, I THOUGHT YOU MIGHT SAY THAT.
LET'S SHOW 'EM WHY YOU DON'T MESS WITH DOOP AND THE DUCK!

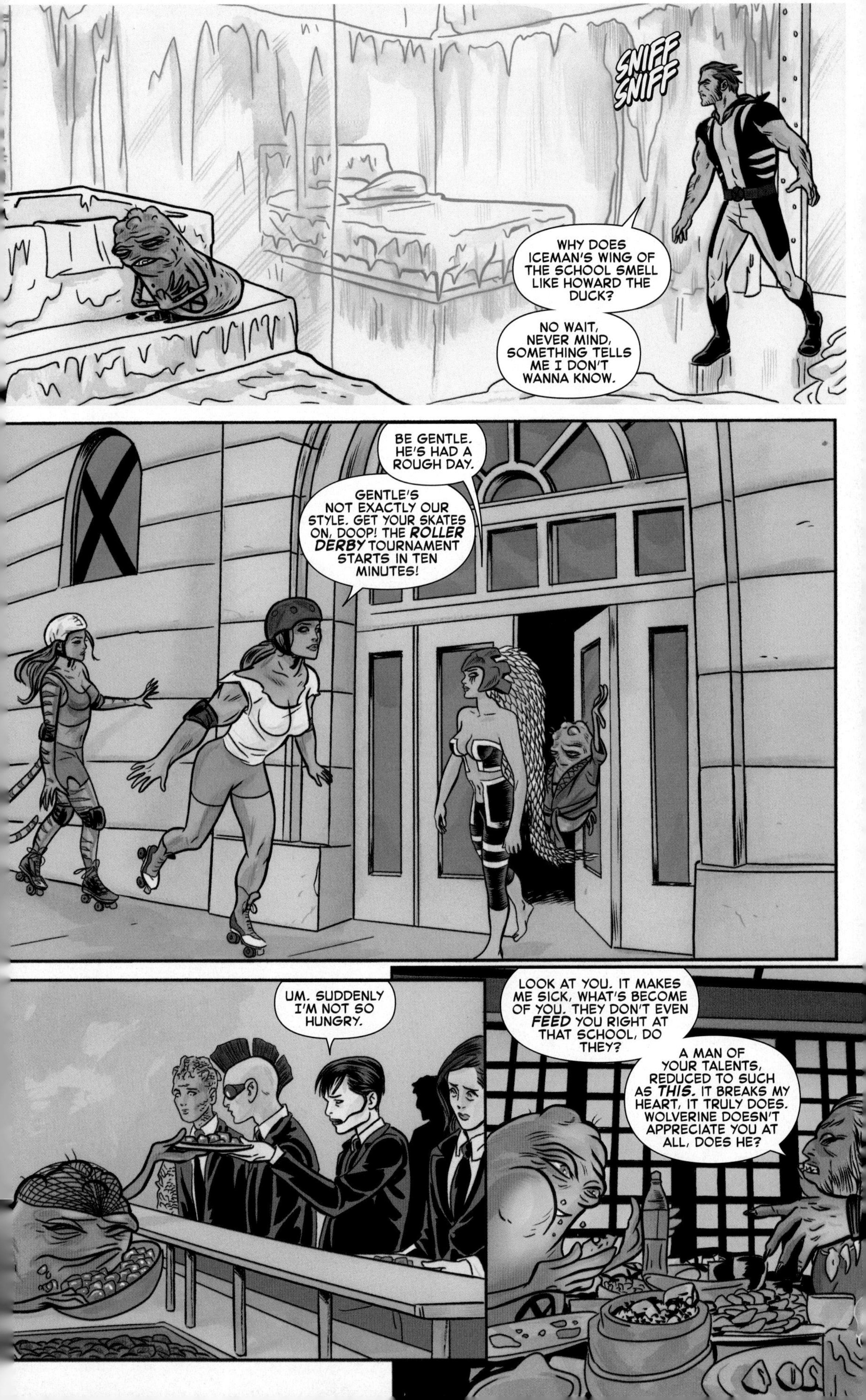

SNIFF SNIFF
WHY DOES ICEMAN'S WING OF THE SCHOOL SMELL LIKE HOWARD THE DUCK?
NO WAIT, NEVER MIND, SOMETHING TELLS ME I DON'T WANNA KNOW.
BE GENTLE. HE'S HAD A ROUGH DAY.
GENTLE'S NOT EXACTLY OUR STYLE. GET YOUR SKATES ON, DOOP! THE ROLLER DERBY TOURNAMENT STARTS IN TEN MINUTES!
UM. SUDDENLY I'M NOT SO HUNGRY.
LOOK AT YOU. IT MAKES ME SICK, WHAT'S BECOME OF YOU. THEY DON'T EVEN FEED YOU RIGHT AT THAT SCHOOL, DO THEY?
A MAN OF YOUR TALENTS, REDUCED TO SUCH AS THIS. IT BREAKS MY HEART, IT TRULY DOES. WOLVERINE DOESN'T APPRECIATE YOU AT ALL, DOES HE?

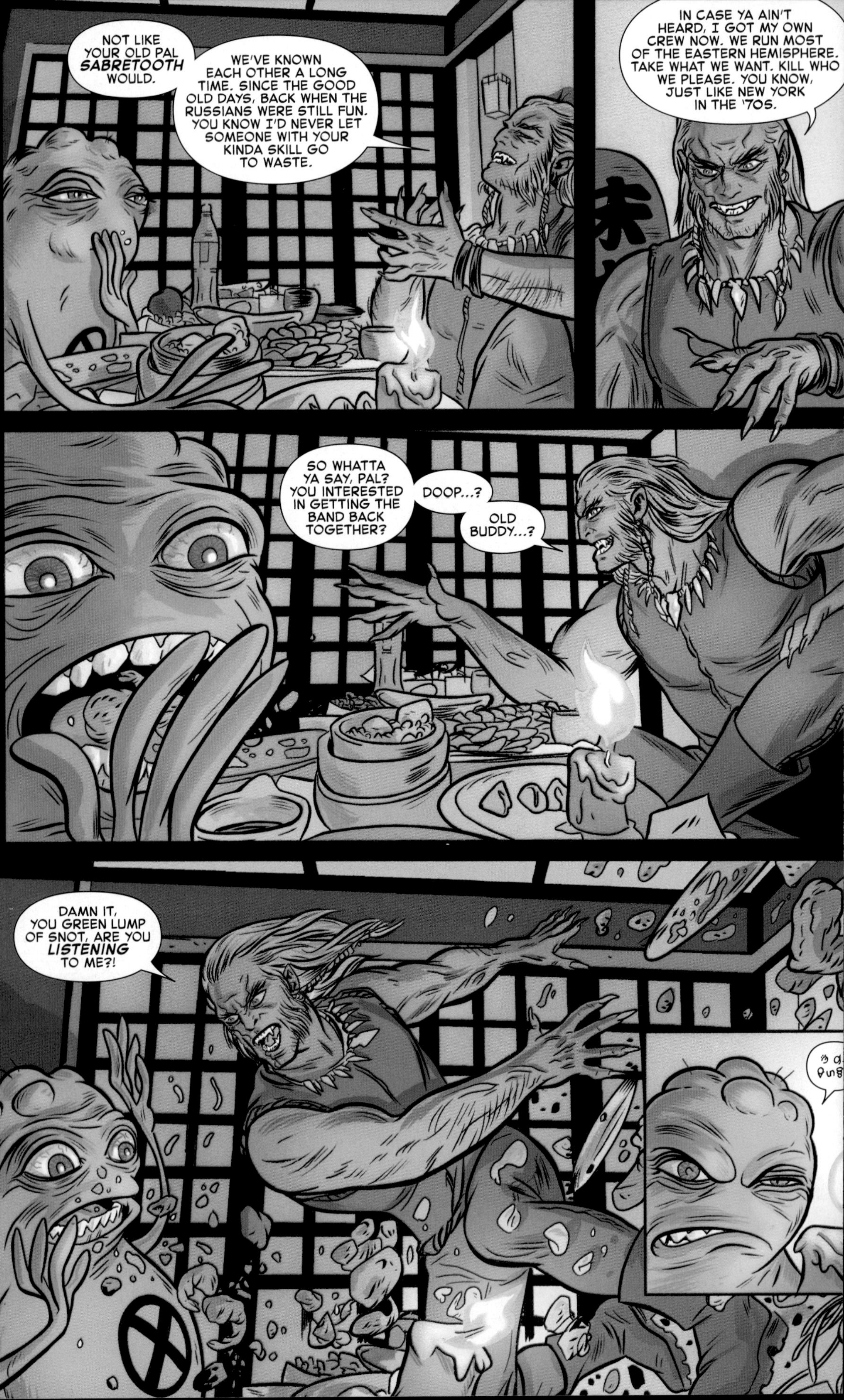
NOT LIKE YOUR OLD PAL SABRETOOTH WOULD.
WE'VE KNOWN EACH OTHER A LONG TIME. SINCE THE GOOD OLD DAYS, BACK WHEN THE RUSSIANS WERE STILL FUN. YOU KNOW I'D NEVER LET SOMEONE WITH YOUR KINDA SKILL GO TO WASTE.
IN CASE YA AIN'T HEARD, I GOT MY OWN CREW NOW. WE RUN MOST OF THE EASTERN HEMISPHERE. TAKE WHAT WE WANT. KILL WHO WE PLEASE. YOU KNOW, JUST LIKE NEW YORK IN THE '70S.
SO WHATTA YA SAY, PAL? YOU INTERESTED IN GETTING THE BAND BACK TOGETHER?
DOOP...?
OLD BUDDY...?
DAMN IT, YOU GREEN LUMP OF SNOT, ARE YOU LISTENING TO ME?!

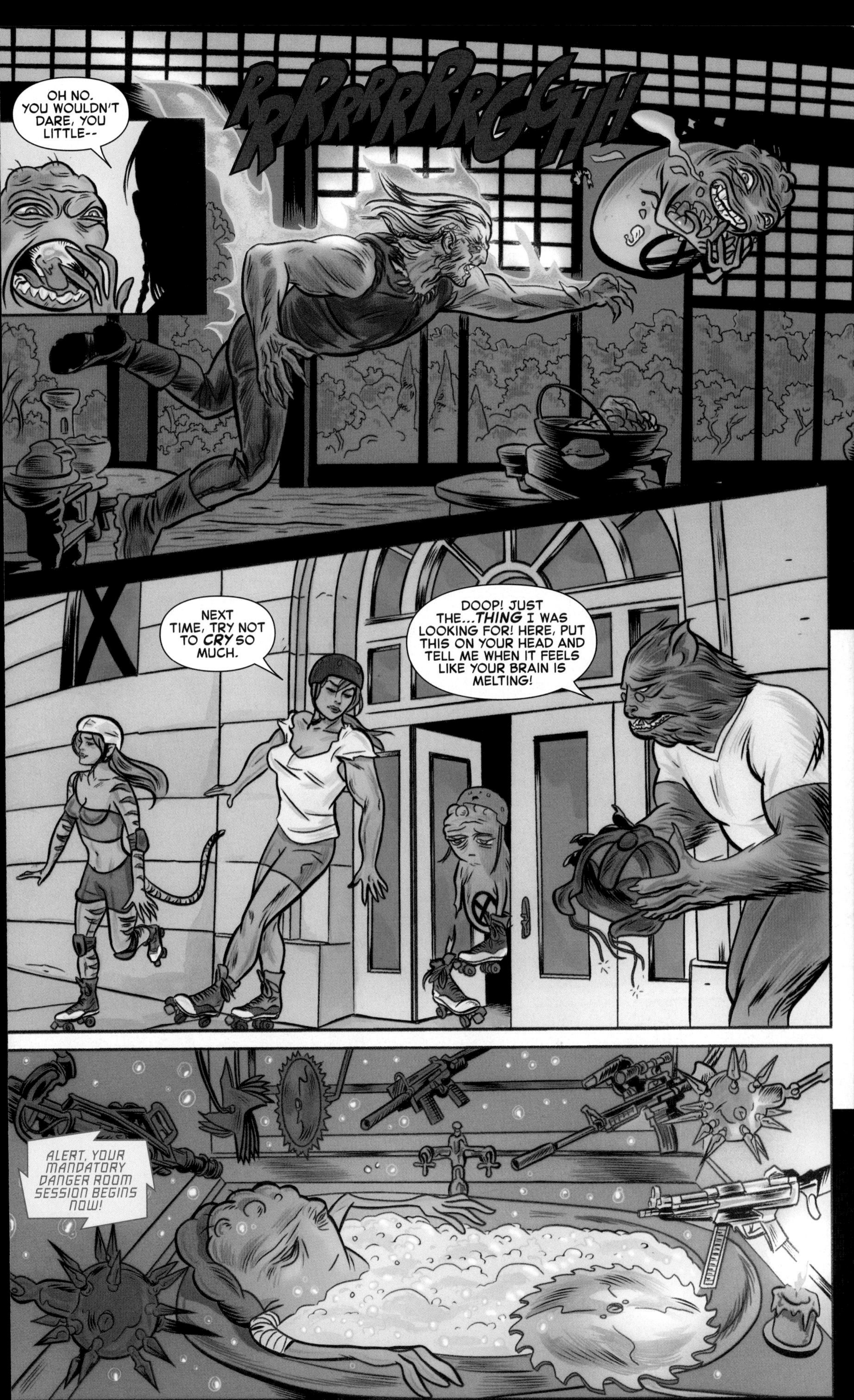
OH NO. YOU WOULDN'T DARE, YOU LITTLE--
RRRRRRRRGGHH
NEXT TIME, TRY NOT TO CRY SO MUCH.
DOOP! JUST THE...THING I WAS LOOKING FOR! HERE, PUT THIS ON YOUR HEAD AND TELL ME WHEN IT FEELS LIKE YOUR BRAIN IS MELTING!
ALERT, YOUR MANDATORY DANGER ROOM SESSION BEGINS NOW!

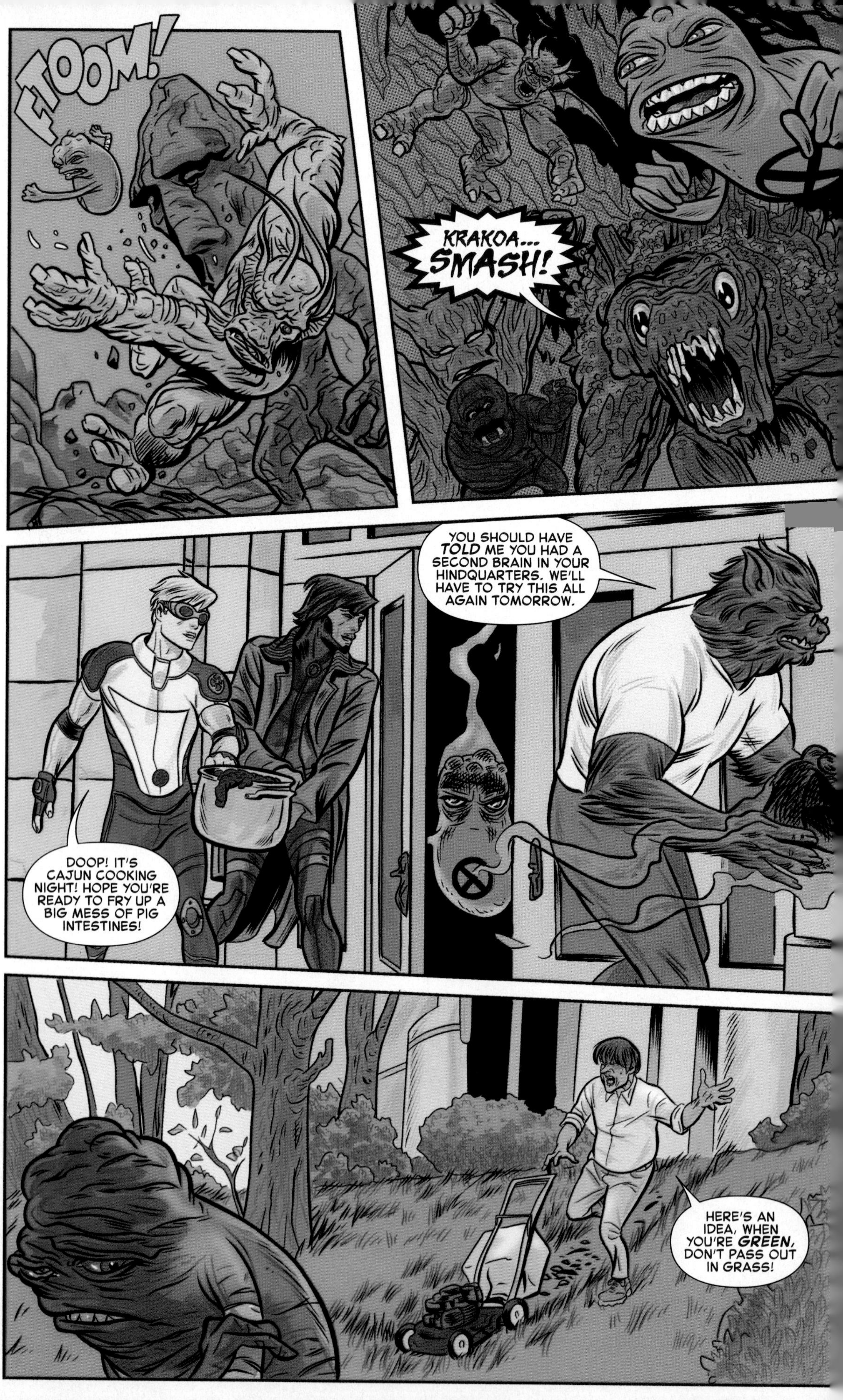
FTOOM!
KRAKOA... SMASH!
YOU SHOULD HAVE TOLD ME YOU HAD A SECOND BRAIN IN YOUR HINDQUARTERS. WE'LL HAVE TO TRY THIS ALL AGAIN TOMORROW.
DOOP! IT'S CAJUN COOKING NIGHT! HOPE YOU'RE READY TO FRY UP A BIG MESS OF PIG INTESTINES!
HERE'S AN IDEA, WHEN YOU'RE GREEN, DON'T PASS OUT IN GRASS!

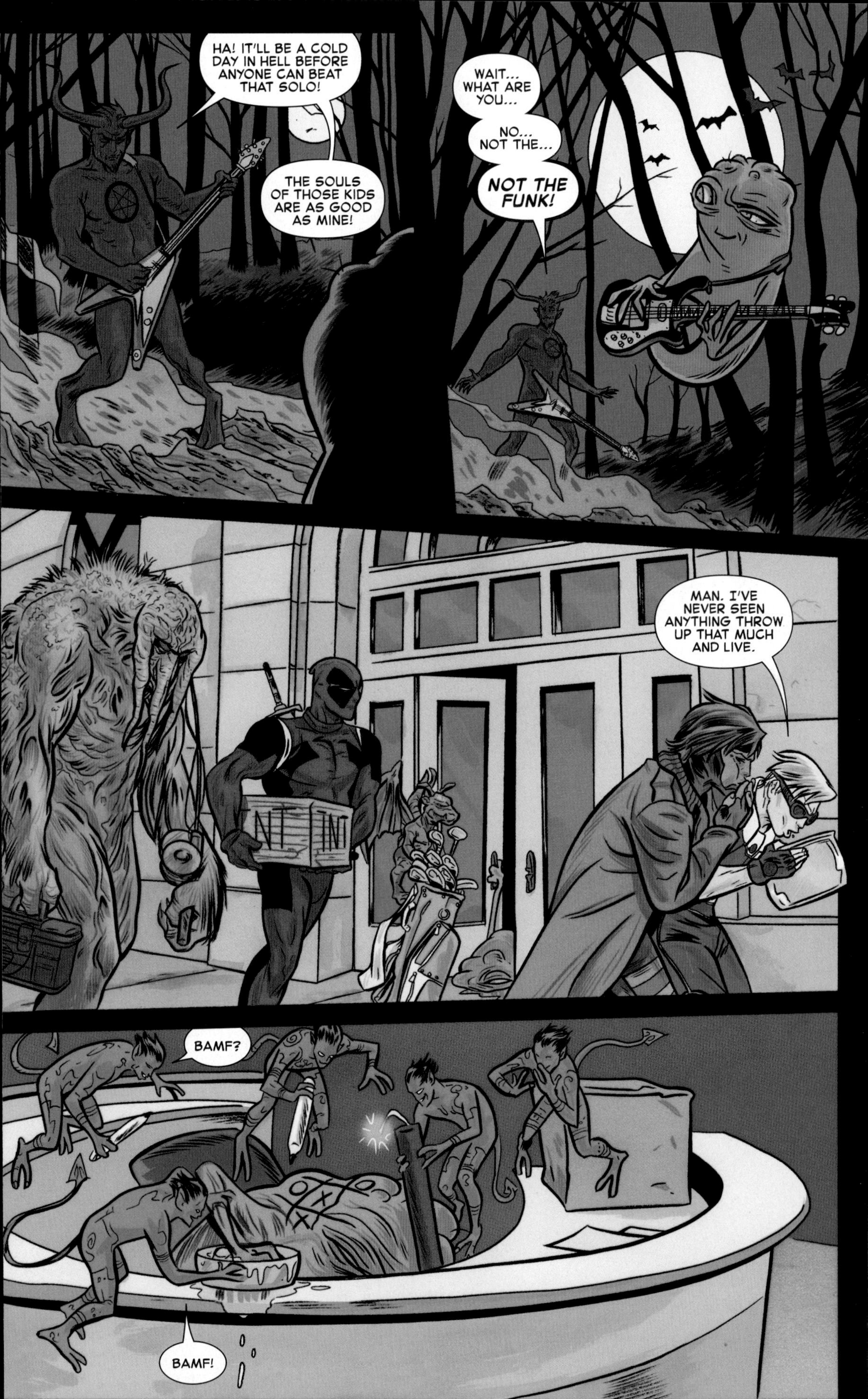
HA! IT'LL BE A COLD DAY IN HELL BEFORE ANYONE CAN BEAT THAT SOLO!
THE SOULS OF THOSE KIDS ARE AS GOOD AS MINE!
WAIT... WHAT ARE YOU...
NO... NOT THE...
NOT THE FUNK!
MAN. I'VE NEVER SEEN ANYTHING THROW UP THAT MUCH AND LIVE.
BAMF?
BAMF!

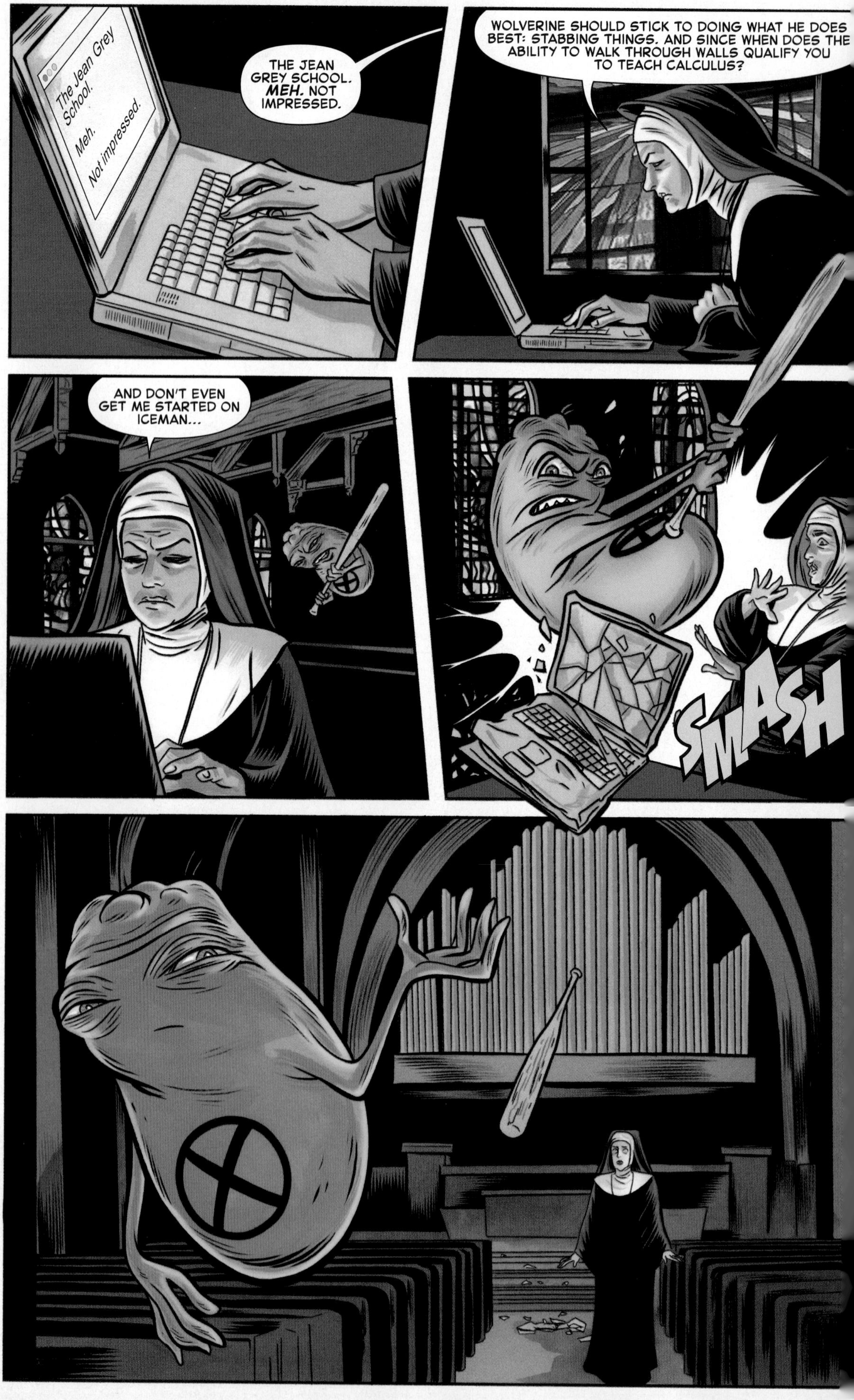

The Jean Grey School.
Meh.
Not impressed.
THE JEAN GREY SCHOOL. MEH. NOT IMPRESSED.
WOLVERINE SHOULD STICK TO DOING WHAT HE DOES BEST: STABBING THINGS. AND SINCE WHEN DOES THE ABILITY TO WALK THROUGH WALLS QUALIFY YOU TO TEACH CALCULUS?
AND DON'T EVEN GET ME STARTED ON ICEMAN...
SMASH

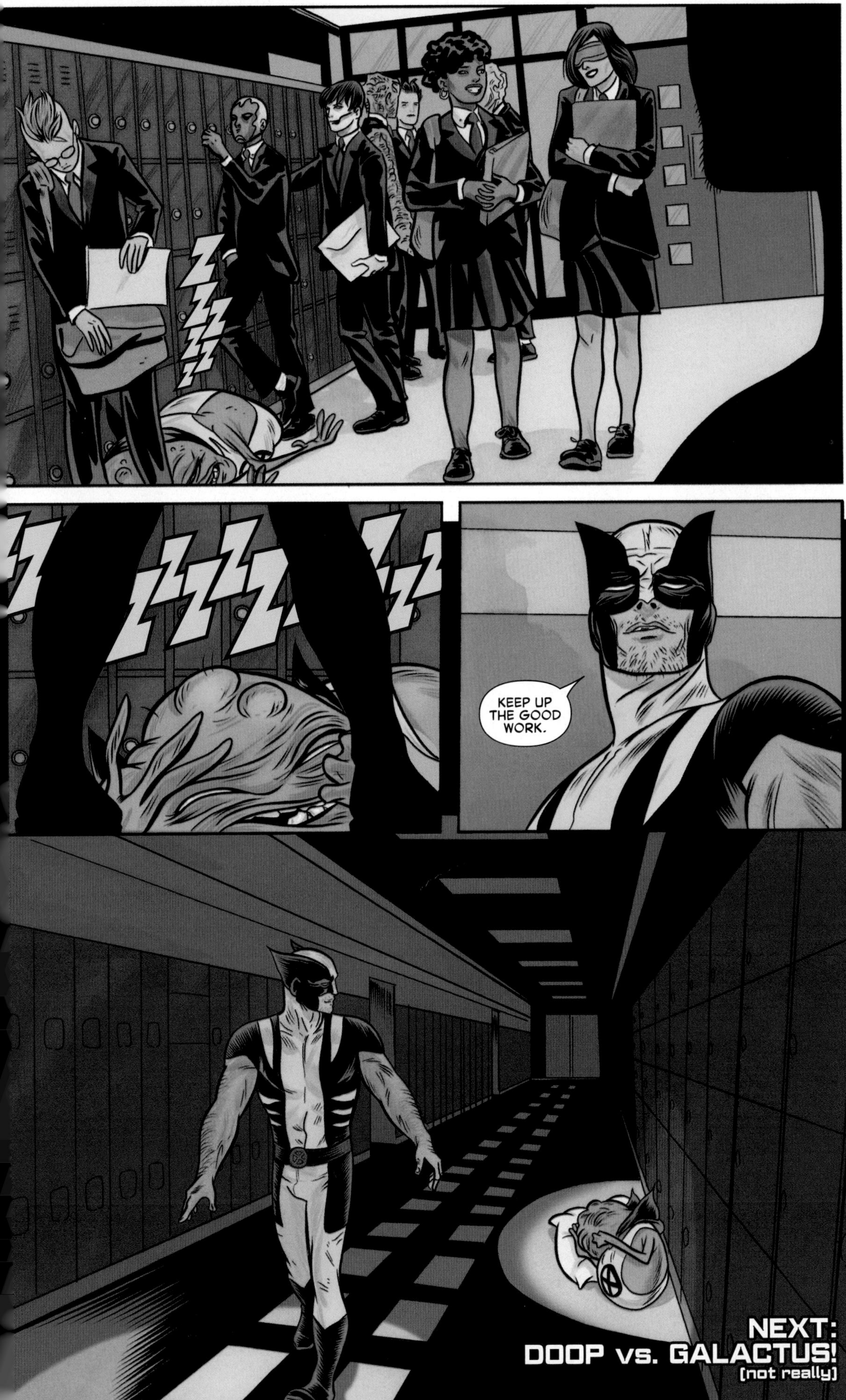
ZZZZZZ
ZZZZZZ
KEEP UP THE GOOD WORK.
NEXT:
DOOP vs. GALACTUS!
[not really]

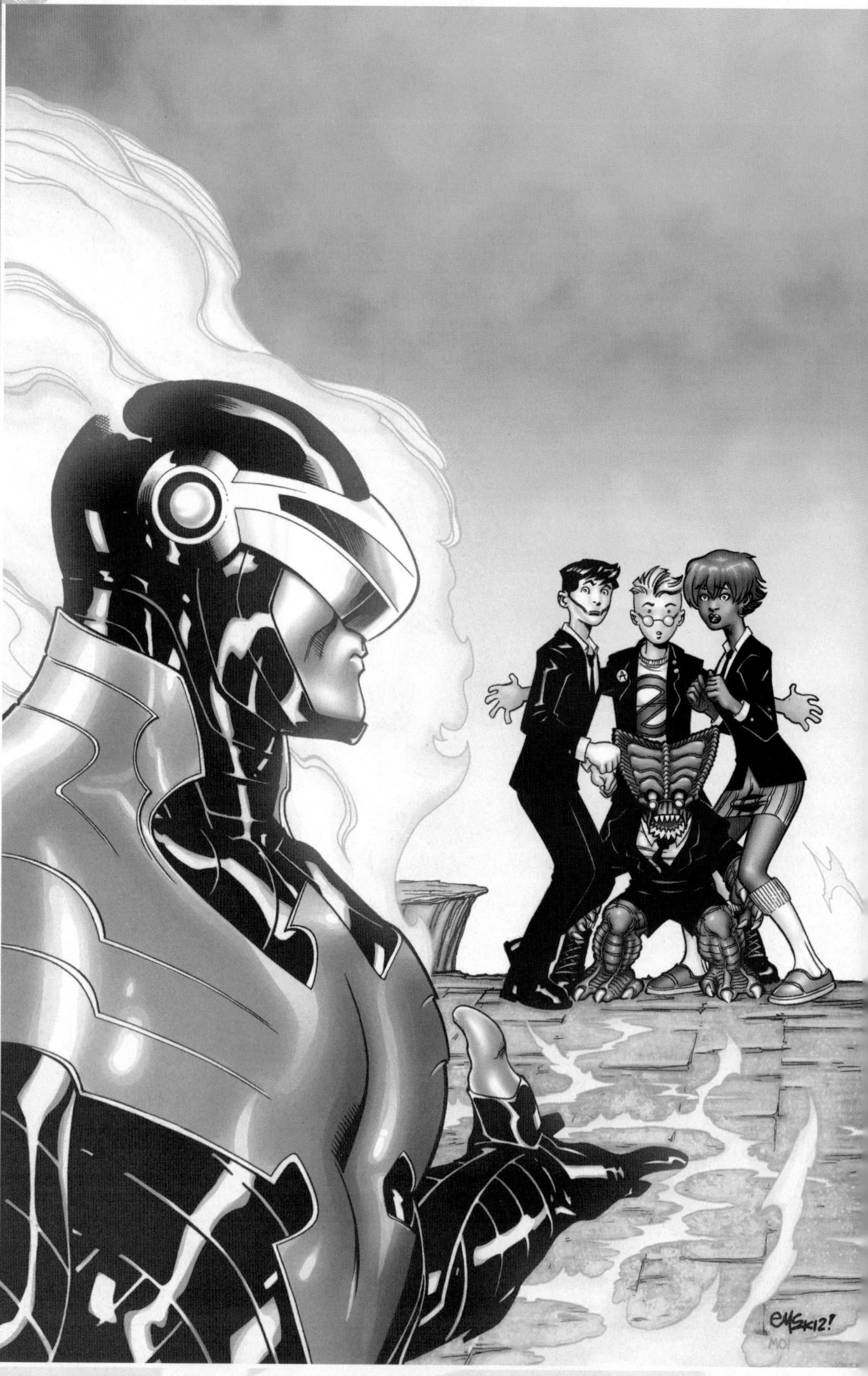
eMSKI2!
MO!

If you were born different with mutant super-powers, the Jean Grey School for Higher Learning is the school for you. Founded by Wolverine and staffed by experienced X-Men, you will learn everything you need to know to survive in a world that hates and fears you.

WOLVERINE and the X-MEN

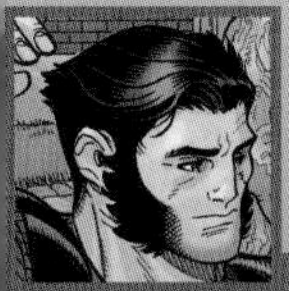

WOLVERINE
Clawed Headmaster

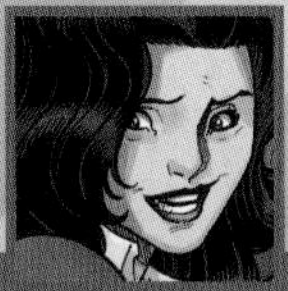

KITTY PRYDE
Phasing Headmistress

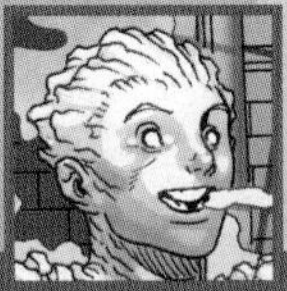

ICEMAN
Ice-Controlling Teacher

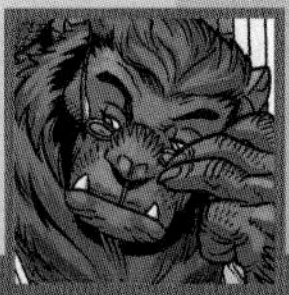

BEAST
Animalistic, Intellectual Vice-Principal

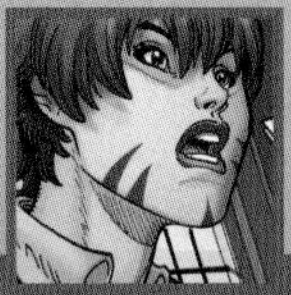

RACHEL GREY
Telekinetic, Telepathic Teacher

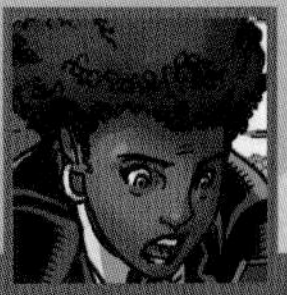

IDIE OKONKWO
Temperature-Controlling Student

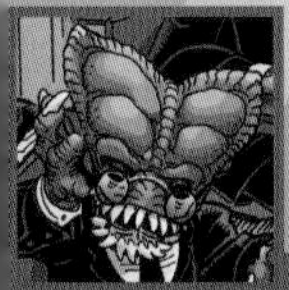

BROO
Alien Student

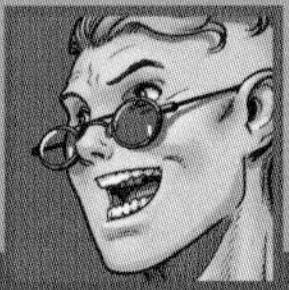

QUENTIN QUIRE
Telepathic Student

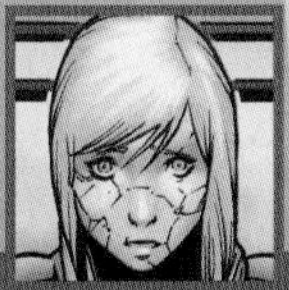

HUSK
Tear-Away Power Shifter Teacher

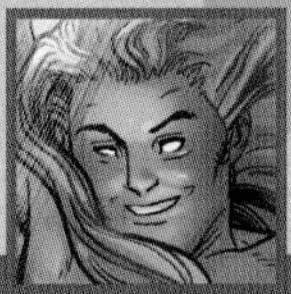

ANGEL
Metal-Winged Student

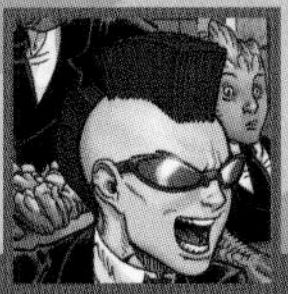

KID GLADIATOR
Superstrong Alien Student

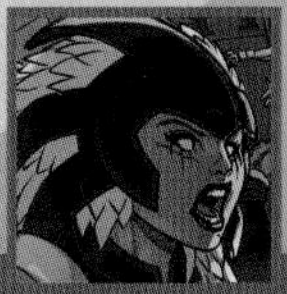

WARBIRD
Shi'ar Bodyguard

PREVIOUSLY

THE CATACLYSMIC PHOENIX FORCE THAT EXPLODED OUT OF THE COSMOS AND DESCENDED TO THE EARTH NOW OCCUPIES JUST ONE X-MAN: CYCLOPS. CORRUPTED BY THE PHOENIX, HE CONTAINS A POWER SO COLOSSAL IT PROMISES GLOBAL ANNIHILATION. WOLVERINE AND HIS X-MEN HAVE JOINED WITH THE AVENGERS AND PROFESSOR X -- FOUNDER OF THE X-MEN AND MENTOR TO CYCLOPS -- AND DEPLOYED FOR WAR TO SAVE THE WORLD FROM ONE OF THEIR OWN.

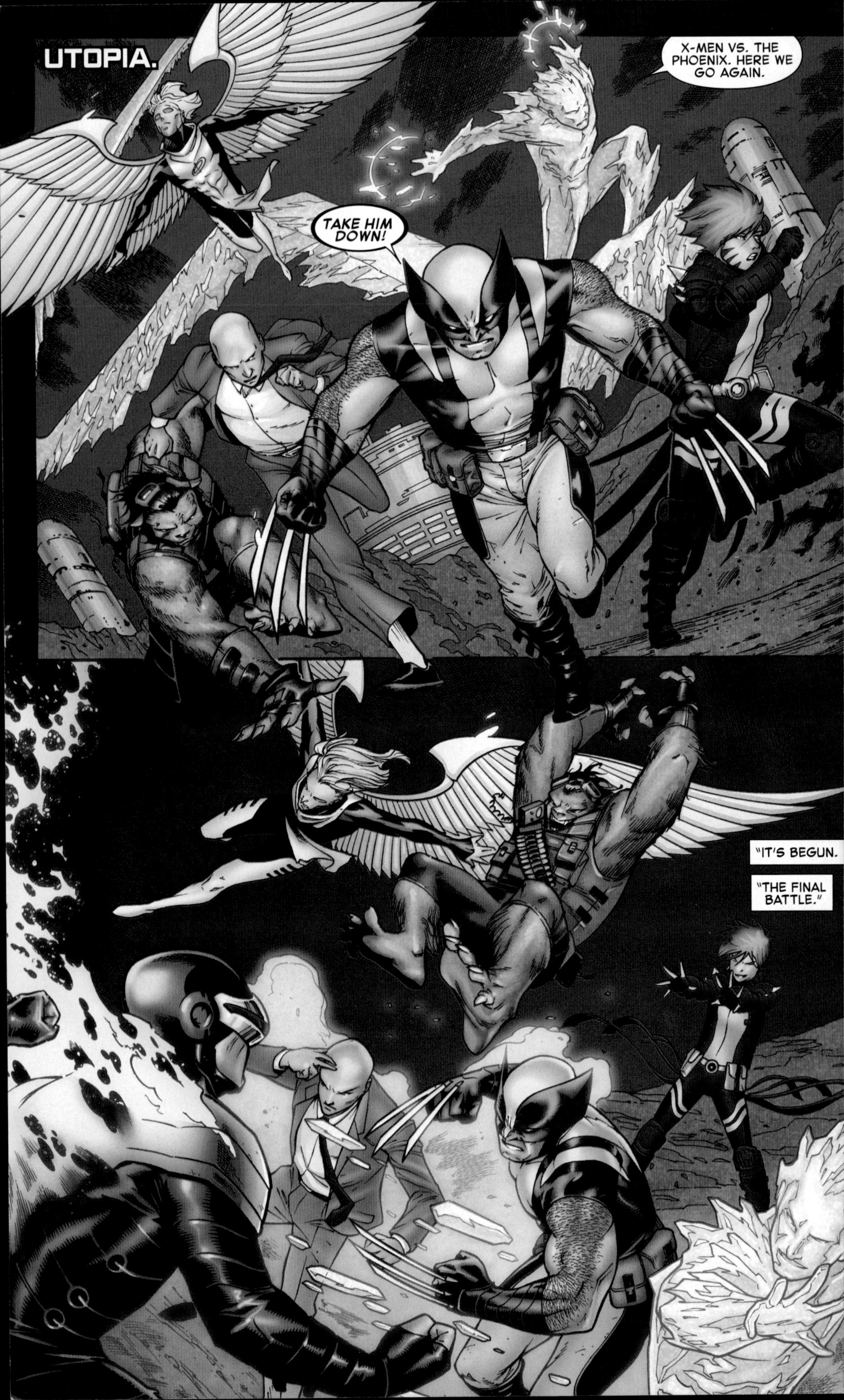
UTOPIA.
X-MEN VS. THE PHOENIX. HERE WE GO AGAIN.
TAKE HIM DOWN!
"IT'S BEGUN.
"THE FINAL BATTLE."

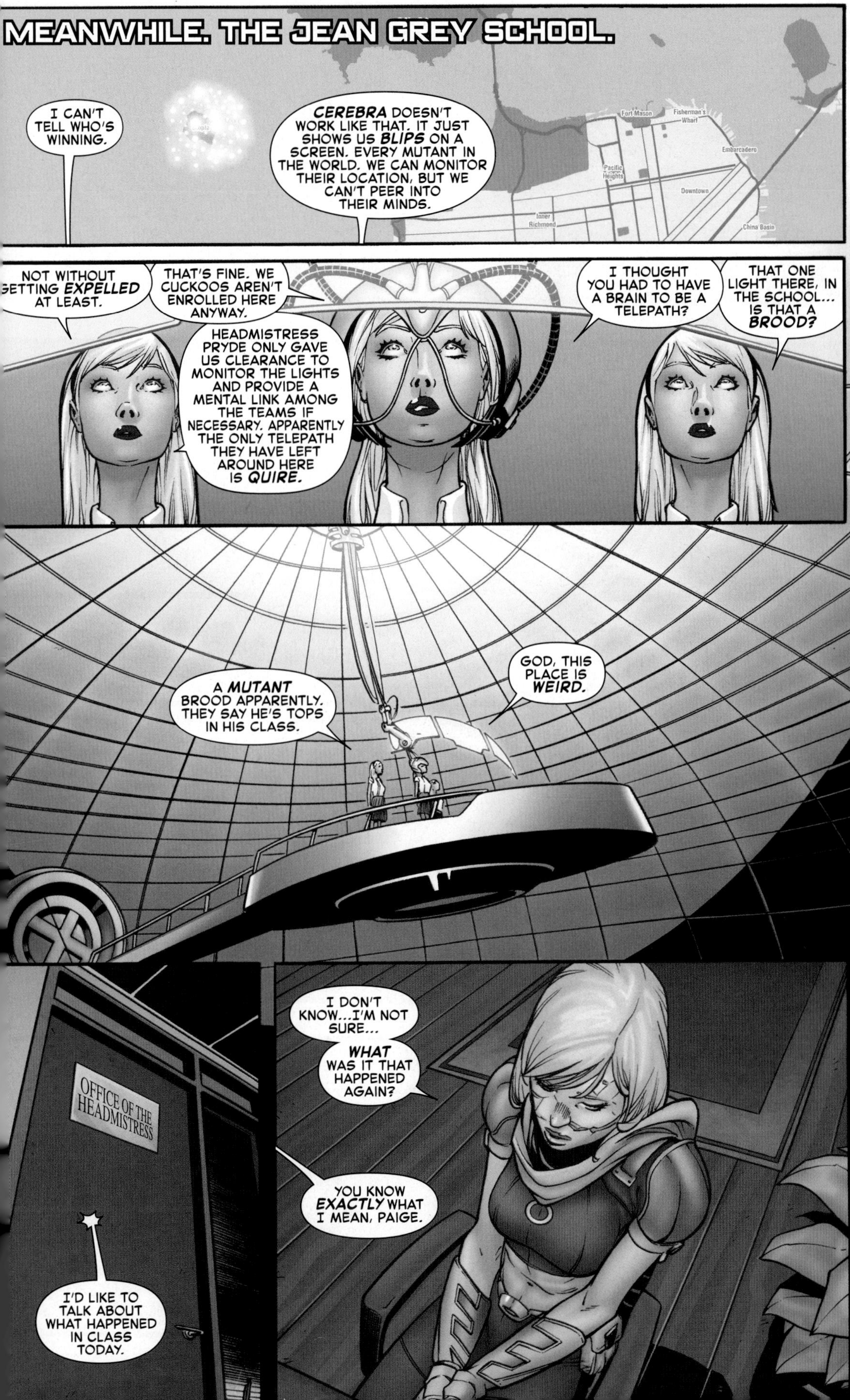
MEANWHILE. THE JEAN GREY SCHOOL.
I CAN'T TELL WHO'S WINNING.
CEREBRA DOESN'T WORK LIKE THAT. IT JUST SHOWS US BLIPS ON A SCREEN. EVERY MUTANT IN THE WORLD. WE CAN MONITOR THEIR LOCATION, BUT WE CAN'T PEER INTO THEIR MINDS.
Fort Mason
Fisherman's Wharf
Embarcadero
Pacific Heights
Downtown
China Basin
NOT WITHOUT GETTING EXPELLED AT LEAST.
THAT'S FINE. WE CUCKOOS AREN'T ENROLLED HERE ANYWAY.
HEADMISTRESS PRYDE ONLY GAVE US CLEARANCE TO MONITOR THE LIGHTS AND PROVIDE A MENTAL LINK AMONG THE TEAMS IF NECESSARY. APPARENTLY THE ONLY TELEPATH THEY HAVE LEFT AROUND HERE IS QUIRE.
I THOUGHT YOU HAD TO HAVE A BRAIN TO BE A TELEPATH?
THAT ONE LIGHT THERE, IN THE SCHOOL... IS THAT A BROOD?
A MUTANT BROOD APPARENTLY. THEY SAY HE'S TOPS IN HIS CLASS.
GOD, THIS PLACE IS WEIRD.
OFFICE OF THE HEADMISTRESS
I'D LIKE TO TALK ABOUT WHAT HAPPENED IN CLASS TODAY.
I DON'T KNOW...I'M NOT SURE...
WHAT WAS IT THAT HAPPENED AGAIN?
YOU KNOW EXACTLY WHAT I MEAN, PAIGE.

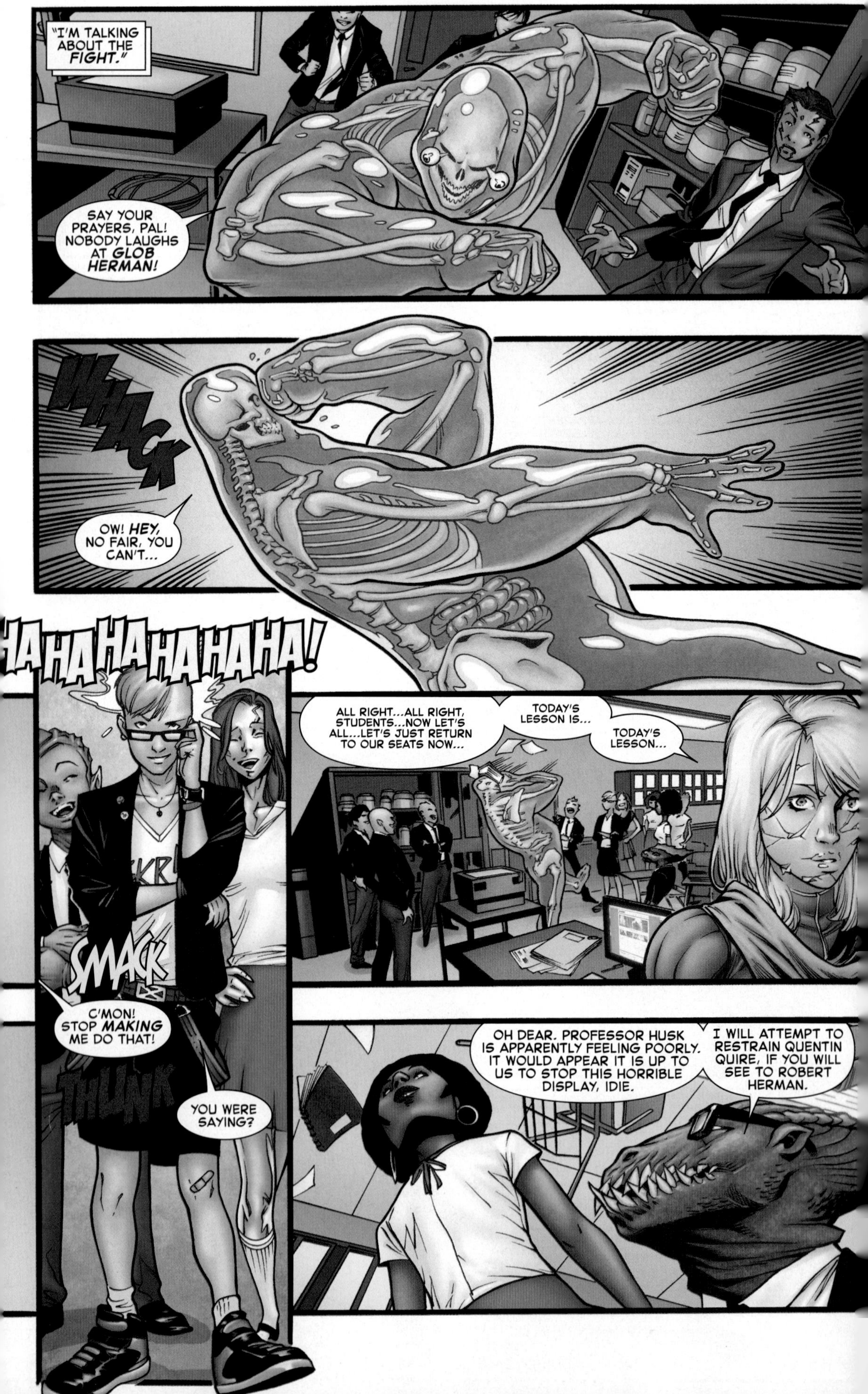
"I'M TALKING ABOUT THE FIGHT."
SAY YOUR PRAYERS, PAL! NOBODY LAUGHS AT GLOB HERMAN!
WHHACK
OW! HEY, NO FAIR, YOU CAN'T...
HAHAHAHAHAHAHA!
ALL RIGHT...ALL RIGHT, STUDENTS...NOW LET'S ALL...LET'S JUST RETURN TO OUR SEATS NOW...
TODAY'S LESSON IS...
TODAY'S LESSON...
SMACK
C'MON! STOP MAKING ME DO THAT!
THUNK
YOU WERE SAYING?
OH DEAR. PROFESSOR HUSK IS APPARENTLY FEELING POORLY. IT WOULD APPEAR IT IS UP TO US TO STOP THIS HORRIBLE DISPLAY, IDIE.
I WILL ATTEMPT TO RESTRAIN QUENTIN QUIRE, IF YOU WILL SEE TO ROBERT HERMAN.

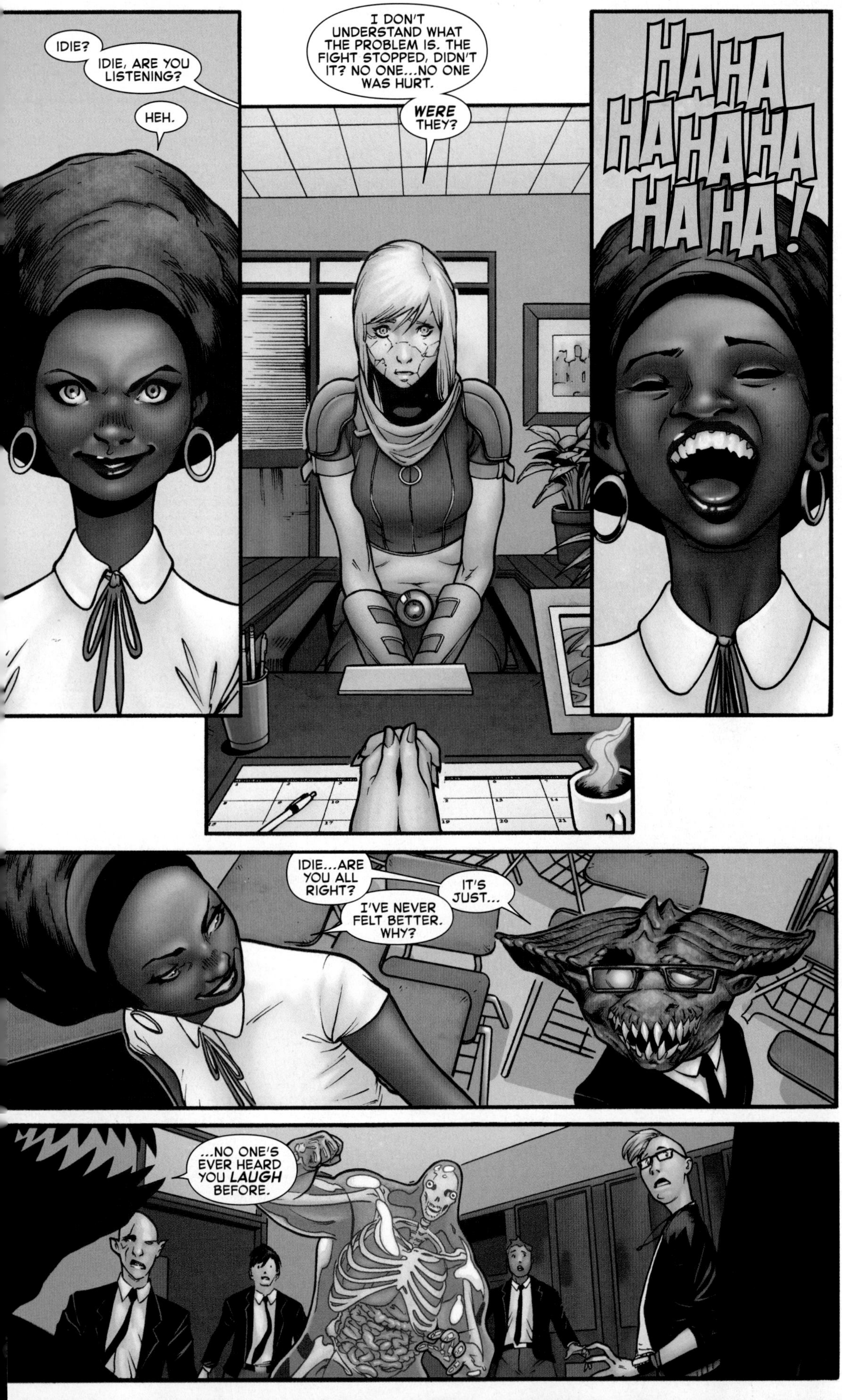
IDIE?
IDIE, ARE YOU LISTENING?
HEH.
I DON'T UNDERSTAND WHAT THE PROBLEM IS. THE FIGHT STOPPED, DIDN'T IT? NO ONE...NO ONE WAS HURT.
WERE THEY?
HAHA HAHAHA HA HA!
IDIE...ARE YOU ALL RIGHT?
I'VE NEVER FELT BETTER. WHY?
IT'S JUST...
...NO ONE'S EVER HEARD YOU LAUGH BEFORE.

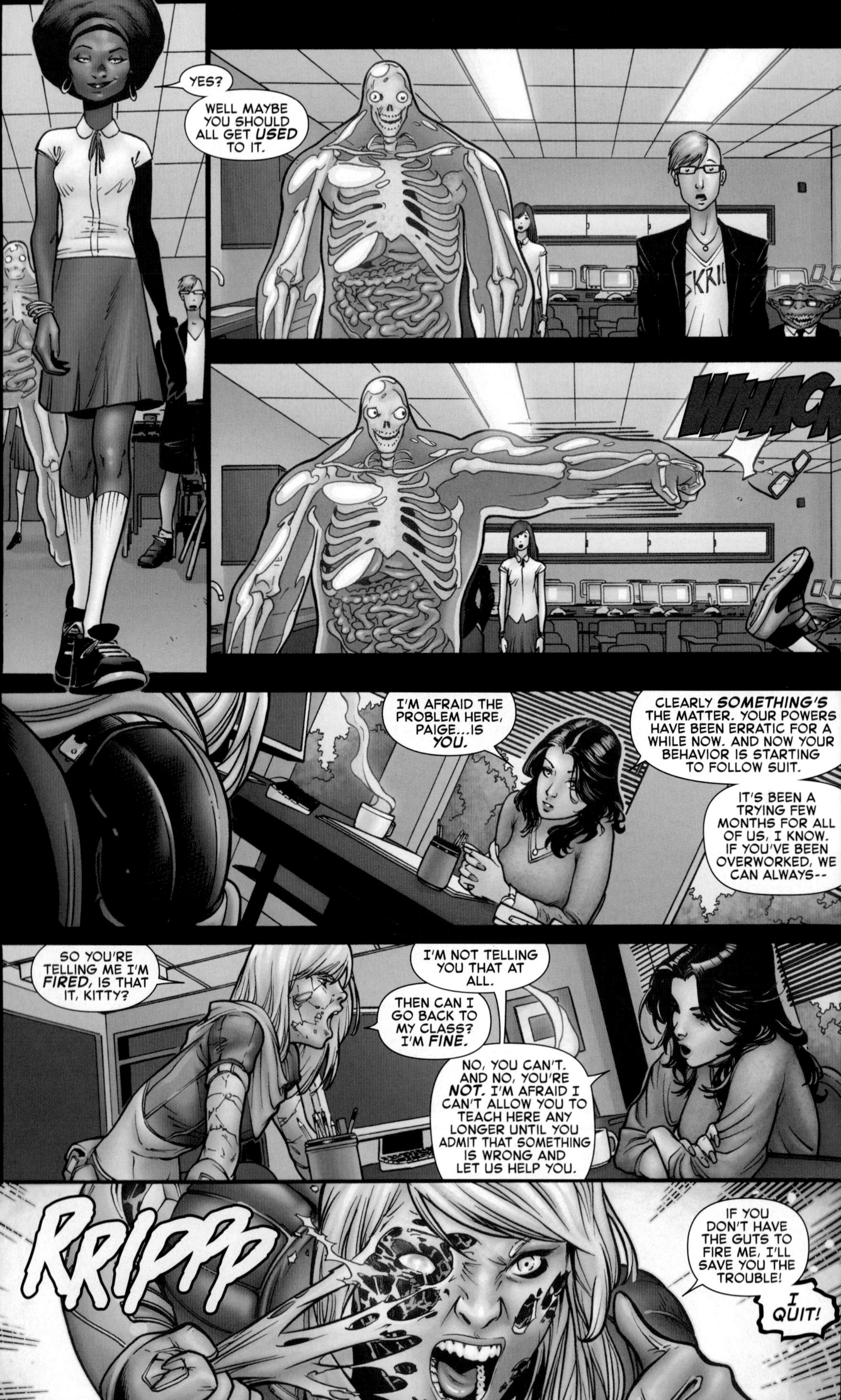

YES?
WELL MAYBE YOU SHOULD ALL GET *USED* TO IT.
WHACK
I'M AFRAID THE PROBLEM HERE, PAIGE...IS *YOU.*
CLEARLY *SOMETHING'S* THE MATTER. YOUR POWERS HAVE BEEN ERRATIC FOR A WHILE NOW. AND NOW YOUR BEHAVIOR IS STARTING TO FOLLOW SUIT.
IT'S BEEN A TRYING FEW MONTHS FOR ALL OF US, I KNOW. IF YOU'VE BEEN OVERWORKED, WE CAN ALWAYS--
SO YOU'RE TELLING ME I'M *FIRED,* IS THAT IT, KITTY?
I'M NOT TELLING YOU THAT AT ALL.
THEN CAN I GO BACK TO MY CLASS? I'M *FINE.*
NO, YOU CAN'T. AND NO, YOU'RE *NOT.* I'M AFRAID I CAN'T ALLOW YOU TO TEACH HERE ANY LONGER UNTIL YOU ADMIT THAT SOMETHING IS WRONG AND LET US HELP YOU.
RRIPPP
IF YOU DON'T HAVE THE GUTS TO FIRE ME, I'LL SAVE YOU THE TROUBLE!
I QUIT!

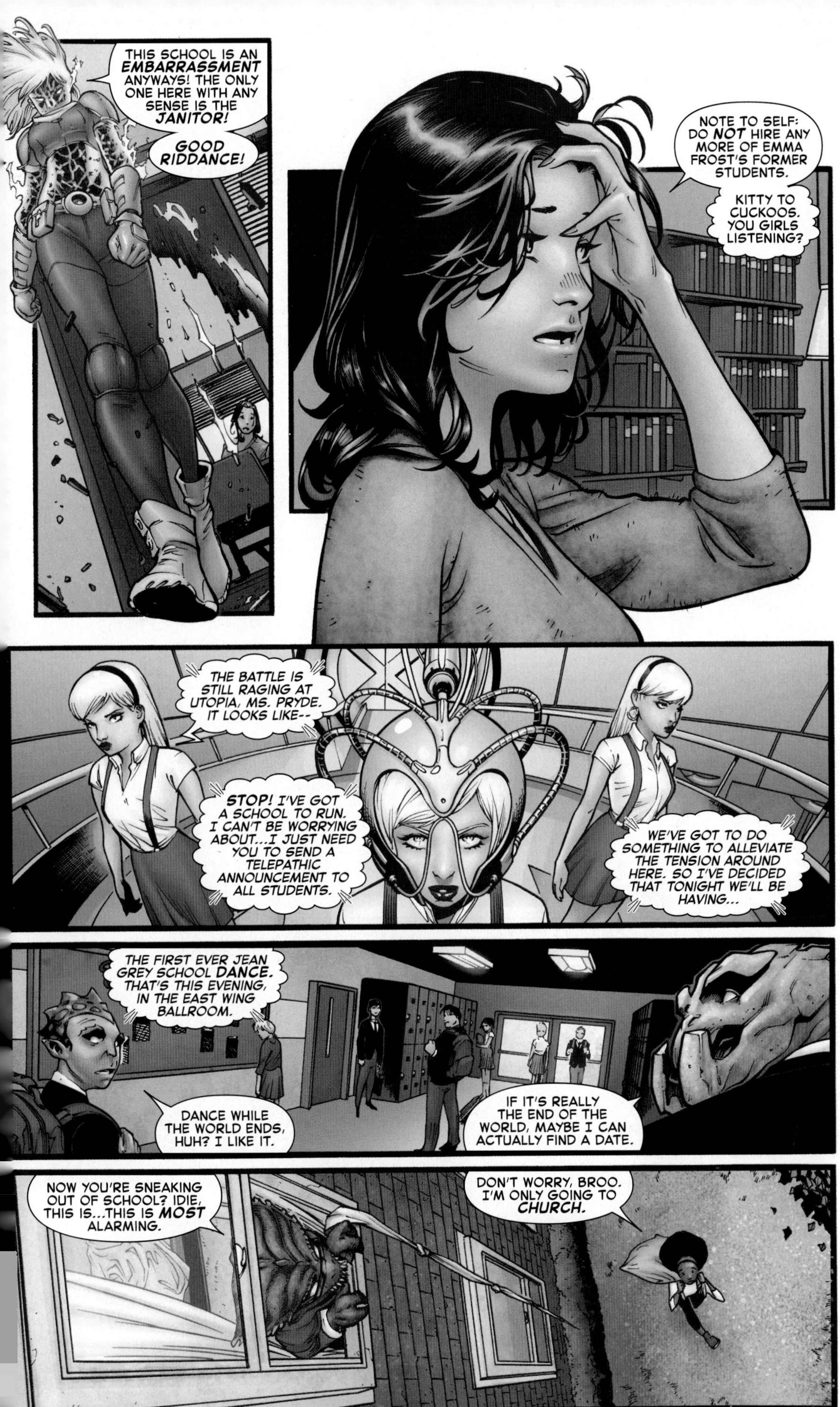

THIS SCHOOL IS AN EMBARRASSMENT ANYWAYS! THE ONLY ONE HERE WITH ANY SENSE IS THE JANITOR!
GOOD RIDDANCE!
NOTE TO SELF: DO NOT HIRE ANY MORE OF EMMA FROST'S FORMER STUDENTS.
KITTY TO CUCKOOS. YOU GIRLS LISTENING?
THE BATTLE IS STILL RAGING AT UTOPIA, MS. PRYDE. IT LOOKS LIKE--
STOP! I'VE GOT A SCHOOL TO RUN. I CAN'T BE WORRYING ABOUT...I JUST NEED YOU TO SEND A TELEPATHIC ANNOUNCEMENT TO ALL STUDENTS.
WE'VE GOT TO DO SOMETHING TO ALLEVIATE THE TENSION AROUND HERE. SO I'VE DECIDED THAT TONIGHT WE'LL BE HAVING...
THE FIRST EVER JEAN GREY SCHOOL DANCE. THAT'S THIS EVENING, IN THE EAST WING BALLROOM.
DANCE WHILE THE WORLD ENDS, HUH? I LIKE IT.
IF IT'S REALLY THE END OF THE WORLD, MAYBE I CAN ACTUALLY FIND A DATE.
NOW YOU'RE SNEAKING OUT OF SCHOOL? IDIE, THIS IS...THIS IS MOST ALARMING.
DON'T WORRY, BROO. I'M ONLY GOING TO CHURCH.

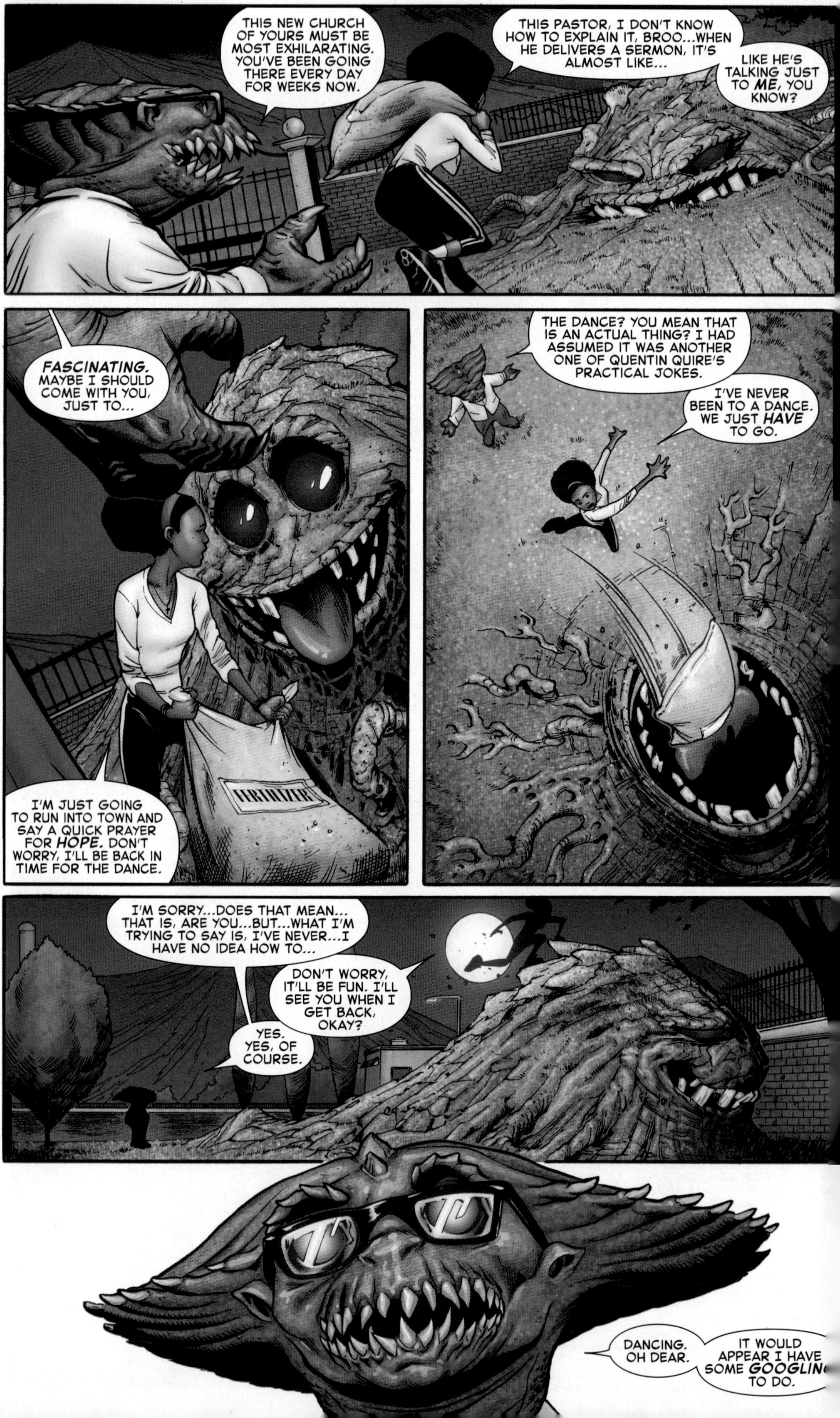
THIS NEW CHURCH OF YOURS MUST BE MOST EXHILARATING. YOU'VE BEEN GOING THERE EVERY DAY FOR WEEKS NOW.
THIS PASTOR, I DON'T KNOW HOW TO EXPLAIN IT, BROO...WHEN HE DELIVERS A SERMON, IT'S ALMOST LIKE...
LIKE HE'S TALKING JUST TO *ME*, YOU KNOW?
FASCINATING. MAYBE I SHOULD COME WITH YOU, JUST TO...
I'M JUST GOING TO RUN INTO TOWN AND SAY A QUICK PRAYER FOR *HOPE.* DON'T WORRY, I'LL BE BACK IN TIME FOR THE DANCE.
FERTILIZER
THE DANCE? YOU MEAN THAT IS AN ACTUAL THING? I HAD ASSUMED IT WAS ANOTHER ONE OF QUENTIN QUIRE'S PRACTICAL JOKES.
I'VE NEVER BEEN TO A DANCE. WE JUST *HAVE* TO GO.
I'M SORRY...DOES THAT MEAN... THAT IS, ARE YOU...BUT...WHAT I'M TRYING TO SAY IS, I'VE NEVER...I HAVE NO IDEA HOW TO...
DON'T WORRY, IT'LL BE FUN. I'LL SEE YOU WHEN I GET BACK, OKAY?
YES. YES, OF COURSE.
DANCING. OH DEAR.
IT WOULD APPEAR I HAVE SOME *GOOGLIN*
TO DO.

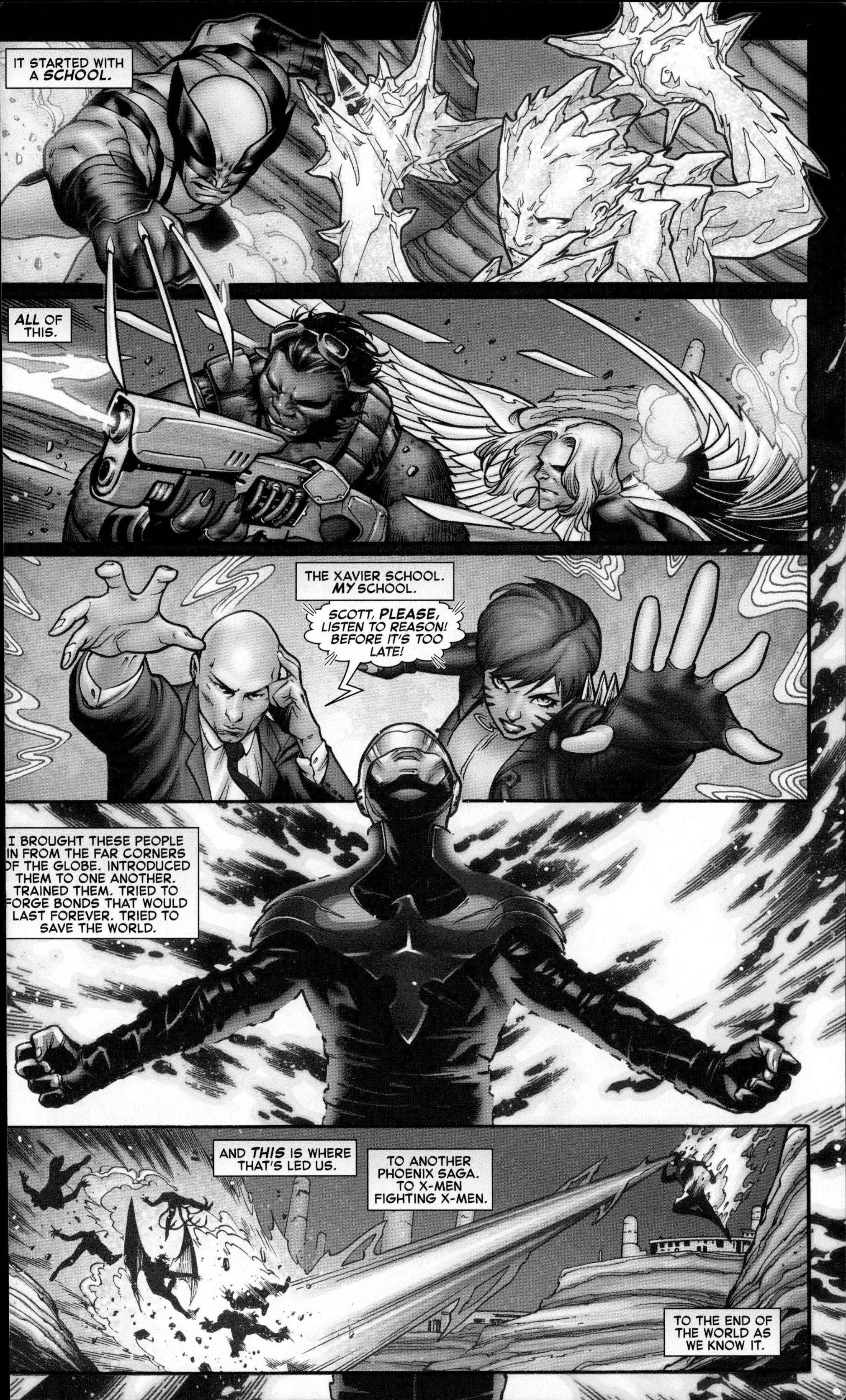
IT STARTED WITH A *SCHOOL.*
ALL OF THIS.
THE XAVIER SCHOOL. *MY* SCHOOL.
SCOTT, **PLEASE,** LISTEN TO REASON! BEFORE IT'S TOO LATE!
I BROUGHT THESE PEOPLE IN FROM THE FAR CORNERS OF THE GLOBE. INTRODUCED THEM TO ONE ANOTHER. TRAINED THEM. TRIED TO FORGE BONDS THAT WOULD LAST FOREVER. TRIED TO SAVE THE WORLD.
AND *THIS* IS WHERE THAT'S LED US.
TO ANOTHER PHOENIX SAGA. TO X-MEN FIGHTING X-MEN.
TO THE END OF THE WORLD AS WE KNOW IT.

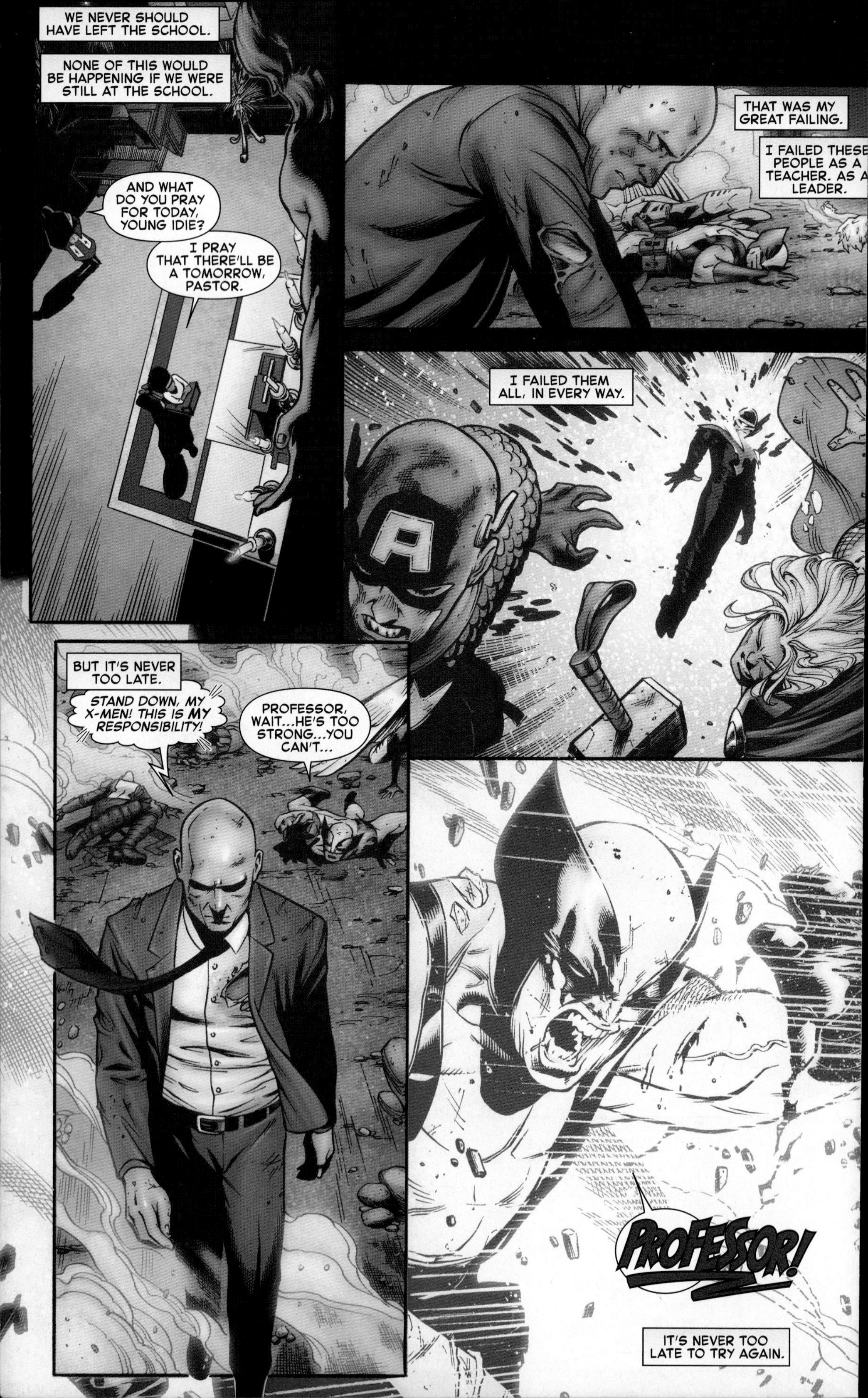
WE NEVER SHOULD HAVE LEFT THE SCHOOL.
NONE OF THIS WOULD BE HAPPENING IF WE WERE STILL AT THE SCHOOL.
AND WHAT DO YOU PRAY FOR TODAY, YOUNG IDIE?
I PRAY THAT THERE'LL BE A TOMORROW, PASTOR.
THAT WAS MY GREAT FAILING.
I FAILED THESE PEOPLE AS A TEACHER. AS A LEADER.
I FAILED THEM ALL, IN EVERY WAY.
BUT IT'S NEVER TOO LATE.
STAND DOWN, MY X-MEN! THIS IS MY RESPONSIBILITY!
PROFESSOR, WAIT...HE'S TOO STRONG...YOU CAN'T...
PROFESSOR!
IT'S NEVER TOO LATE TO TRY AGAIN.

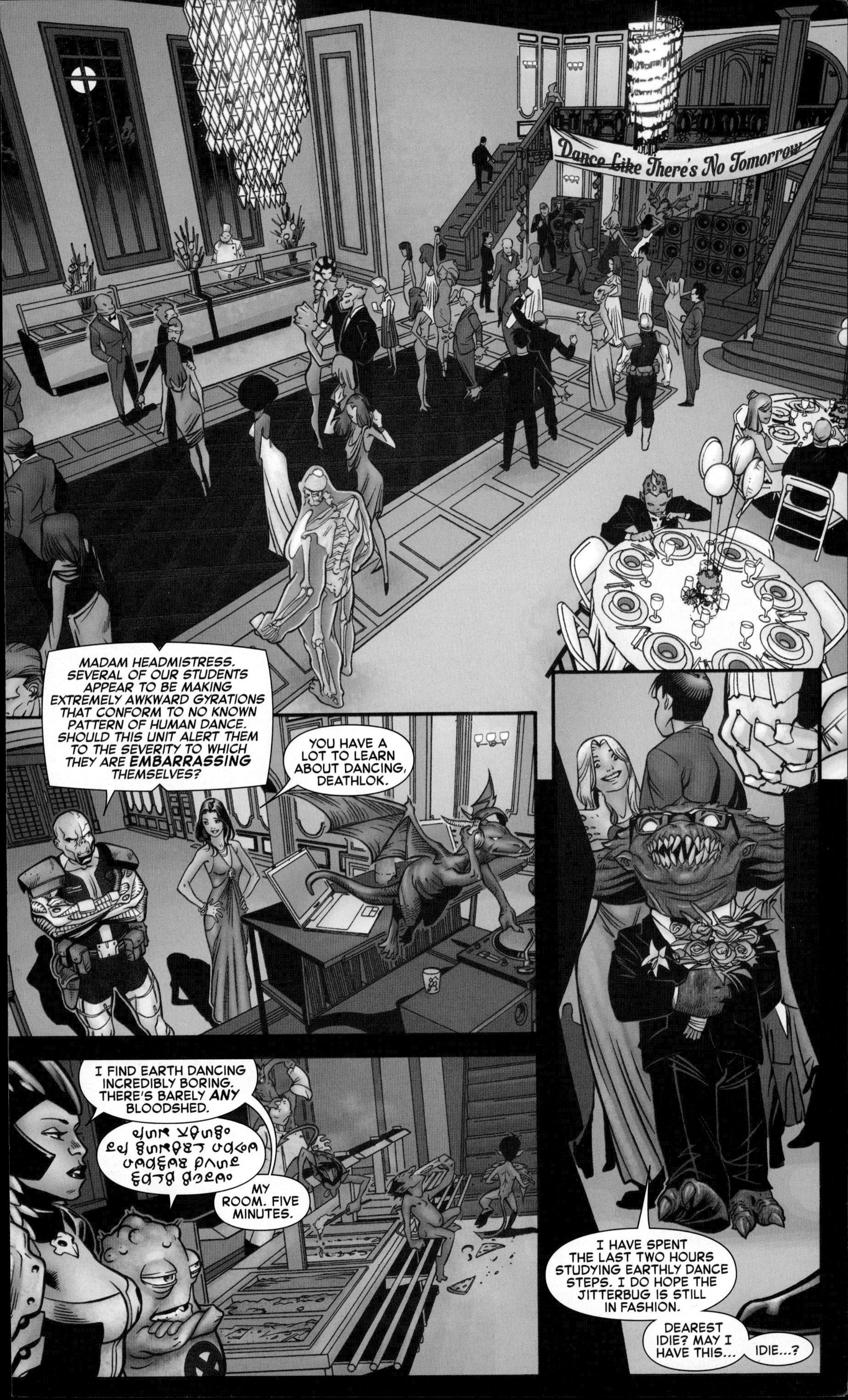
Dance Like There's No Tomorrow
MADAM HEADMISTRESS. SEVERAL OF OUR STUDENTS APPEAR TO BE MAKING EXTREMELY AWKWARD GYRATIONS THAT CONFORM TO NO KNOWN PATTERN OF HUMAN DANCE. SHOULD THIS UNIT ALERT THEM TO THE SEVERITY TO WHICH THEY ARE EMBARRASSING THEMSELVES?
YOU HAVE A LOT TO LEARN ABOUT DANCING, DEATHLOK.
I HAVE SPENT THE LAST TWO HOURS STUDYING EARTHLY DANCE STEPS. I DO HOPE THE JITTERBUG IS STILL IN FASHION.
DEAREST IDIE? MAY I HAVE THIS...
IDIE...?
I FIND EARTH DANCING INCREDIBLY BORING. THERE'S BARELY ANY BLOODSHED.
MY ROOM. FIVE MINUTES.

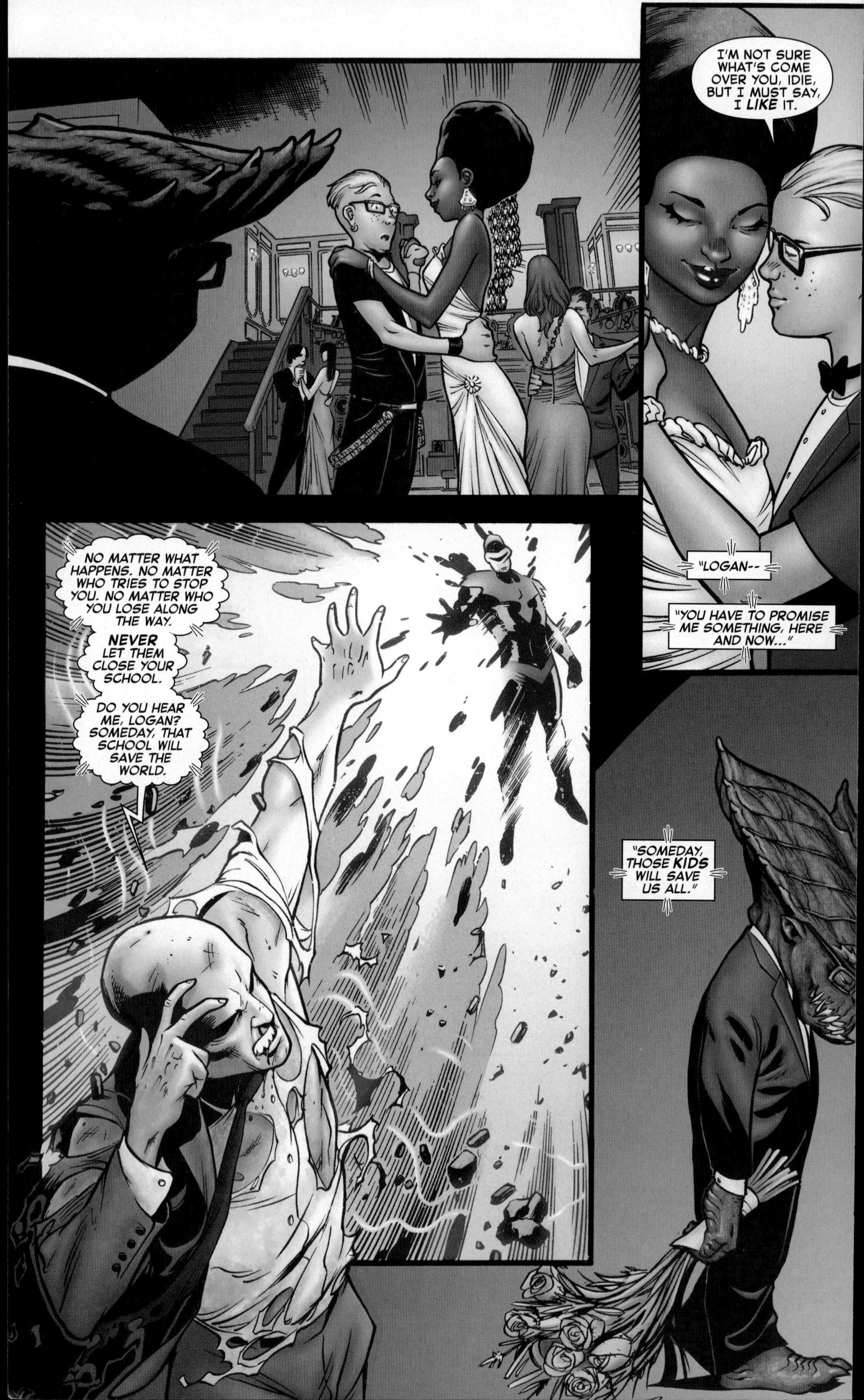
I'M NOT SURE WHAT'S COME OVER YOU, IDIE, BUT I MUST SAY, I *LIKE* IT.
"LOGAN--
"YOU HAVE TO PROMISE ME SOMETHING, HERE AND NOW..."
NO MATTER WHAT HAPPENS. NO MATTER WHO TRIES TO STOP YOU. NO MATTER WHO YOU LOSE ALONG THE WAY.
NEVER LET THEM CLOSE YOUR SCHOOL.
DO YOU HEAR ME, LOGAN? SOMEDAY, THAT SCHOOL WILL SAVE THE WORLD.
"SOMEDAY, THOSE **KIDS** WILL SAVE US ALL."

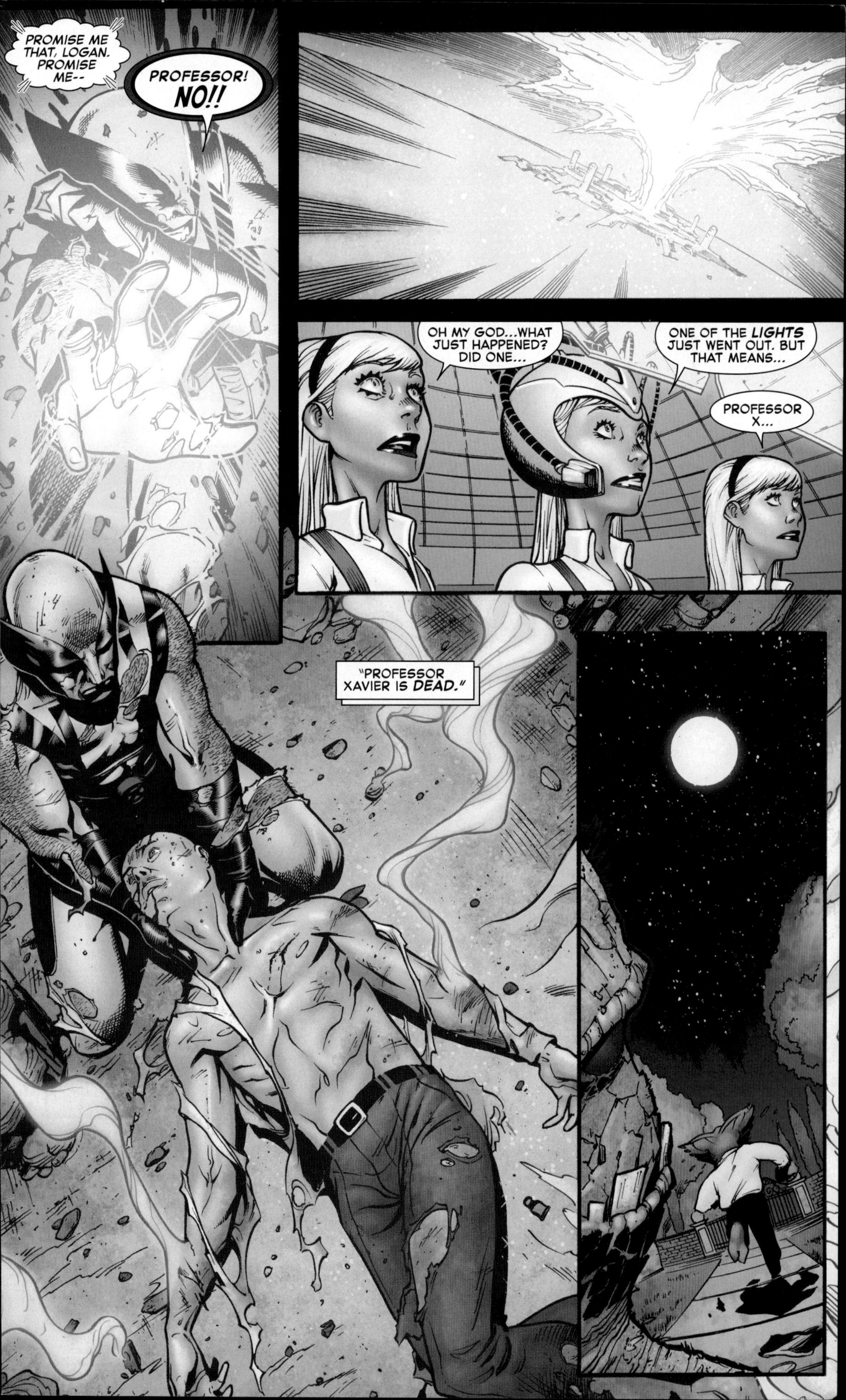
PROMISE ME THAT, LOGAN. PROMISE ME--
PROFESSOR! NO!!
OH MY GOD...WHAT JUST HAPPENED? DID ONE...
ONE OF THE LIGHTS JUST WENT OUT. BUT THAT MEANS...
PROFESSOR X...
"PROFESSOR XAVIER IS DEAD."

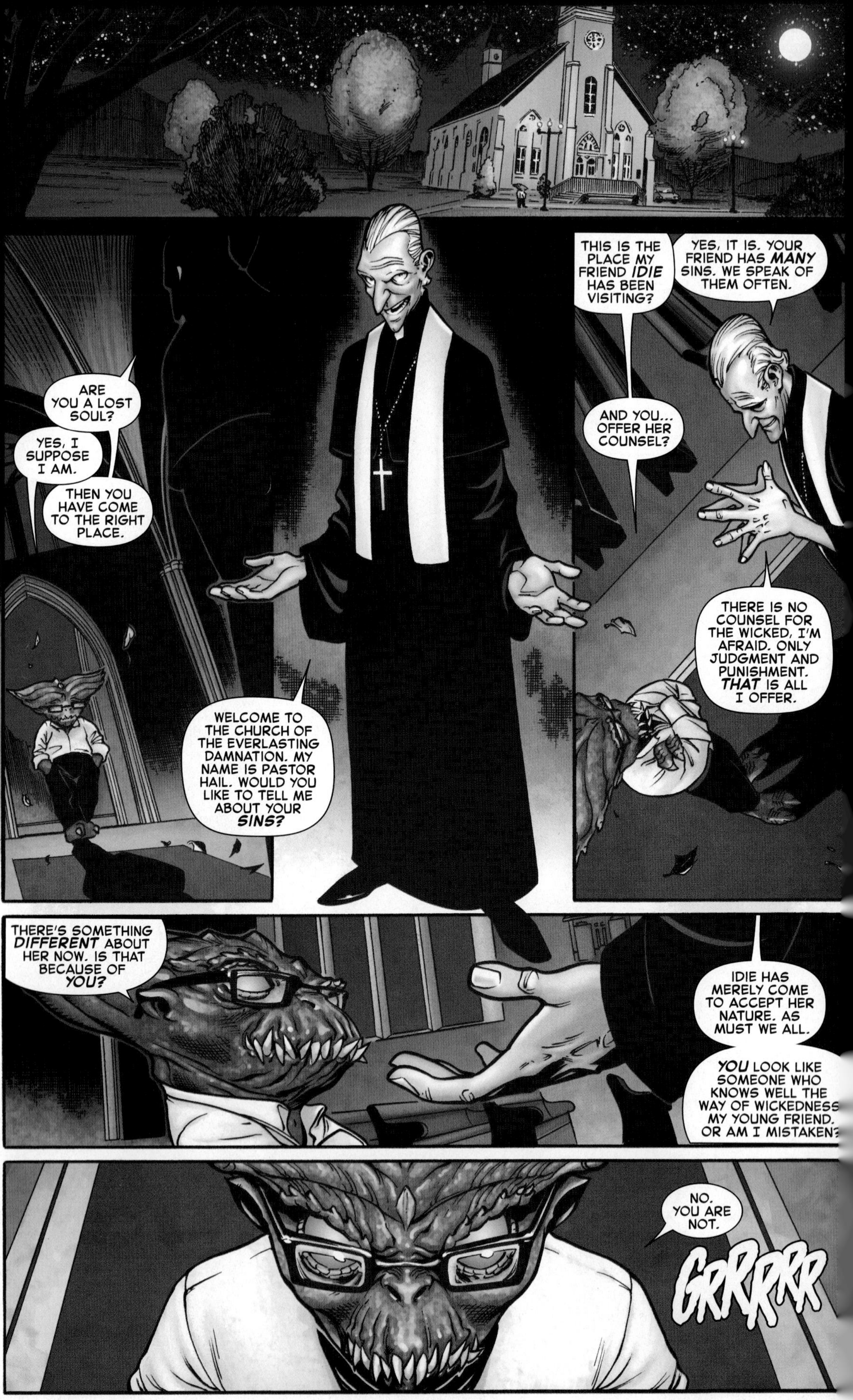
ARE YOU A LOST SOUL?
YES, I SUPPOSE I AM.
THEN YOU HAVE COME TO THE RIGHT PLACE.
WELCOME TO THE CHURCH OF THE EVERLASTING DAMNATION. MY NAME IS PASTOR HAIL. WOULD YOU LIKE TO TELL ME ABOUT YOUR SINS?
THIS IS THE PLACE MY FRIEND IDIE HAS BEEN VISITING?
YES, IT IS. YOUR FRIEND HAS MANY SINS. WE SPEAK OF THEM OFTEN.
AND YOU... OFFER HER COUNSEL?
THERE IS NO COUNSEL FOR THE WICKED, I'M AFRAID. ONLY JUDGMENT AND PUNISHMENT. THAT IS ALL I OFFER.
THERE'S SOMETHING DIFFERENT ABOUT HER NOW. IS THAT BECAUSE OF YOU?
IDIE HAS MERELY COME TO ACCEPT HER NATURE. AS MUST WE ALL.
YOU LOOK LIKE SOMEONE WHO KNOWS WELL THE WAY OF WICKEDNESS MY YOUNG FRIEND. OR AM I MISTAKEN?
NO. YOU ARE NOT.
GRRRRR

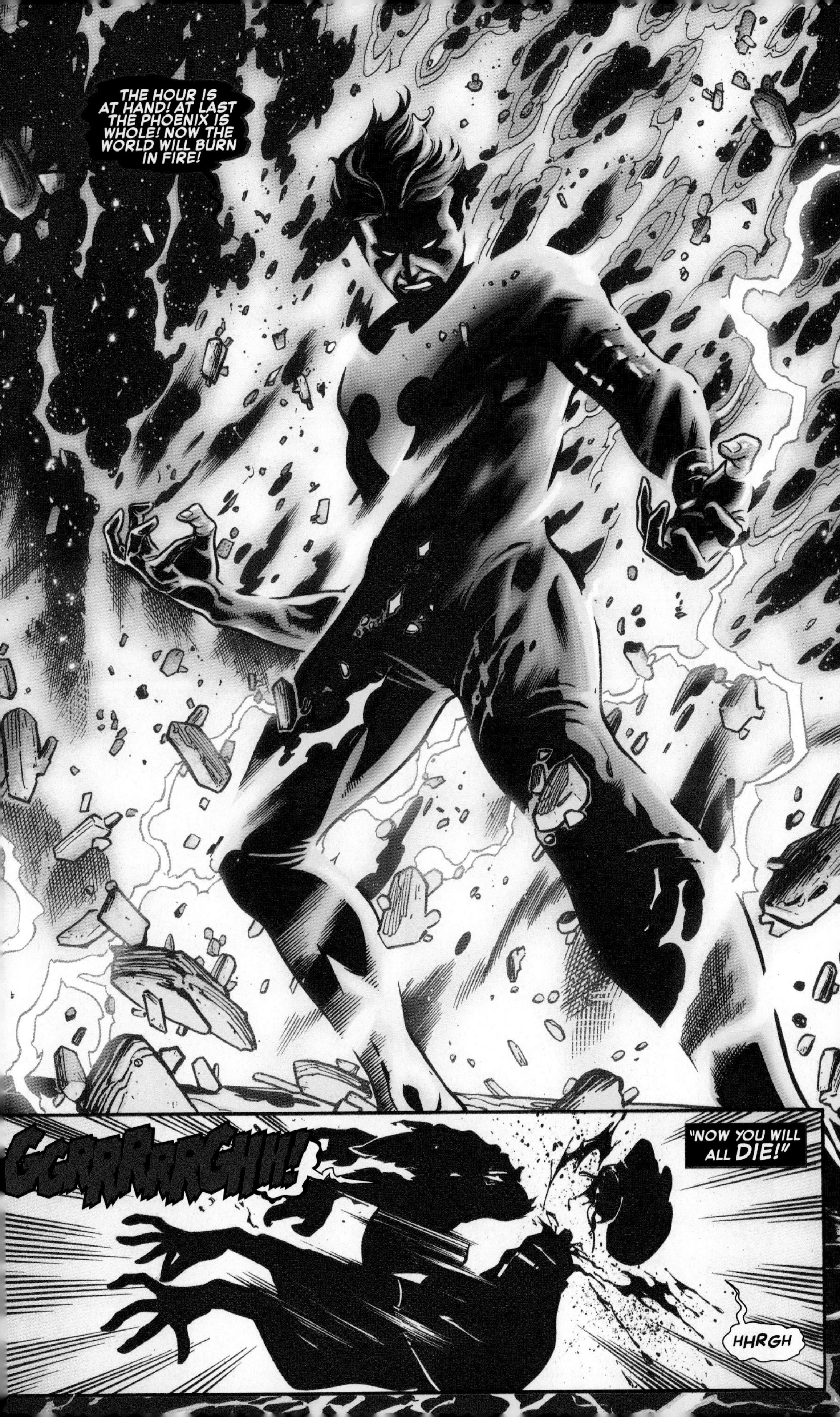
THE HOUR IS AT HAND! AT LAST THE PHOENIX IS WHOLE! NOW THE WORLD WILL BURN IN FIRE!
GGRRRRRGHH!
"NOW YOU WILL ALL DIE!"
HHRGH

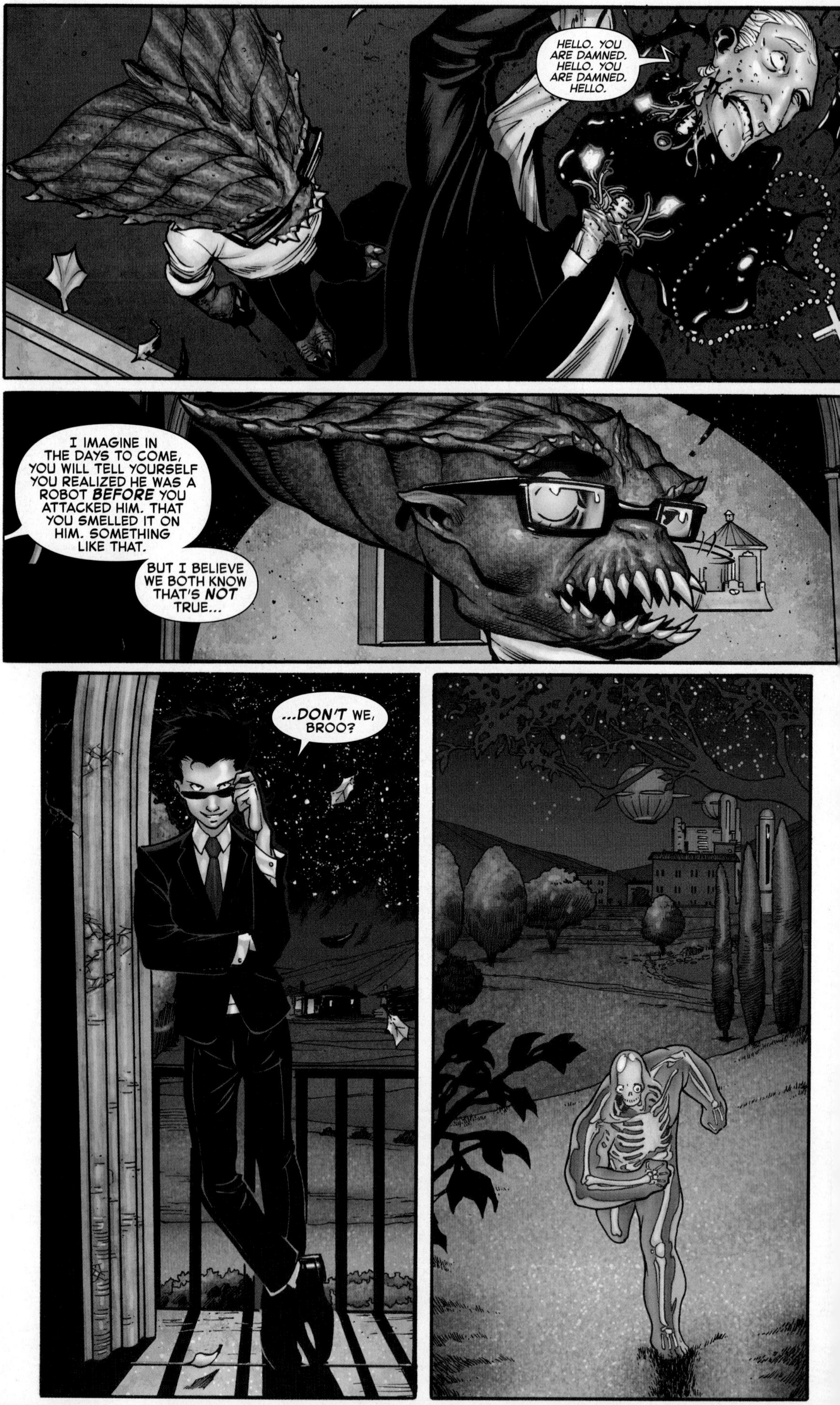
HELLO. YOU ARE DAMNED. HELLO. YOU ARE DAMNED. HELLO.
I IMAGINE IN THE DAYS TO COME, YOU WILL TELL YOURSELF YOU REALIZED HE WAS A ROBOT BEFORE YOU ATTACKED HIM. THAT YOU SMELLED IT ON HIM. SOMETHING LIKE THAT.
BUT I BELIEVE WE BOTH KNOW THAT'S NOT TRUE...
...DON'T WE, BROO?

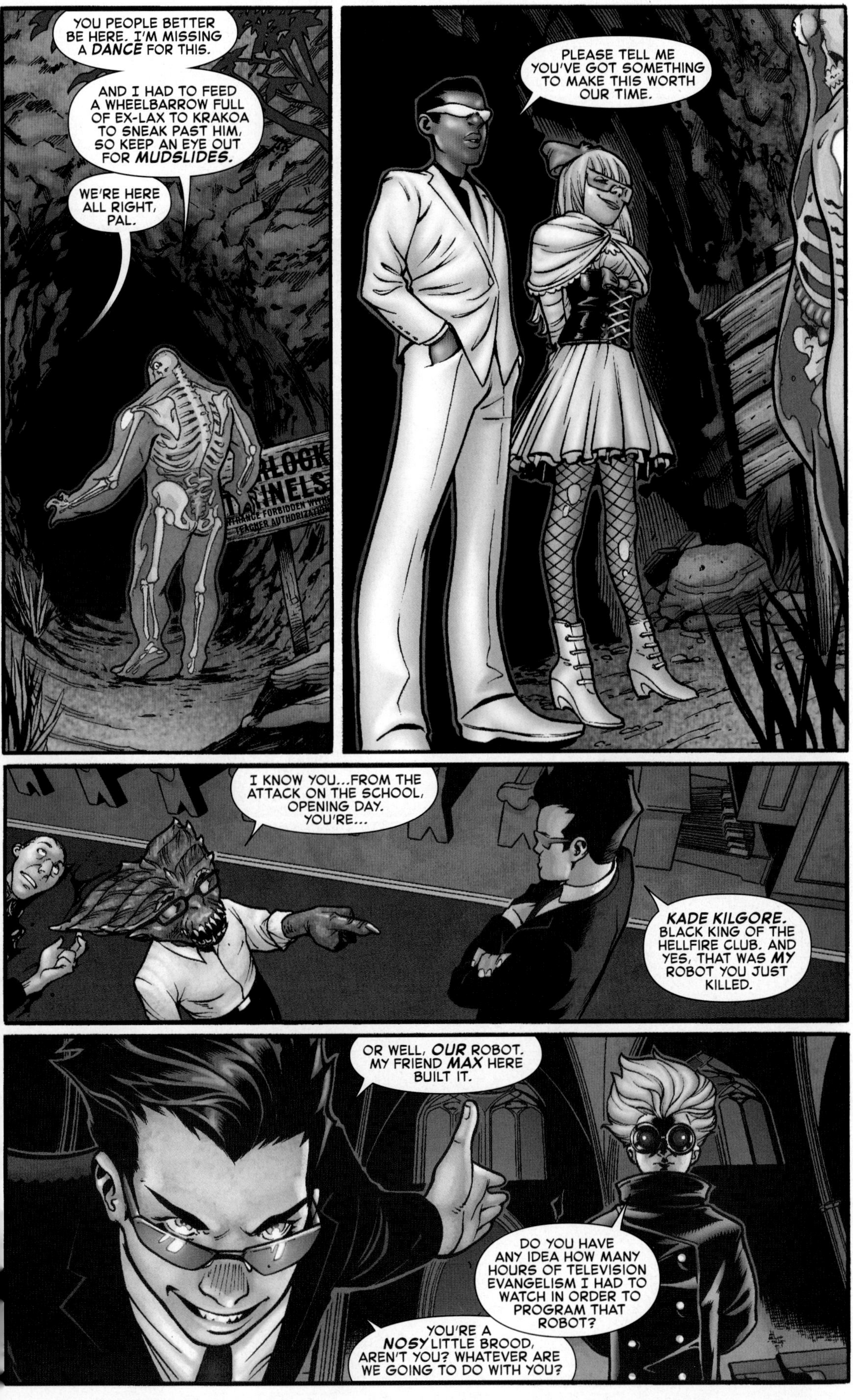

YOU PEOPLE BETTER BE HERE. I'M MISSING A DANCE FOR THIS.
AND I HAD TO FEED A WHEELBARROW FULL OF EX-LAX TO KRAKOA TO SNEAK PAST HIM, SO KEEP AN EYE OUT FOR MUDSLIDES.
WE'RE HERE ALL RIGHT, PAL.
PLEASE TELL ME YOU'VE GOT SOMETHING TO MAKE THIS WORTH OUR TIME.
I KNOW YOU...FROM THE ATTACK ON THE SCHOOL, OPENING DAY. YOU'RE...
KADE KILGORE. BLACK KING OF THE HELLFIRE CLUB. AND YES, THAT WAS MY ROBOT YOU JUST KILLED.
OR WELL, OUR ROBOT. MY FRIEND MAX HERE BUILT IT.
DO YOU HAVE ANY IDEA HOW MANY HOURS OF TELEVISION EVANGELISM I HAD TO WATCH IN ORDER TO PROGRAM THAT ROBOT?
YOU'RE A NOSY LITTLE BROOD, AREN'T YOU? WHATEVER ARE WE GOING TO DO WITH YOU?

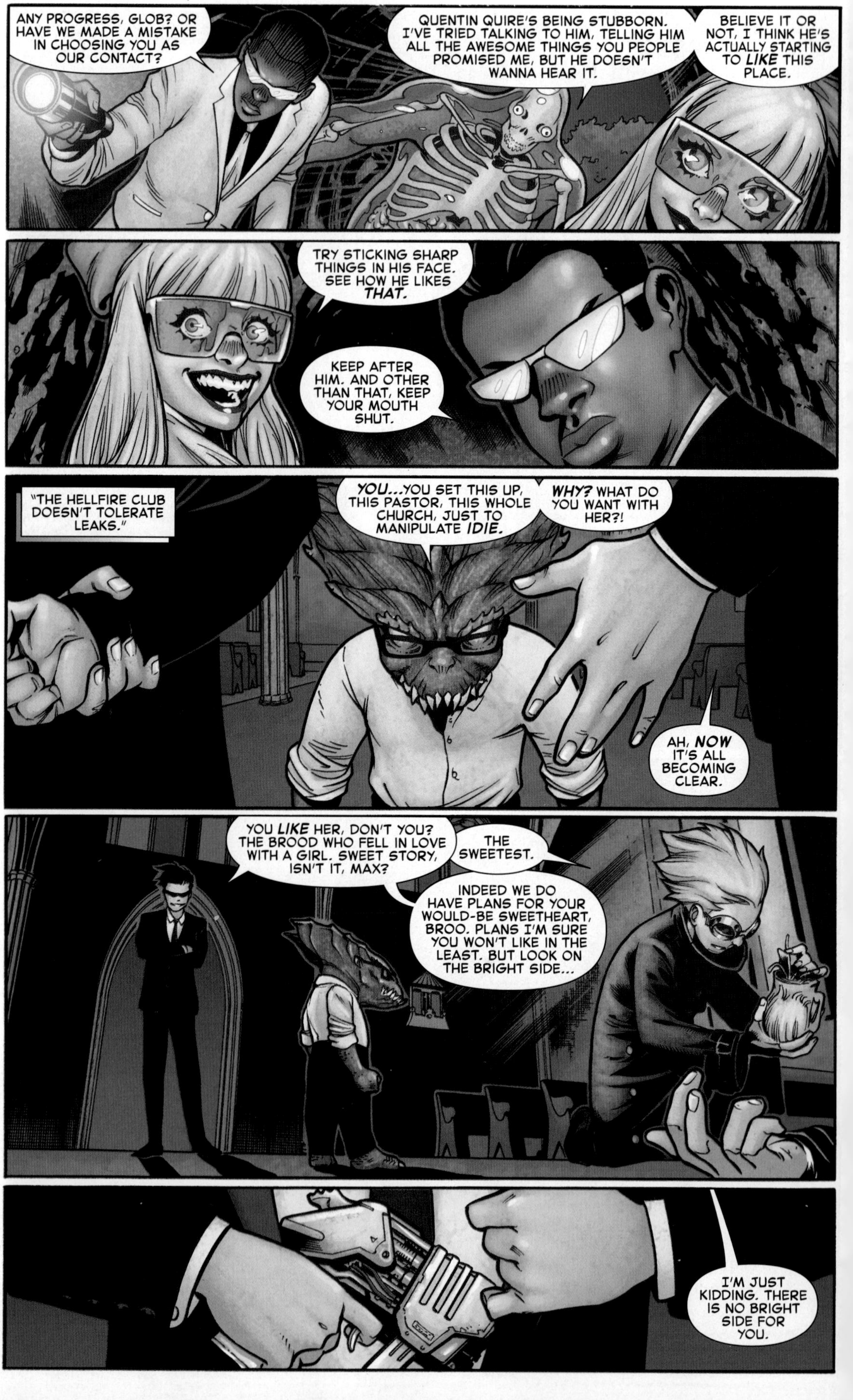

ANY PROGRESS, GLOB? OR HAVE WE MADE A MISTAKE IN CHOOSING YOU AS OUR CONTACT?
QUENTIN QUIRE'S BEING STUBBORN. I'VE TRIED TALKING TO HIM, TELLING HIM ALL THE AWESOME THINGS YOU PEOPLE PROMISED ME, BUT HE DOESN'T WANNA HEAR IT.
BELIEVE IT OR NOT, I THINK HE'S ACTUALLY STARTING TO *LIKE* THIS PLACE.
TRY STICKING SHARP THINGS IN HIS FACE. SEE HOW HE LIKES *THAT.*
KEEP AFTER HIM. AND OTHER THAN THAT, KEEP YOUR MOUTH SHUT.
"THE HELLFIRE CLUB DOESN'T TOLERATE LEAKS."
*YOU...*YOU SET THIS UP, THIS PASTOR, THIS WHOLE CHURCH, JUST TO MANIPULATE *IDIE.*
WHY? WHAT DO YOU WANT WITH HER?!
AH, *NOW* IT'S ALL BECOMING CLEAR.
YOU *LIKE* HER, DON'T YOU? THE BROOD WHO FELL IN LOVE WITH A GIRL. SWEET STORY, ISN'T IT, MAX?
THE SWEETEST.
INDEED WE DO HAVE PLANS FOR YOUR WOULD-BE SWEETHEART, BROO. PLANS I'M SURE YOU WON'T LIKE IN THE LEAST. BUT LOOK ON THE BRIGHT SIDE...
I'M JUST KIDDING. THERE IS NO BRIGHT SIDE FOR YOU.

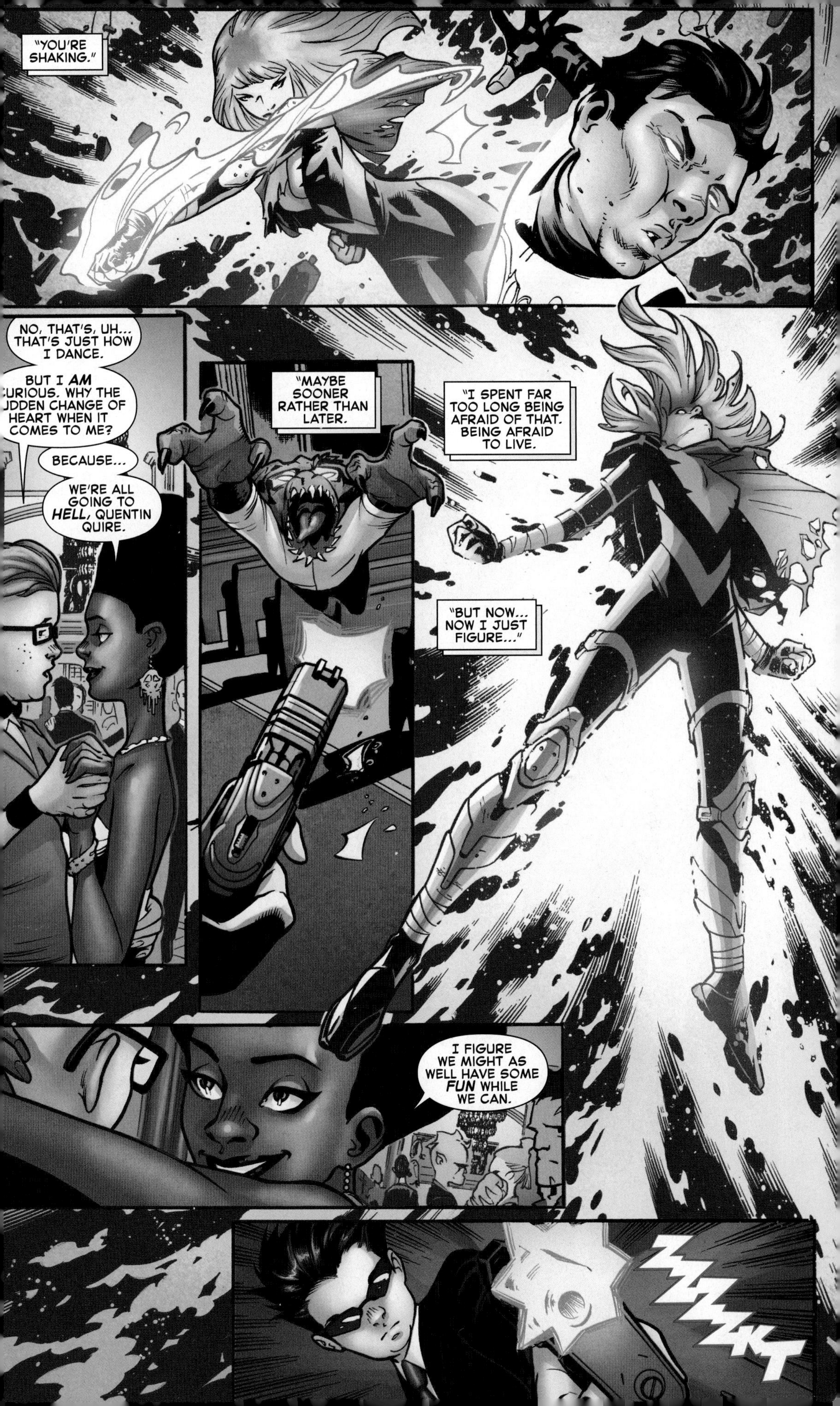

"YOU'RE SHAKING."
NO, THAT'S, UH... THAT'S JUST HOW I DANCE.
BUT I AM CURIOUS. WHY THE SUDDEN CHANGE OF HEART WHEN IT COMES TO ME?
BECAUSE...
WE'RE ALL GOING TO HELL, QUENTIN QUIRE.
"MAYBE SOONER RATHER THAN LATER.
"I SPENT FAR TOO LONG BEING AFRAID OF THAT. BEING AFRAID TO LIVE.
"BUT NOW... NOW I JUST FIGURE..."
I FIGURE WE MIGHT AS WELL HAVE SOME FUN WHILE WE CAN.
ZZZZKT

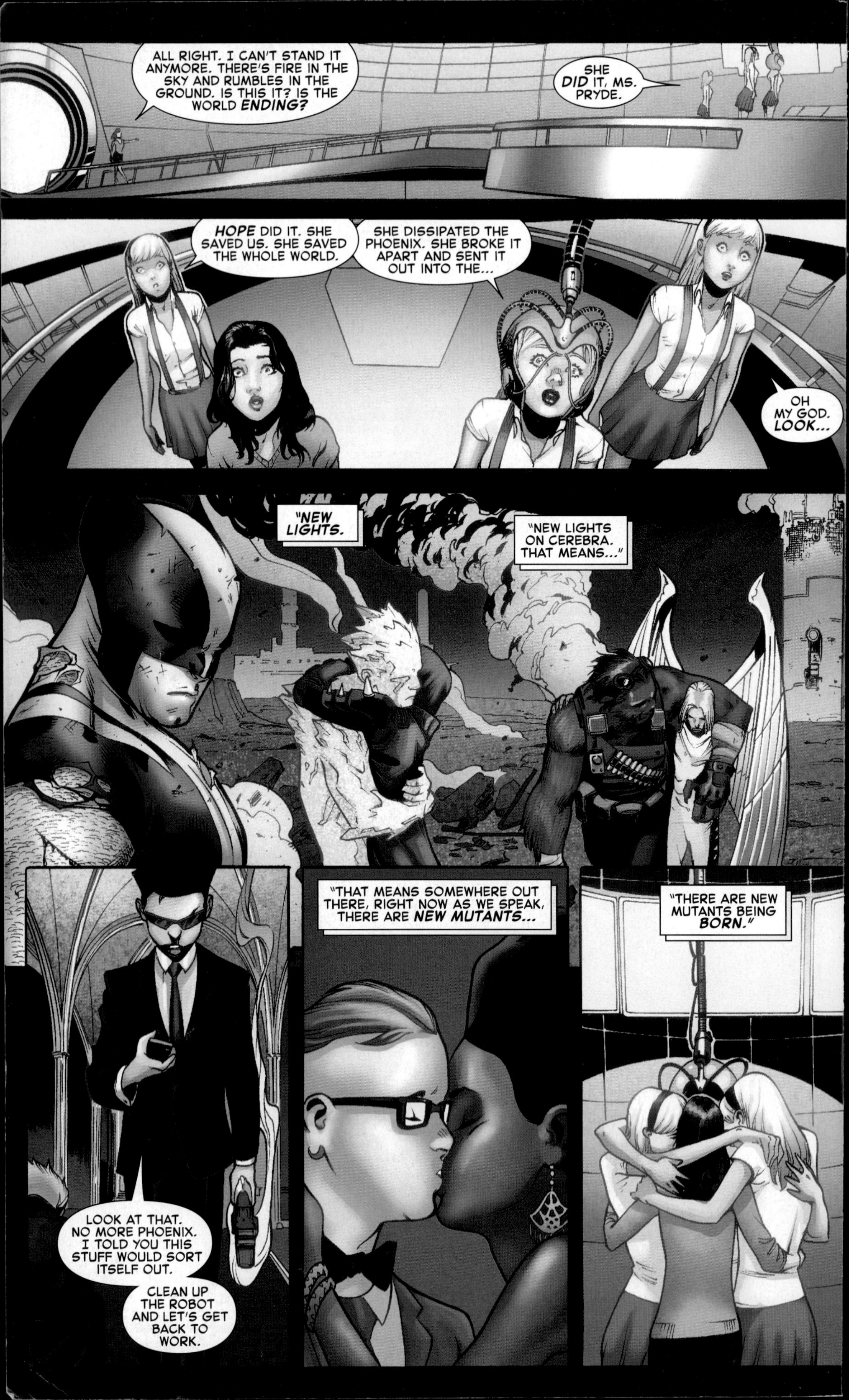
ALL RIGHT. I CAN'T STAND IT ANYMORE. THERE'S FIRE IN THE SKY AND RUMBLES IN THE GROUND. IS THIS IT? IS THE WORLD ENDING?
SHE DID IT, MS. PRYDE.
HOPE DID IT. SHE SAVED US. SHE SAVED THE WHOLE WORLD.
SHE DISSIPATED THE PHOENIX. SHE BROKE IT APART AND SENT IT OUT INTO THE...
OH MY GOD. LOOK...
"NEW LIGHTS.
"NEW LIGHTS ON CEREBRA. THAT MEANS..."
"THAT MEANS SOMEWHERE OUT THERE, RIGHT NOW AS WE SPEAK, THERE ARE NEW MUTANTS...
LOOK AT THAT. NO MORE PHOENIX. I TOLD YOU THIS STUFF WOULD SORT ITSELF OUT.
CLEAN UP THE ROBOT AND LET'S GET BACK TO WORK.
"THERE ARE NEW MUTANTS BEING BORN."

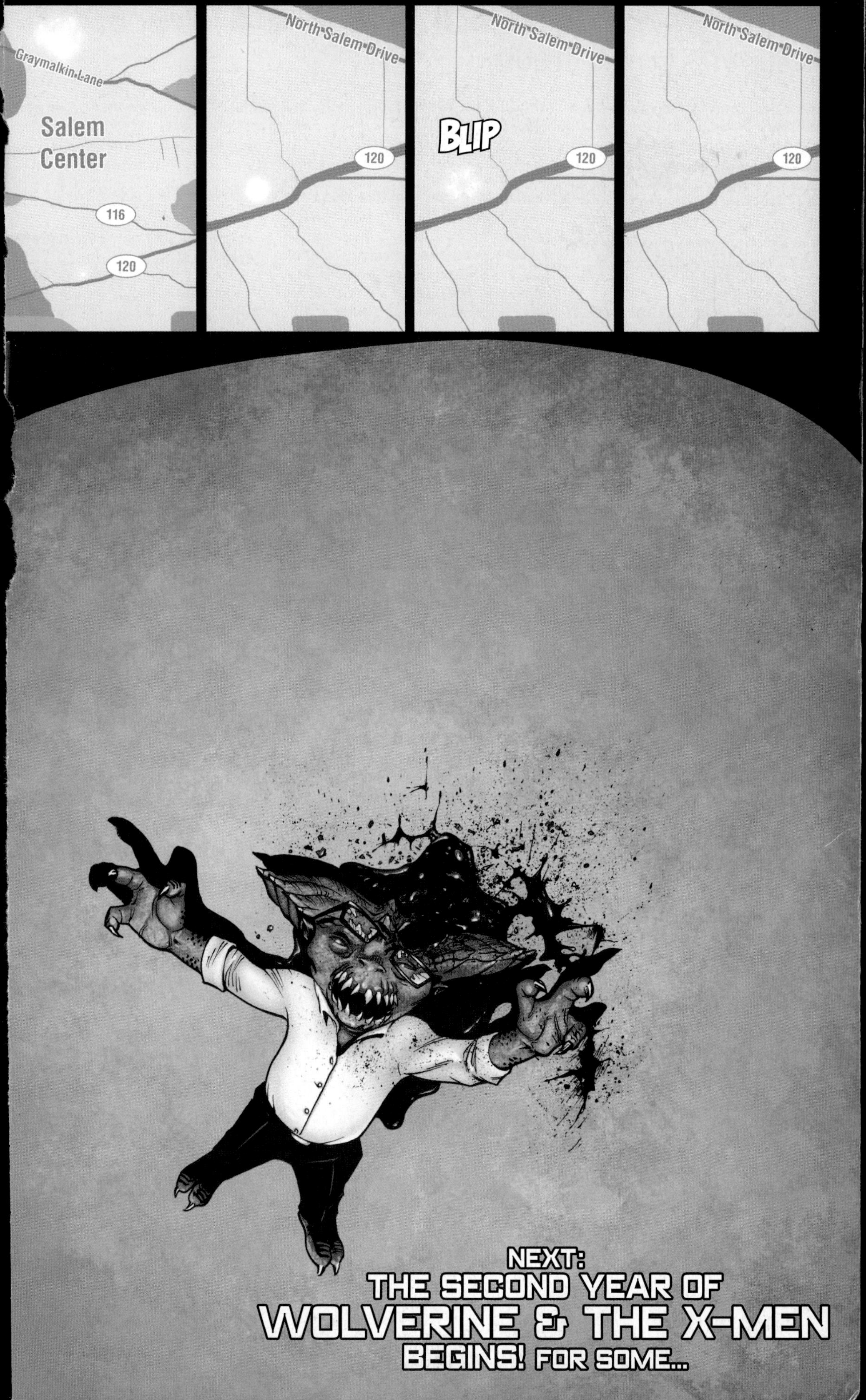
Graymalkin Lane
Salem Center
116
120
North Salem Drive
120
North Salem Drive
BLIP
120
North Salem Drive
120
NEXT:
THE SECOND YEAR OF
WOLVERINE & THE X-MEN
BEGINS! FOR SOME...

ISSUE #16 LETTERS COLUMN

Well hello there. I'm Kade Kilgore, president and CEO of Kilgore Arms and former inmate of Rykers Island. And, yes, I've hacked into the shabby security of the Jean Grey School and taken the pathetic mailbag. I never knew that this ridiculous school had fans. You sad people and your sad lives. I do, however, plan on using the school's mailing list for Kilgore marketing purposes (not that any of you can afford our products). Now what do you dolts have to say for yourselves?

I've been keeping up with the Jean Grey School for Higher Learning since day one, and I just want to wish my congratulations to Mr. Howlett, Miss Pryde, and Mr. Drake as well as all the other staff for keeping the school going despite the attacks from the Hellfire Club and now more recently one of the Phoenix Five!

I do, however, question one thing: why don't I see any human staff/students? I mean I'm not trying to raise a fuss but I think the students can learn a valuable perspective if they had Homo sapiens teaching a class or two.

I also notice you have no school newsletter!

Well, I'd like to offer my services as both a Sapiens Studies teacher as well as a journalism teacher. I only have a Bachelor's in English, however I almost have a year's worth of experience in journalism-- writing is writing my friends.

I know the headmaster and headmistress are a little preoccupied with protecting the world from Scott Summers--never liked that guy, just saying--but when they get a chance, have them think it over. I'd be more than happy to send in my resume too.

Thank you for your time and keep up the good work!

-Vince Mancuso

Vince—may I call you Vince? Wait, I forgot, I don't care. Anyway, Vince, your credibility as an educator is called into question merely by your "appreciation" of the Jean Grey School. Unless, of course, you're following in the footsteps of so many proles and lying like you're in a job interview. And the reason why there aren't more humans at the school is because Wolverine only kills humans. Don't you feel like you need a Sentinel to protect yourself from that stubby Canadian?

Hi Guys,

What's the likelihood of you guys making a Janitor Toad t-shirt ?

The guy gets a lot of stick, about time he got some glory.

"I clean up the mess" on the back or "It's a living."

Thanks,
Chris M
Sydney, Australia

Who wears T-Shirts, Chris? I'll tell you who: non-billionaires. NEXT!

I'm really loving all the adventures and such especially from the last issue. Did I just see Piotr Rasputin giving flowers to Kitty Pryde? Is he trying to get her back again? Tell me, how many times have they broken up and gotten back together? I'm actually enjoying the Kitty and Bobby kisses and slight romance, but they never really show much of it. I think that Piotr and Kitty's romance is cute but I'm still not feeling it, sorry about that! You know what will make me happy? If you have Pete Wisdom back in Kitty's life. How long has it been since Excalibur? Long time, I guess. I don't know how Marvel will put Wisdom in this comic but you'll figure something out, I hope.

 -Dannie Pablo, CA

Here's what I heard in my head when I was reading this letter: BLAH BLAH BLAH NER NER NER GUB GUB. But I think it is important to discuss one topic of your letter. Piotr Rasputin certainly did visit the school while possessed by a cosmic force of destruction. That's what mutants do, Dannie. They make horribly ill-conceived and dangerous decisions. It leaves intelligent people like you and… well, it leaves intelligent people like me to construct death machines to exterminate them.

Hello all,

I just wanted to say that I am very glad that Toad decided to "work" at the school. I have always liked him. Sure, he was never the strongest...or the fastest...or even the smartest of villains. BUT, he ALWAYS makes me smile. I think it would be cool if everyone at the school got into something that only Toad could get them out of... and I don't mean falling in the toilet.

Che' McCrary

You know this school is terrible if most of the letters are in regards to the janitor. NEXT!

Dear So Called Educators,
 I hope this is the truth. I just received word that Doop shall make his triumphant return to the Mutant world. You wanna know what my dream is? That my letter will be published and perhaps, answered by the Doopster himself! Forget Thor, Spidey, Deadpool, and Iron Man... we want Doop! He's a lovable green blob of astonishing excitement. Maximum Doopage, bro!!!

Does Kitty Pryde get a lot of marriage proposals in the mail? Does Toad smell as bad as he looks? Also, when will Logan ever get around to actually teaching and providing structure for the students? I bet Broo is upset by the lack of structure and small animals to feed on.

Daniel Bellay,
Fairmont, WV

A letter to Doop. I'm going to have to look into this Doop character. As for the rest of your questions, Dani there's really no point in answering them as we plan destroy the school in the near future.

To whichever Jean Grey School staff membe stumbles onto this,

We are now deep into a rift amongst mutants an other heroes. I am so excited to see this progress and know how this turns out. I must say, though, th emotional scars that will result leave me a little sad f each of them. Friend vs. Friend. Teacher vs. Studen Family members and loved ones battling each other fo what they believe is right. There seems to be one th good coming out of all of this, and that's Iceman. I h never seen him be so impressive. Really, he has b such a second rate character in my view with a nice s of humor here and there. But now I can see his amaz powers that I hope are not peaking but on a very go incline. He is one of my favorites. Top notch work the

Good luck, X-Men. Take down those bully Avengers, just don't blame the headmaster when all said and done.

Lee
Ottawa, Canada

Good luck, X-Men? Another letter from another buffoo The one thing I agree on here is that I'm excited abo the progress of the war because it means PROFIT Well, that's enough fun for one day! I better get bac to every twelve-year-old's favorite pastime--releasing positive quarterly statement for my corporation.

Worst of luck,

Kade